About the 2012 Standard

The ISF's Standard of Good Practice is **the Standard** for information security. Updated regularly to reflect the latest findings from our research programme, input from our global Member organisations, trends from the ISF **Benchmark** and major external developments, **the Standard** is used by many organisations as their *de facto* standard or primary reference for information security.

The sources used in developing the 2012 version of **the Standard** are:

The Standard is updated annually, reflecting: the rapid pace of change in technology and its use (and the 'surprises' this can sometimes present); and organisations' need to respond to escalating threats from activities such as cybercrime, 'hacktivism', insiders and espionage. As a result, **the Standard** helps the ISF and its Members to maintain their position at the leading edge of good practice in information security.

The Standard incorporates the most up-to-date thinking in information risk management; reflects actual practice of leading global organisations (particularly as results from the ISF **Benchmark** are used to inform and validate the 2012 updates); and remains tightly aligned with other information security-related standards.

Consequently, **the Standard** represents **the** international reference for information security. Implementing **the Standard** helps organisations to:

- be agile and exploit new opportunities – while providing confidence that the associated information risks are managed to acceptable levels
- respond to fast-changing threats, using current information to increase cyber resilience
- simplify the way in which regulatory and compliance requirements can be satisfied.

www.securityforum.org   Information Security Forum • 2012 Standard of Good Practice

Using the Standard to manage risk

Managing information risk is relevant to all organisations, in the public and private sectors, in the context of their strategy, initiatives and goals. Information risk management must focus on enabling the organisation and ensuring it is well positioned to succeed and is resilient to unexpected events.

An organisation's management cycle will typically consist of: *Defining* objectives and strategy; *Implementing* operational plans; *Evaluating* ongoing progress; and *Enhancing* performance and responding to internal and external factors, although different models and terms may be used.

The management cycle depicted below emphasises how *the Standard* and related tools and services can assist ISF Members in managing information risk as part of their enterprise risk management approach or as a stand-alone activity.

❶ DEFINE

Establishing the 'tone from the top' and commitment towards sound information security governance, assessing the organisation's 'risk appetite', aligning security strategy with the organisation's strategy and developing information security policy accordingly.

The Standard offers comprehensive material on which information security governance and information security policy can be based. *The Standard* covers the requirements of other significant information security standards and regulations (ie ISO, COBIT, PCI DSS) and so can be used where these apply. Many Members have adopted *the Standard* 'as is' as the detailed part of their information security policy.

❷ IMPLEMENT

Defining the means by which the policy will be implemented, how risk will be assessed, and implementing controls consistent with risk appetite.

The ISF's *Information Risk Analysis Methodology (IRAM)* is designed to assess risks at application, business process or business unit level and select appropriate controls to mitigate risk consistent with risk appetite. *The Standard* defines potential information security controls. Once risk and security requirements are identified using *IRAM*, the 'Control Framework' in *the Standard* can be used to select appropriate controls.

❹ ENHANCE

Enhancing controls and activities where alignment of risk, policy and implementation requires improvement.

Where the ISF *Benchmark* has highlighted weaknesses / gaps in controls, Members can use *the Standard* and other ISF reports to identify and select controls to better align arrangements. Reports on new emerging topics enable Members to respond to changes in threats and business activities.

❸ EVALUATE

Assessing the effectiveness of controls implemented against policy and regulatory requirements.

The ISF's *Benchmark* is a powerful service that enables Members to assess the extent to which controls are implemented. It also allows areas of control weakness / gaps (and strengths) to be identified and provides comparisons to peers. The *Benchmark* enables assessment using a high level *Security Healthcheck* for lower risk activities, and more detailed assessments at the level of *the Standard* for higher risk areas and critical business applications. The Benchmark reports results in many formats, including ISO, COBIT and PCI DSS formats, and so can also be used to assess performance and gaps against those standards.

These ISF tools and services should be used in the context of the organisation's business strategy and other detailed enabling strategies that set context for managing information risk. For example, strategies that introduce implications for risk include establishing new routes to market, changing ways of doing business or delivering services, adopting new technologies, developing new products or services and mergers and acquisitions. The information risks emerging from organisational strategies can also be compounded by political, regulatory and socio-cultural factors.

In addition to helping Members manage information risk effectively, **the Standard** provides Members with a powerful tool to help meet the requirements of many common information security-related standards, such as those published by ISO (eg 27001 & 27002), ISACA (eg COBIT 5 for Information Security) and the Payment Card Industry Security Standards Council (PCI DSS).

When implemented comprehensively, **the Standard** enables Members to build an Information Security Management System (ISMS) as set out in ISO/IEC 27001, perform information risk assessments according to ISO/IEC 27005 and implement security controls beyond those defined in ISO/IEC 27002, including recent developments / topics not addressed by ISO 27002, such as cloud computing, cybercrime attacks and consumer devices. **The Standard** is therefore an ideal tool to help enable ISO 27001 certification.

The ISF provides a highly integrated set of tools and services to help Members manage information risk. These are founded on **the Standard**, the *Information Risk Analysis Methodology (IRAM)* and the **Benchmark**. When applied as part of a business cycle for improvement, these tools and services support a typical business process to manage information risk.

An overview of these tools and services is provided below.

Information Risk Analysis Methodology (IRAM)
IRAM provides an approach to analyse information risk in all types of systems or processes. *IRAM* can be used to: assess the business impact of potential security breaches; assess threats and vulnerabilities; determine information risks; and help identify controls that can be implemented to mitigate risks.

Benchmark service
The *Benchmark* service enables Members to assess the extent to which controls are implemented in key processes and activities. It helps identify areas of control weakness / gaps (and strengths) and provides comparisons to peers. The service enables assessments to be performed at the level of the:

- *Healthcheck* for low risk activities or high level risk assessments / gap analyses
- *Full Benchmark* for high risk business processes / environments and critical business applications.

The *Benchmark* presents results in many formats (eg ISO 27002 and COBIT 5 for Information Security) and can be used to assess performance and gaps against those standards. Additionally, Members using the *Benchmark* can draw meaningful comparisons with the status of information security in other organisations (eg in the same industry sector).

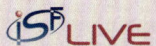

Implementation Support via ISF Live
ISF Live offers a vibrant environment for Member collaboration. Offering groups dedicated to sharing information about implementing *the Standard*, *IRAM* and the *Benchmark*, it provides implementation support in the form of additional guidance, scenarios, case studies and discussions between Members and with the ISF Global Team.

Target audience

The Standard is primarily developed for major national and international organisations that recognise information security as a key business challenge. However, **the Standard** is also of value to any type of organisations, such as small- to medium-sized enterprises – as it presents latest thinking on good information security practice described in clear, accessible language.

Good practice described in **the Standard** will typically be incorporated into an organisation's information security policy and other arrangements by a range of key individuals or external parties, including:

- **Chief Information Security Officers** (or equivalent), responsible for developing policy and implementing sound Information Security Governance and Information Security Assurance
- **Information Security managers** (local security co-ordinators and information protection champions), responsible for promoting or implementing an information security assurance programme
- **Business managers** responsible for ensuring that critical business applications, processes and local environments on which their organisation's success depends are well controlled
- **IT managers and technical staff** responsible for designing, planning, developing, deploying and maintaining key business applications, information systems or facilities
- **Internal and external auditors** responsible for conducting security audits
- **IT service providers** responsible for managing critical facilities (eg computer installations and networks) on behalf of the organisation.

The ISF Security Model

The ISF has developed a security model to support organisations in designing their approach to addressing information security and to give them a basis for identifying the key aspects of an information security programme. The ISF provides insights, best practice standards and tools which address each aspect of the model to aid organisations in enhancing their information security environment.

Within the ISF Security Model, **The Standard of Good Practice for Information Security** forms part of the Research and Reports service. Using a rating from very high to very low, the way in which this report aligns with the ISF Security Model is shown below.

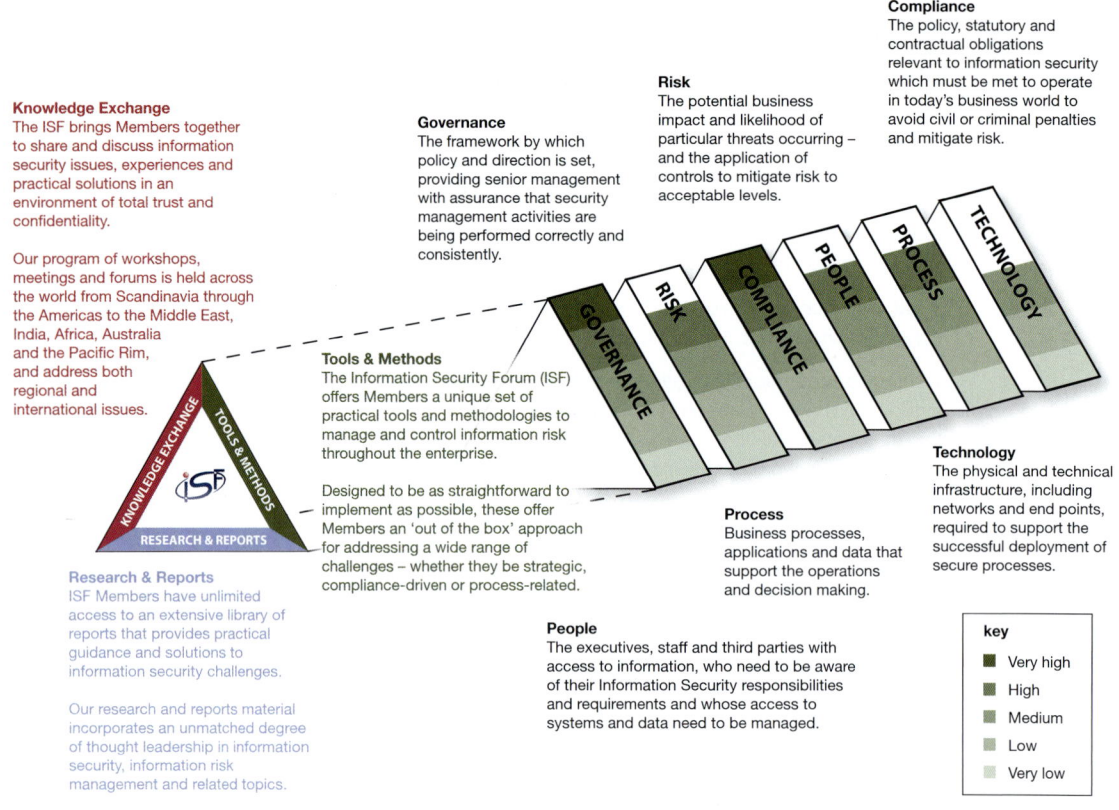

Knowledge Exchange
The ISF brings Members together to share and discuss information security issues, experiences and practical solutions in an environment of total trust and confidentiality.

Our program of workshops, meetings and forums is held across the world from Scandinavia through the Americas to the Middle East, India, Africa, Australia and the Pacific Rim, and address both regional and international issues.

Research & Reports
ISF Members have unlimited access to an extensive library of reports that provides practical guidance and solutions to information security challenges.

Our research and reports material incorporates an unmatched degree of thought leadership in information security, information risk management and related topics.

Tools & Methods
The Information Security Forum (ISF) offers Members a unique set of practical tools and methodologies to manage and control information risk throughout the enterprise.

Designed to be as straightforward to implement as possible, these offer Members an 'out of the box' approach for addressing a wide range of challenges – whether they be strategic, compliance-driven or process-related.

Governance
The framework by which policy and direction is set, providing senior management with assurance that security management activities are being performed correctly and consistently.

Risk
The potential business impact and likelihood of particular threats occurring – and the application of controls to mitigate risk to acceptable levels.

Compliance
The policy, statutory and contractual obligations relevant to information security which must be met to operate in today's business world to avoid civil or criminal penalties and mitigate risk.

People
The executives, staff and third parties with access to information, who need to be aware of their Information Security responsibilities and requirements and whose access to systems and data need to be managed.

Process
Business processes, applications and data that support the operations and decision making.

Technology
The physical and technical infrastructure, including networks and end points, required to support the successful deployment of secure processes.

key
- Very high
- High
- Medium
- Low
- Very low

A copy of the ISF Security Model can be downloaded by Members from the ISF **Member only website** (ISF Live), which can be used to clearly describe to your team and others (management, potential Supply Chain or other Membership prospects) the key aspects of the information security environment within your organisation.

Contents

Topics in the Standard of Good Practice ... 2

Key features and structure
Relationship between the Standard and other major information security standards ... 4
Fundamental and Specialised controls ... 4
Structure ... 5
Topic layout ... 6
About the Index ... 7

The 2012 Standard
SECURITY GOVERNANCE	9
SECURITY REQUIREMENTS	21
CONTROL FRAMEWORK	41
SECURITY MONITORING AND IMPROVEMENT	233

Appendix A: The ISF Business Impact Reference Table ... 250

Appendix B: The ISF Threat List ... 251

Appendix C: Description of external standards ... 255

Appendix D: Templates ... 256

Index ... 263

Topics in the Standard of Good Practice

SECURITY GOVERNANCE

		TYPE	PAGE
SG1 Security Governance Approach			
SG1.1	Security Governance Framework	S	10
SG1.2	Security Direction	F	12
SG2 Security Governance Components			
SG2.1	Information Security Strategy	S	14
SG2.2	Stakeholder Value Delivery	S	16
SG2.3	Information Security Assurance Programme	F	18

SECURITY REQUIREMENTS

		TYPE	PAGE
SR1 Information Risk Assessment			
SR1.1	Managing Information Risk Assessment	F	22
SR1.2	Information Risk Assessment Methodologies	F	25
SR1.3	Confidentiality Requirements	F	28
SR1.4	Integrity Requirements	F	30
SR1.5	Availability Requirements	F	32
SR1.6	Information Risk Treatment	F	34
SR2 Compliance			
SR2.1	Legal and Regulatory Compliance	F	36
SR2.2	Information Privacy	F	38

CONTROL FRAMEWORK

		TYPE	PAGE
CF1 Security Policy and Organisation			
CF1.1	Information Security Policy	F	44
CF1.2	Information Security Function	F	46
CF2 Human Resource Security			
CF2.1	Staff Agreements	F	49
CF2.2	Security Awareness Programme	F	51
CF2.3	Security Awareness Messages	F	53
CF2.4	Security Education / Training	F	55
CF2.5	Roles and Responsibilities	F	58
CF3 Asset Management			
CF3.1	Information Classification	S	60
CF3.2	Document Management	S	62
CF3.3	Sensitive Physical Information	F	64
CF3.4	Asset Register	F	66

KEY
TYPE: F Fundamental topic   S Specialised topic
Topics that have been subject to significant change since the 2011 Standard of Good Practice

CONTROL FRAMEWORK (continued)

		TYPE	PAGE
CF4 Business Applications			
CF4.1	Application Protection	S	68
CF4.2	Browser-based Application Protection	S	70
CF4.3	Information Validation	F	72
CF5 Customer Access			
CF5.1	Customer Access Arrangements	F	73
CF5.2	Customer Contracts	S	76
CF5.3	Customer Connections	F	78
CF6 Access Management			
CF6.1	Access Control	F	80
CF6.2	User Authorisation	F	82
CF6.3	Access Control Mechanisms	F	83
CF6.4	Access Control Mechanisms – Password	S	85
CF6.5	Access Control Mechanisms – Token	S	87
CF6.6	Access Control Mechanisms – Biometric	S	89
CF6.7	Sign-on Process	F	91
CF7 System Management			
CF7.1	Computer and Network Installations	F	92
CF7.2	Server Configuration	F	94
CF7.3	Virtual Servers	S	96
CF7.4	Network Storage Systems	S	98
CF7.5	Back-up	F	100
CF7.6	Change Management	F	102
CF7.7	Service Level Agreements	F	104
CF8 Technical Security Infrastructure			
CF8.1	Security Architecture	S	106
CF8.2	Identity and Access Management	S	109
CF8.3	Critical Infrastructure	S	111
CF8.4	Cryptographic Solutions	S	113
CF8.5	Cryptographic Key Management	S	115
CF8.6	Public Key Infrastructure	S	117
CF8.7	Information Leakage Protection	S	120
CF8.8	Digital Rights Management	S	122
CF9 Network Management			
CF9.1	Network Device Configuration	F	124
CF9.2	Physical Network Management	F	126
CF9.3	External Network Connections	F	127
CF9.4	Firewalls	F	129
CF9.5	Remote Maintenance	S	131
CF9.6	Wireless Access	F	132

CONTROL FRAMEWORK (continued)

CF9 Network Management (continued)

		TYPE	PAGE
CF9.7	Voice over IP (VoIP) Networks	S	134
CF9.8	Telephony and Conferencing	S	135

CF10 Threat and Vulnerability Management

		TYPE	PAGE
CF10.1	Patch Management	F	136
CF10.2	Malware Awareness	F	138
CF10.3	Malware Protection Software	F	139
CF10.4	Security Event Logging	F	141
CF10.5	System / Network Monitoring	F	143
CF10.6	Intrusion Detection	F	145

CF11 Incident Management

		TYPE	PAGE
CF11.1	Information Security Incident Management	F	147
CF11.2	Cybercrime Attacks	S	150
CF11.3	Emergency Fixes	F	152
CF11.4	Forensic Investigations	S	154

CF12 Local Environments

		TYPE	PAGE
CF12.1	Local Environment Profile	S	156
CF12.2	Local Security Co-ordination	S	158
CF12.3	Office Equipment	S	160

CF13 Desktop Applications

		TYPE	PAGE
CF13.1	Inventory of Desktop Applications	S	162
CF13.2	Protection of Spreadsheets	S	164
CF13.3	Protection of Databases	S	166
CF13.4	Desktop Application Development	S	168

CF14 Mobile Computing

		TYPE	PAGE
CF14.1	Remote Environments	S	170
CF14.2	Mobile Device Configuration	F	172
CF14.3	Mobile Device Connectivity	F	175
CF14.4	Portable Storage Devices	S	177
CF14.5	Consumer Devices	S	179

CF15 Electronic Communications

		TYPE	PAGE
CF15.1	Email	F	181
CF15.2	Instant Messaging	S	183

CF16 External Supplier Management

		TYPE	PAGE
CF16.1	External Supplier Management Process	F	184
CF16.2	Hardware / Software Acquisition	F	187
CF16.3	Outsourcing	S	189
CF16.4	Cloud Computing Policy	S	191
CF16.5	Cloud Service Contracts	S	194

CONTROL FRAMEWORK (continued)

CF17 System Development Management

		TYPE	PAGE
CF17.1	System Development Methodology	F	196
CF17.2	System Development Environments	F	198
CF17.3	Quality Assurance	F	199

CF18 Systems Development Lifecycle

		TYPE	PAGE
CF18.1	Specifications of Requirements	F	200
CF18.2	System Design	F	202
CF18.3	System Build	F	204
CF18.4	Systems Testing	F	206
CF18.5	Security Testing	F	209
CF18.6	System Promotion Criteria	F	211
CF18.7	Installation Process	F	213
CF18.8	Post-implementation Review	F	214

CF19 Physical and Environmental Security

		TYPE	PAGE
CF19.1	Physical Protection	F	215
CF19.2	Power Supplies	F	217
CF19.3	Hazard Protection	F	218

CF20 Business Continuity

		TYPE	PAGE
CF20.1	Business Continuity Strategy	S	219
CF20.2	Business Continuity Programme	S	221
CF20.3	Resilience	S	223
CF20.4	Crisis Management	S	225
CF20.5	Business Continuity Planning	F	227
CF20.6	Business Continuity Arrangements	F	229
CF20.7	Business Continuity Testing	F	231

SECURITY MONITORING AND IMPROVEMENT

SI1 Security Audit

		TYPE	PAGE
SI1.1	Security Audit Management	F	234
SI1.2	Security Audit Process – Planning	F	236
SI1.3	Security Audit Process – Fieldwork	F	238
SI1.4	Security Audit Process – Reporting	F	240
SI1.5	Security Audit Process – Monitoring	F	242

SI2 Security Performance

		TYPE	PAGE
SI2.1	Security Monitoring	F	243
SI2.2	Information Risk Reporting	S	245
SI2.3	Monitoring Information Security Compliance	S	247

KEY

TYPE: F Fundamental topic   S Specialised topic

Topics that have been subject to significant change since the 2011 Standard of Good Practice

Key features and structure

Relationship between the Standard and other major information security standards

The Standard covers the complete spectrum of security arrangements that need to be considered to keep business risks associated with information systems within acceptable limits, by presenting good practice in practical, clear statements. As a result, not only does it contribute towards improving the quality and efficiency of information security that might be applied, it can also contribute to information security compliance. As *the Standard* is closely aligned to the structures of ISO 27001[1], ISO 27002[1], ISO 27005[1] and COBIT 5 for Information Security, using *the Standard* to comply with these standards can greatly reduce the complexity of compliance (and certification) activities. Further, as *the Standard* is aligned with other regulatory requirements and guidance such as the Payment Card Industry Data Security Standard (PCI DSS), Sarbanes Oxley Act, Basel III Accord and Cloud Security Alliance (CSA) Cloud Controls Matrix, it can contribute to harmonising information security compliance activities across the board.

The relationship between *the Standard* and the relevant ISO information security-related standards is shown below.

How the Standard is aligned with the ISO '27000 suite' of Standards

Fundamental and Specialised controls

The Standard makes a distinction between those topics that are considered 'Fundamental' and those that are considered 'Specialised'. This classification is used to make it easier to identify essential security arrangements likely to be relevant for most organisations and distinguished from those that depend on other factors that are not universal.

FUNDAMENTAL topics are the information security arrangements that are generally applied by Members to form the foundation of their information security programme.

SPECIALISED topics are those that depend on how or in what environment the business operates and are not typically relevant to most organisations, or topics that do not apply to all environments – such as Server Virtualisation or Cloud Computing.

A clear indicator at the top of each topic page in *the Standard* shows whether the controls presented in that topic are 'Fundamental' or 'Specialised'.

 The Standard also provides coverage of COBIT 5 for Information Security and PCI DSS, and will be a useful aid to organisations implementing this framework

---

[1] Full titles and descriptions of the relevant standards in the ISO 27000 'suite' are provided in *Appendix C*.

Structure

The information security good practice presented in *the Standard* is divided into four categories:

- Security Governance
- Security Requirements
- Control Framework
- Security Monitoring and Improvement.

The Standard sets out statements of good practice as a series of 118 'topics' or business activities, which are grouped into 26 higher level 'areas' and then 4 high level 'categories'. Each topic is designed to 'stand alone' and addresses that particular aspect of business activity from an information security perspective. The categories reflect the typical approach taken to Security Governance and Security Assurance in many organisations.

The structure of *the Standard* enables organisations to 'dip' into it to address specific areas of concern (such as Information Classification or Office Equipment) if they wish. *The Standard* is also consistent with the structure and flow of the ISO 27000 'suite' of standards, and is appropriate for those organisations that wish to use *the Standard* as an enabler to ISO compliance or certification, or to implement one or more Information Security Management Systems (ISMS).

The overall structure of *the Standard* is illustrated below. Each category is composed of a number of areas, each covering an information security-related subject. An area is broken down further into topics, each of which contains a set of statements.

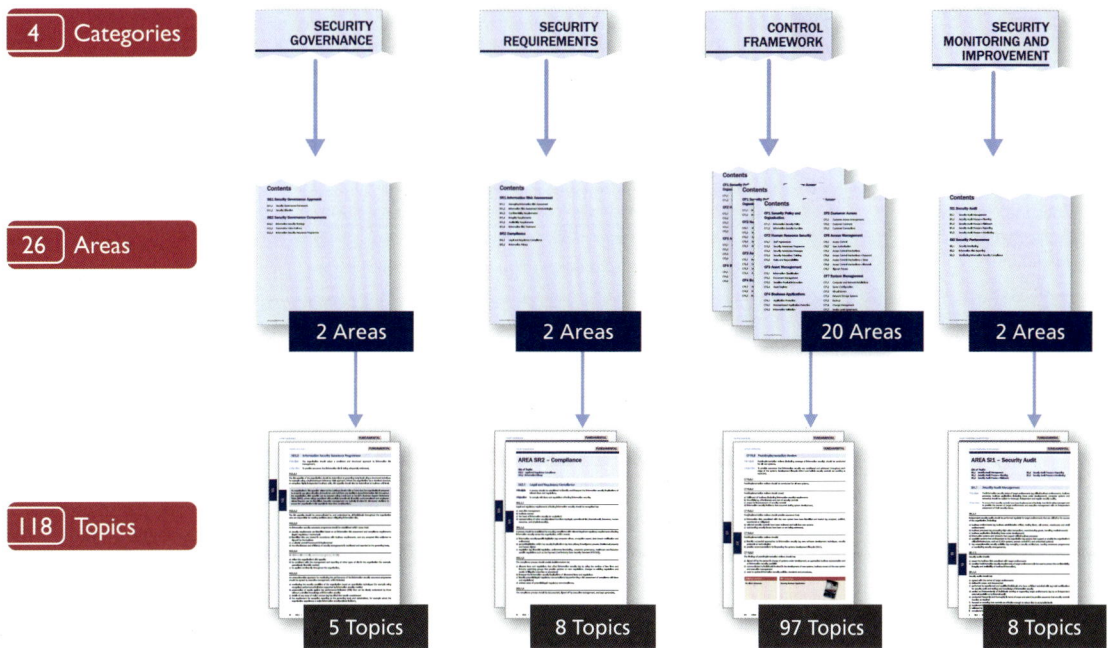

Structure of the 2012 Standard

Introduction

Topic layout

Each of the 118 topics in *the Standard* is set out as shown below.

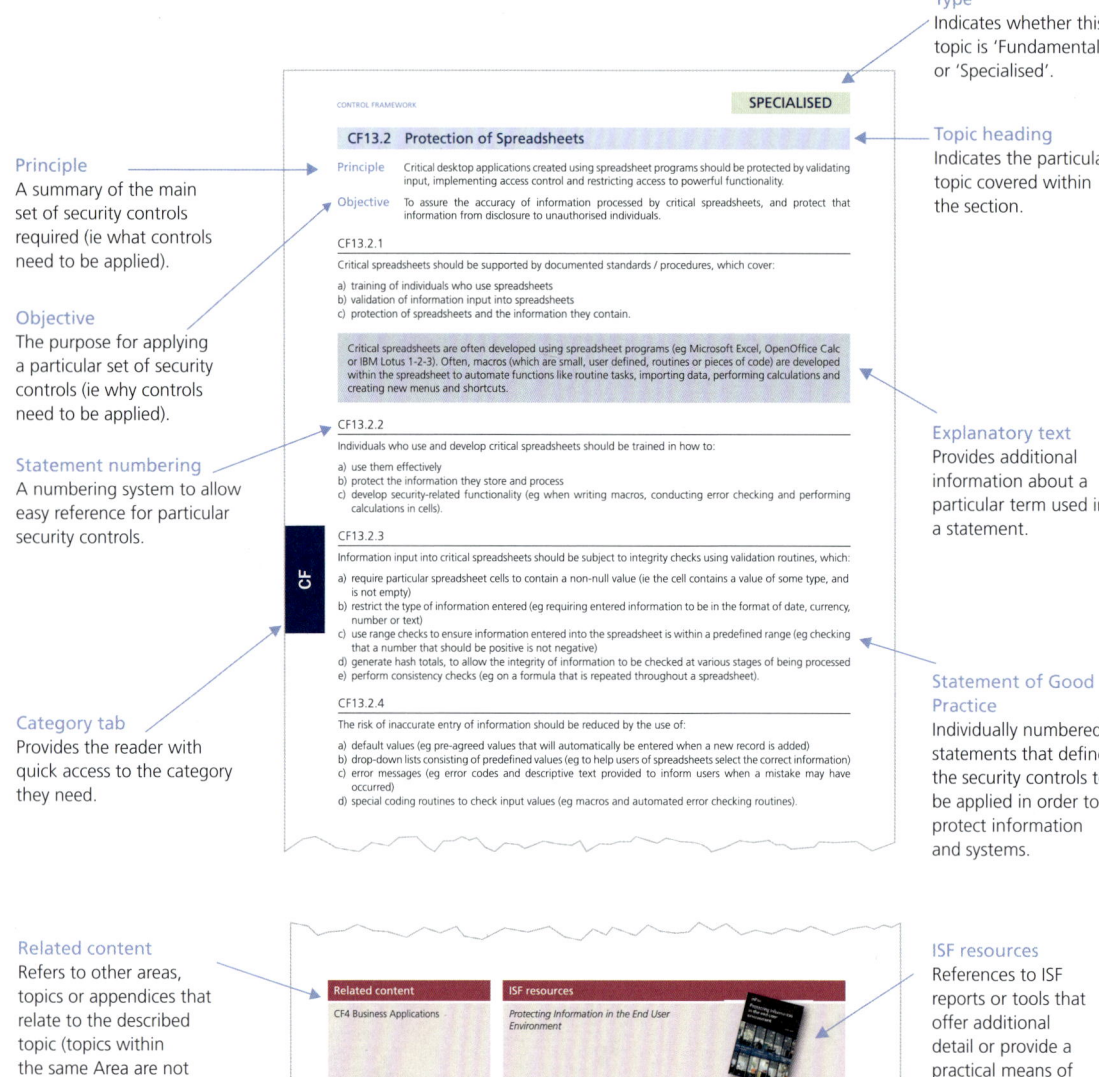

Principle
A summary of the main set of security controls required (ie what controls need to be applied).

Objective
The purpose for applying a particular set of security controls (ie why controls need to be applied).

Statement numbering
A numbering system to allow easy reference for particular security controls.

Category tab
Provides the reader with quick access to the category they need.

Related content
Refers to other areas, topics or appendices that relate to the described topic (topics within the same Area are not necessarily shown).

Type
Indicates whether this topic is 'Fundamental' or 'Specialised'.

Topic heading
Indicates the particular topic covered within the section.

Explanatory text
Provides additional information about a particular term used in a statement.

Statement of Good Practice
Individually numbered statements that define the security controls to be applied in order to protect information and systems.

ISF resources
References to ISF reports or tools that offer additional detail or provide a practical means of implementation.

Topic number
Provides quick access to the required topic of the Standard.

Example of how each topic in the Standard is presented

Introduction

About the Index

The Index presents an extensive alphabetical list of information security-related terms, concepts and topics, and provides a reference to relevant topics in which they are covered in *the Standard* (as shown below).

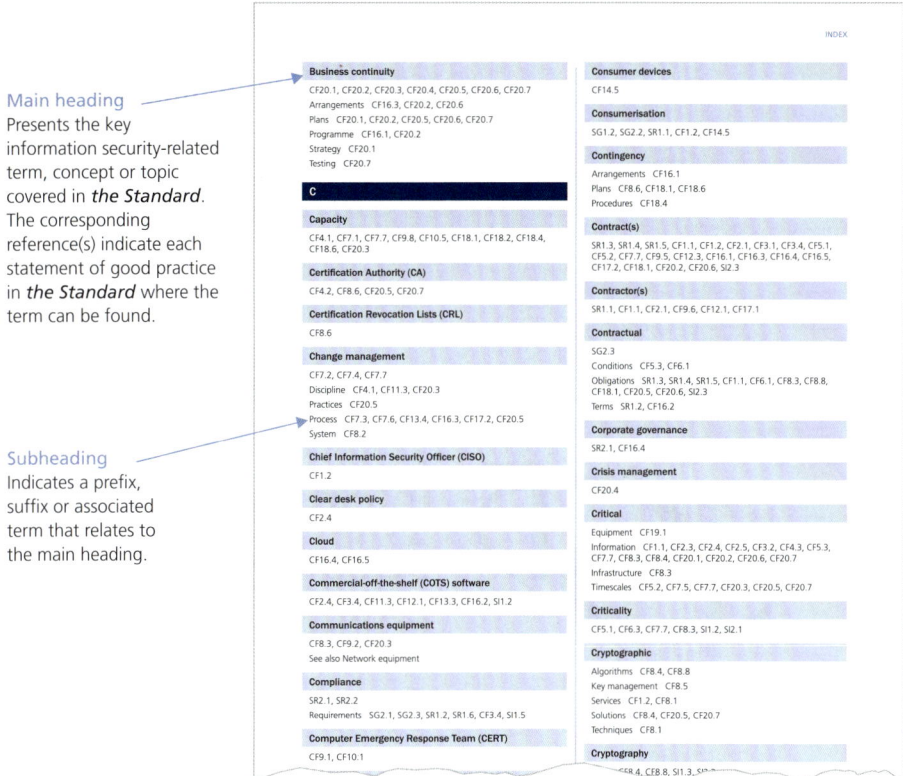

Main heading
Presents the key information security-related term, concept or topic covered in *the Standard*. The corresponding reference(s) indicate each statement of good practice in *the Standard* where the term can be found.

Subheading
Indicates a prefix, suffix or associated term that relates to the main heading.

Example of the Index

SECURITY GOVERNANCE

Contents

SG1 Security Governance Approach

SG1.1   Security Governance Framework

SG1.2   Security Direction

SG2 Security Governance Components

SG2.1   Information Security Strategy

SG2.2   Stakeholder Value Delivery

SG2.3   Information Security Assurance Programme

SECURITY GOVERNANCE

SPECIALISED

AREA SG1 – Security Governance Approach

List of Topics
SG1.1 Security Governance Framework
SG1.2 Security Direction

SG1.1   Security Governance Framework

Principle   A framework for information security governance should be established, and commitment demonstrated by the organisation's governing body.

Objective   To ensure that the organisation's overall approach to information security supports high standards of governance.

SG1.1.1

The organisation's governing body (eg members of the board or equivalent) should establish, direct, monitor and communicate an information security governance framework.

> The governing body of an organisation is typically the group of individuals that is responsible for running that organisation (eg members of the board or equivalent). It is typically supported by executive management, which is made up of senior individuals responsible for running operational business units (eg a trading floor, sales order processing function, manufacturing plant, call centre, large department or retail outlet) or specialist functions (eg major IT functions, information security, operational risk, internal audit, finance, legal or human resources).

SG1.1.2

The governing body should:

a) treat information security as a critical business issue
b) appoint a board-level executive or equivalent to take overall responsibility for the information security governance framework
c) ensure that the information security governance framework is supported by an information security strategy and security assurance programme.

SG1.1.3

The governing body should define the objectives of the information security governance framework, which include:

a) aligning the information security strategy with the business strategy
b) delivering value to stakeholders (eg reduced cost and enhanced reputation)
c) providing assurance that information risks are being adequately addressed.

SPECIALISED

SG1.1 Security Governance Framework (continued)

SG1.1.4

The information security governance framework should address the need to:

a) co-ordinate information security activities throughout the organisation
b) make investment decisions about information security that reflect business objectives
c) ensure that decisions about information security activities are based on risk, reflect the organisation's overall risk appetite and are made in a timely manner
d) promote a security-positive environment
e) support compliance with applicable legislation and regulation
f) measure its success in terms of contribution to the objectives of the organisation.

SG1.1.5

The information security governance framework should include a process that requires the governing body to:

a) evaluate the extent to which the information security strategy is meeting the needs of the business, and respond accordingly
b) direct information security activity overall by determining the organisation's overall risk appetite, endorsing the information security strategy and policy, and allocating sufficient resources
c) monitor the success of information security management arrangements, the extent of overall compliance with information security-related legislation and regulation, and overall implications of the changing threat landscape
d) communicate the status of high-level information security-related activity to external stakeholders, and inform information security management where corrective action is required.

> An organisation's information risk appetite may be subject to frequent change, often as a result of:
>
> - developments in the enterprise's business strategy
> - changes in stakeholder expectations
> - growth, mergers and acquisitions
> - increased competition or difficult economic circumstances
> - evolving threats to information
> - major incidents experienced
> - new product or service development.

SG1.1.6

The information security governance framework should require the governing body to monitor and review the organisation's information risk appetite on a regular basis.

SG1.1.7

The governing body should demonstrate their commitment by signing off the:

a) overall approach to information security governance
b) strategy for information security
c) information security assurance programme
d) information security policy
e) security architecture for the organisation.

Related content	ISF resources	
SG2 Security Governance Components	ISF Briefing: Information Security Governance Information Security Governance: Raising the game	

SECURITY GOVERNANCE

FUNDAMENTAL

SG1.2 Security Direction

Principle Control over information security should be provided by a high-level working group, committee or equivalent body, and managed by a senior executive.

Objective To provide a top-down management structure and mechanism for co-ordinating security activity and supporting the information security governance approach.

SG1.2.1

A full-time Chief Information Security Officer (or equivalent) should be appointed at executive management level, with overall responsibility for the organisation's information security programme.

> Ideally, the Chief Information Security Officer (CISO) should report either directly to the governing body, or via a senior member of an independent risk management function.

SG1.2.2

The Chief Information Security Officer should implement the organisation's overall approach to information security by:

a) developing and maintaining an information security strategy and policy that supports the security governance framework
b) focusing on information, business and compliance risks
c) concentrating on the protection of critical business processes and applications
d) protecting sensitive information from disclosure to unauthorised individuals
e) taking responsibility for developing and maintaining an information security architecture that provides a framework for the application of standard security controls throughout the organisation
f) ensuring that new information systems are developed securely.

SG1.2.3

The Chief Information Security Officer should adopt a business-focused approach to information security throughout the organisation by:

a) establishing a rapport with business and technical communities throughout the organisation to promote the value and importance of information security
b) organising the delivery of risk-based security solutions that address people, process and technology
c) developing information security staff to be 'advisors' that have expertise in delivering security solutions in a business context
d) delivering solutions to be implemented and owned by relevant business and IT functions.

SG1.2.4

A high-level working group, committee or equivalent body should be established, which:

a) co-ordinates information security activity across the organisation
b) is chaired by a member of the governing body (ie a board-level executive or equivalent)
c) meets on a regular basis (eg three or more times a year) and documents actions agreed at those meetings.

SG1.2.5

Membership of the high-level working group should include:

a) the Chief Information Security Officer
b) one or more business owners (ie heads of business units / departments or people in charge of particular business applications or processes)
c) representatives of specialist functions (eg legal, operational risk, internal audit, human resources and physical security)
d) the head of IT (or equivalent).

FUNDAMENTAL

SECURITY GOVERNANCE

SG1.2 Security Direction (continued)

SG1.2.6

The high-level working group should support the Chief Information Security Officer (or equivalent) in establishing the organisation's overall approach to information security by:

a) adopting an agile, business-oriented perspective (ie forward-looking, dynamic, and flexible enough to scale in size and respond to business demands and challenges)
b) reviewing the overall information security strategy, policy and architecture prior to sign-off by the governing body
c) promoting continuous improvement in information security throughout the organisation
d) emphasising the importance of information security to the organisation
e) ensuring information security is addressed in the organisation's business planning processes
f) embedding information security in the organisation's system development methodology.

SG1.2.7

The high-level working group should ensure the ongoing effectiveness and efficiency of information security arrangements by:

a) approving key decisions affecting the information security status of the organisation
b) reviewing threat intelligence and making recommendations to the governing body (where appropriate) on how to respond to new and changing threats
c) promoting timely decision-making about information risk by monitoring the organisation's exposure to current and emerging information security threats (eg the cyber environment, cloud adoption, external suppliers and consumerisation)
d) approving new information security policies, standards and procedures
e) monitoring security performance using information that is timely and accurate
f) promoting resilience against the potential and actual high business impacts of major incidents, such as those typically associated with targeted cyber attacks
g) reporting to stakeholders (eg about risks identified and progress of information security-related projects and initiatives).

Related content	ISF resources
CF1.2 Information Security Function	ISF Briefing: Information Security Governance
SI2.1 Security Monitoring	Role of Information Security in the Enterprise (RISE): Workshop Report
	Information Security Governance: Raising the game
	Cyber Security Strategies: Achieving cyber resilience

AREA SG2 – Security Governance Components

List of Topics
SG2.1 Information Security Strategy
SG2.2 Stakeholder Value Delivery
SG2.3 Information Security Assurance Programme

SG2.1 Information Security Strategy

Principle All information security projects and initiatives should be demonstrably aligned with the organisation's strategic objectives.

Objective To ensure that the information security programme contributes to the organisation's success.

SG2.1.1

Information security governance should be supported by a documented information security strategy that states how information security activity will be aligned with the organisation's overall objectives.

SG2.1.2

The information security strategy should support the organisation's overall objectives by outlining:

a) how information security will add value to the organisation (eg in terms of reduced cost and enhanced reputation) and protect the interests of stakeholders
b) the role of individual information security projects in enabling specific strategic initiatives
c) the importance of information security in addressing market and regulation-related risks; legal and compliance-related risks; and technology-related risks
d) a balanced approach to information security that takes into account the need to manage information risk (eg according to the organisation's risk appetite) and meet legal and regulatory compliance requirements
e) how information security activity will help establish resilience against high-impact incidents and ensure the continuity of business operations.

SG2.1.3

The information security strategy should help defend the organisation against threats by:

a) outlining how the information security programme will enable the organisation to maintain its strategic direction (eg by responding to the evolving threat landscape)
b) describing how individual information security projects will protect the organisation against the possible adverse business impact associated with specific strategic initiatives (such as new business ventures involving external parties via the Internet or cross-border business relationships)
c) incorporating information security incident management as a key element of the strategy.

SG2.1.4

The information security strategy should describe how the value of the information security function, and therefore its profile in the organisation, will be raised over time.

SPECIALISED

SECURITY GOVERNANCE

SG2.1   Information Security Strategy (continued)

SG2.1.5

The high-level working group or committee responsible for co-ordinating information security activity overall should:

a) review the information security strategy on a regular basis to ensure it continues to support delivery of the organisation's objectives
b) approve changes to the information security strategy where appropriate
c) ensure the current version of the information security strategy is disseminated throughout the organisation.

Related content	ISF resources
SG1.2 Security Direction	*Information Security Strategy: Workshop Report*
CF20.1 Business Continuity Strategy	*ISF Digest: Managing a Security Function*
SI2.1 Security Monitoring	*ISF Briefing: Information Security Governance*
Appendix A: The ISF Business Impact Reference Table	*Information Security Governance: Raising the game*
Appendix B: The ISF Threat List	

SECURITY GOVERNANCE

SPECIALISED

SG2.2 Stakeholder Value Delivery

Principle The organisation should implement processes to measure the value delivered by information security initiatives and report the results to all stakeholders.

Objective To ensure that the information security programme delivers value to stakeholders.

SG2.2.1

The governing body (eg members of the board or equivalent) should identify and record the requirements of stakeholders (such as shareholders, regulators, auditors and customers) for protecting their interests and delivering value through information security activity, and set direction accordingly.

SG2.2.2

The role of information security in enhancing the 'agility' of the organisation should be promoted by the governing body – for example by enabling initiatives that deliver value.

> Information security can play a leading role in removing barriers to added-value activities or services. Examples of information security as an enabler include:
>
> - two-factor authentication to enable secure online banking services to be delivered
> - public key infrastructure to help establish trust between organisations trading over the Internet
> - virtualisation, MDM and VPN technology to support consumerisation (or a Bring Your Own Device initiative).

SG2.2.3

The value delivered to stakeholders by key information security initiatives should be optimised by calculating return on security investment (ROSI) using recognised techniques that:

a) measure the likely financial return from the investment, taking into account financial benefits and the cost of security (typically the cost of controls in addition to the cost of incidents)
b) estimate the likely non-financial benefits resulting from the initiative, such as brand protection, favourable media coverage and increased customer satisfaction.

SG2.2.4

The value actually delivered to stakeholders by key information security initiatives should be:

a) recorded in a way that can be clearly understood by those without a detailed knowledge of information security, for example in a business-focused case study or financial benefits statement
b) reported to executive management.

SG2.2.5

To facilitate the most efficient use of existing information security-related assets throughout the organisation, an inventory of resources that can be used to reduce cost and add value should be maintained. These resources include:

a) information security specialists / staff, whose knowledge can be leveraged across different parts of the organisation
b) sources of information security knowledge available throughout the organisation
c) information security-related products and services (that have been purchased externally or developed internally).

SPECIALISED

SECURITY GOVERNANCE

SG2.2 Stakeholder Value Delivery (continued)

SG2.2.6

Information security-related initiatives (including recruitment and / or procurement) should be supported by a business case that:

a) clearly states how the project / initiative contributes to achievement of the organisation's strategic objectives, and delivery of the information security strategy
b) includes details regarding the need to recruit additional information security staff or purchase new information security-related products or services
c) is signed off by a business manager
d) provides an indication of the return on investment expected (ie the value expected to be delivered), in both tangible (financial) and intangible (non-financial) terms.

SG2.2.7

Business cases for information security-related initiatives (including recruitment and / or procurement) should:

a) indicate how the initiative will make best possible use of the information security resources available
b) explain why existing resources are insufficient.

SG2.2.8

Information security-related initiatives should be supported by a business case that is subject to an escalation procedure where:

a) alignment between the initiative and business objectives is not apparent
b) effective use of existing information security resources is not apparent.

Related content	ISF resources
SI2.1 Security Monitoring	ROSI – Return on Security Investment: Workshop Report
	RO$I – Return on Security Investment Tool
	Role of Information Security in the Enterprise (RISE): Workshop Report
	Information Security Governance: Raising the game

SECURITY GOVERNANCE

FUNDAMENTAL

SG2.3 Information Security Assurance Programme

Principle   The organisation should adopt a consistent and structured approach to information risk management.

Objective   To provide assurance that information risk is being adequately addressed.

SG2.3.1

The risk appetite of the organisation should be determined at governing body level using a structured technique, for example using a *Business Impact Reference Table* approach. Where the organisation has a devolved structure, or comprises highly independent business units, risk appetite should also be determined at business unit level.

> An organisation's 'risk appetite' relates to the maximum level of risk or harm that the organisation is prepared to accept in any given situation. It should be used to inform any decisions about information risk throughout the organisation. Risk appetite can be assessed using a tool such as the ISF's *Business Impact Reference Table (BIRT)*, where ratings associated with possible operational, financial, customer-related and employee-related impacts can be identified (see *Appendix A*). Executive management are typically involved in risk-based decisions to ensure the organisation's risk appetite is taken into consideration.

SG2.3.2

The risk appetite should be communicated to, and understood by, all individuals throughout the organisation who are responsible for making decisions about mitigating information risk.

SG2.3.3

An information security assurance programme should be established which states that:

a) security requirements are identified based on an information risk assessment and compliance requirements (legal / regulatory / contractual)
b) identified risks are treated in accordance with business requirements, and any accepted risks subjected to sign-off by the business
c) a suitable control framework is implemented
d) the effectiveness and efficiency of security arrangements is monitored and reported to the governing body.

SG2.3.4

The information security assurance programme should:

a) reflect the organisation's risk appetite
b) be consistent with the management and reporting of other types of risk in the organisation (for example, operational, financial, market)
c) be applied consistently throughout the organisation.

SG2.3.5

An enterprise-wide approach for monitoring the performance of the information security assurance programme should be agreed by executive management, which includes:

a) monitoring the security condition of the organisation based on quantitative techniques (eg using recognised performance indicators supported by information security metrics)
b) presentation of results against key performance indicators (KPIs) that can be clearly understood by those without a detailed knowledge of information security
c) details of any areas of major concern (eg key risks) that remain unaddressed
d) the requirement for exception reporting to the governing body and stakeholders, for example where the organisation experiences a major information security-related incident.

FUNDAMENTAL

SECURITY GOVERNANCE

SG2.3 Information Security Assurance Programme (continued)

SG2.3.6

The high-level working group or committee responsible for co-ordinating information security activity overall should review the effectiveness of performance monitoring techniques on a regular basis and make adjustments when and where necessary.

Related content	ISF resources
SR1 Information Risk Assessment	*ISF Briefing: Information Security Governance*
SR2 Compliance	*Information Security Assurance: An overview for implementing an information security assurance programme*
SI2 Security Performance	
Appendix A: The ISF Business Impact Reference Table	*ISF Briefing: Key Performance Indicators for Information Security*
	Information Risk Analysis Methodology (IRAM) – Business Impact Reference Table (BIRT)
	Information Security Governance: Raising the game

SECURITY REQUIREMENTS

Contents

SR1 Information Risk Assessment

SR1.1   Managing Information Risk Assessment
SR1.2   Information Risk Assessment Methodologies
SR1.3   Confidentiality Requirements
SR1.4   Integrity Requirements
SR1.5   Availability Requirements
SR1.6   Information Risk Treatment

SR2 Compliance

SR2.1   Legal and Regulatory Compliance
SR2.2   Information Privacy

SECURITY REQUIREMENTS   **FUNDAMENTAL**

AREA SR1 – Information Risk Assessment

List of Topics
SR1.1 Managing Information Risk Assessment
SR1.2 Information Risk Assessment Methodologies
SR1.3 Confidentiality Requirements
SR1.4 Integrity Requirements
SR1.5 Availability Requirements
SR1.6 Information Risk Treatment

SR1.1 Managing Information Risk Assessment

Principle Information risk assessments should be performed for target environments (eg critical business environments, business processes, business applications (including those under development), information systems and networks) on a regular basis.

Objective To enable individuals who are responsible for target environments to identify key information risks and determine the controls required to keep those risks within acceptable limits.

SR1.1.1

There should be formal, documented standards / procedures for performing information risk assessments, which apply across the organisation. Standards / procedures should cover the:

a) need for information risk assessments to be performed
b) types of target environment that should be assessed for information risks
c) circumstances in which information risk assessments should be performed
d) individuals who need to be involved, and their specific responsibilities
e) method of managing and responding to the results of information risk assessments.

> Information risk assessment (sometimes referred to as risk analysis) is the identification, measurement and prioritisation of risk.

SR1.1.2

Information risk assessments should be performed for target environments, including:

a) business environments (eg business administration offices, trading floors, call centres, warehouses and retail environments)
b) business processes (eg processing high value transactions, manufacturing goods, handling medical records)
c) business applications (including those under development)
d) information systems and networks that support critical business processes
e) specialist systems that are important to the organisation (eg systems that support or enable critical infrastructure, such as SCADA systems, process control PCs and embedded systems).

FUNDAMENTAL

SECURITY REQUIREMENTS

SR1.1   Managing Information Risk Assessment (continued)

SR1.1.3

Decision-makers (including: executive management; heads of business units / departments; and owners of business applications, information systems, networks and systems under development) should be aware of the need to carry out information risk assessments for target environments within the organisation.

> Traditional information risk assessment has typically focussed on business applications and information systems. However, in recent years some organisations have expanded the target of risk assessments to encompass environments such as business processes (eg processing high value transactions, manufacturing goods, handling medical records) or even business environments (eg business administration offices, trading floors, call centres, warehouses and retail environments). Accordingly, the term target environments has been used to refer to those business environments, business processes, business applications (including those under development), information systems and networks that are critical to the organisation.

SR1.1.4

Target environments should be subject to an information risk assessment:

a) at an early stage in their development
b) prior to significant change (at an early stage in the change management process)
c) when considering if they should be outsourced to an external party, such as a managed security service provider (eg through the cloud).

SR1.1.5

Information risk assessments should be performed regularly and prior to:

a) the introduction of major new technologies (eg mobile applications, HTML5, consumerisation, RFID and IPv6 networking)
b) using the services of external service providers (eg when outsourcing, offshoring or using cloud service providers)
c) permitting access to the organisation's critical systems (including those under development) by external individuals (eg consultants, contractors and employees of external parties)
d) granting access from external locations (eg employees' homes, external party premises or public places).

SR1.1.6

Information risk assessments should involve:

a) business owners (eg owners of business applications and business environments)
b) experts in risk assessment (eg a member of staff or an external party specialist who has significant experience as an information risk assessment practitioner)
c) IT specialists
d) key user representatives
e) information security specialists (eg a member of staff or an external party specialist who has significant experience as an information security practitioner).

SR1.1.7

Information risk assessments should be supported by reviewing intelligence information about:

a) emerging and changing threats (eg cybercrime, identity theft, spear phishing and cyber-espionage attacks)
b) known vulnerabilities and exploits associated with key operating systems, applications and other software (eg using vendor websites and mailing lists)
c) information security incidents affecting major organisations (including type of incidents, frequency of occurrence and preceding events)
d) impacts being experienced by major organisations (eg including those associated with brand, reputational, legal and financial impact).

SECURITY REQUIREMENTS

FUNDAMENTAL

SR1.1   Managing Information Risk Assessment (continued)

SR1.1.8

Results from information risk assessments conducted across the organisation should be:

a) reported to owners of business environments and executive management (or equivalent)
b) used to help determine programmes of work in information security (eg developing an information security management system (ISMS), performing remedial actions and establishing new security initiatives, such as consumerisation, digital rights management (DRM) and federated identity and access management (FIAM))
c) integrated with wider risk management activities (eg managing operational risk).

Related content	ISF resources
SR1.6 Information Risk Treatment	*Risk Convergence: Implications for Information Risk Management*
SI2.2 Information Risk Reporting	*Reporting Information Risk*
Appendix A: The ISF Business Impact Reference Table	*IRAM – Risk Analyst Workbench (RAW)*
Appendix B: The ISF Threat List	*ISF Briefing: Insider threats*
	Cyber Security Strategies: Achieving cyber resilience

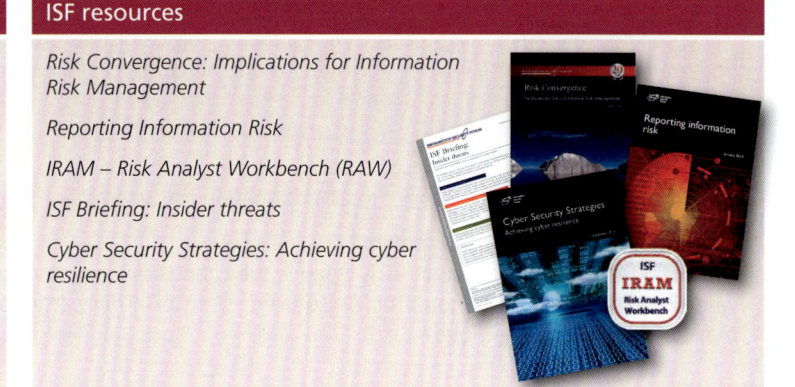

FUNDAMENTAL   SECURITY REQUIREMENTS

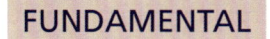

SR1.2 Information Risk Assessment Methodologies

Principle   Information risk assessments should be undertaken using structured methodologies.

Objective   To make information risk assessments consistent throughout the organisation, effective, easy to conduct, and produce a clear picture of key risks.

SR1.2.1

Information risks associated with the organisation's information and systems should be assessed using structured information risk assessment methodologies (eg the ISF's *Information Risk Analysis Methodology (IRAM)*).

SR1.2.2

Information risk assessment methodologies should be:

a) documented, and approved by executive management
b) performed consistently across the organisation
c) automated (eg using specialist software tools such as the ISF's *Risk Analyst Workbench (RAW)*)
d) reviewed regularly to ensure that they meet business needs
e) applicable to business environments, business processes and systems of various sizes and types
f) easy to understand by non-security specialists (eg business representatives).

SR1.2.3

Information risk assessment methodologies should require all risk assessments to have a clearly defined scope.

SR1.2.4

Information risk assessments should determine risk by assessing:

a) the potential level of business impact associated with the business environment, business process, business information and systems, should business information be compromised
b) the likelihood of business information being compromised (ie by assessing levels of threat and vulnerability).

SR1.2.5

The likelihood of business information being compromised should be assessed by evaluating threats to the confidentiality, integrity and availability of critical systems, including:

a) deliberate threats (eg carrying out denial of service attacks, malware, installing unauthorised software, disclosing sensitive information to unauthorised individuals or organisations for financial gain and misusing systems to commit fraud)
b) accidental threats (eg information leakage when sending emails, exchanging electronic documents and sharing paper-based documents, making mistakes in data input, inadvertently deleting database records and failing to back-up information)
c) threats posed by internal staff (the insider threat)
d) threats posed by external parties / individuals
e) man-made disasters (eg loss of power, system or software malfunctions, fire or explosions)
f) natural disasters (eg hurricane, storm or flood damage).

SECURITY REQUIREMENTS

FUNDAMENTAL

SR1.2 Information Risk Assessment Methodologies (continued)

SR1.2.6

Vulnerabilities that increase the likelihood of business information being compromised should be assessed by performing:

a) a control analysis (ie an assessment of the weaknesses of existing controls in an information system, such as lack of information classification, poorly protected portable storage devices or unprotected critical desktop applications)
b) an environment analysis (ie an analysis of the external macro-environment in which an information system operates (eg using the PLEST model covering political, legal and regulatory, economic, socio-cultural and technological factors))
c) a system analysis (ie an analysis of the key characteristics of an information system (eg Internet connectivity, scale and complexity of system, number of transactions))
d) technical analysis (ie an analysis of the technical weaknesses inherent in an information system, such as configuration errors, operating system weaknesses and known software bugs).

SR1.2.7

Vulnerabilities should be assessed for each stage of the information lifecycle, including:

a) creation (eg lack of security requirements, classifications and centralised control)
b) processing (eg excessive privileges, user inexperience and unapproved use of equipment)
c) transmission (eg lack of encryption or restrictions on distribution of information such as email)
d) storage (eg storing sensitive files on mobile devices, consumer devices and unencrypted external hard disk drives)
e) destruction (eg poor disposal practices or accidental destruction of critical information).

SR1.2.8

Information risk assessments should take into account factors that may influence the likelihood of threats materialising, including:

a) service level agreements (SLAs) associated with business applications, information systems and networks
b) the different formats of information (including paper documents, electronic files, verbal communications and physical objects)
c) information classification requirements
d) previous risk assessments conducted on the information or system being assessed
e) incidents previously experienced (including frequency and magnitude)
f) supporting technology that uses makes / models of hardware and software that are proprietary, obsolete or unsupported.

SR1.2.9

Information risk assessments should take into account factors related to business operations, including:

a) compliance requirements (eg with legislation, regulation, contractual terms, industry standards and internal policies)
b) objectives of the organisation (eg those identified in the organisation's business and security strategies)
c) characteristics of the operating environment of information and systems being assessed (eg number and diversity of users, their level of access to information, their attitude to handling business information, resistance to control and influence by the organisation)
d) the physical locations associated with the target environments (eg conventional offices within the organisation, remote parts of the organisation such as satellite offices, industrial environments and customer facing locations such as retail stores and airports)
e) the organisation's presence in and – dependence on – cyberspace (eg brand, reputation and market share).

FUNDAMENTAL

SECURITY REQUIREMENTS

SR1.2   Information Risk Assessment Methodologies (continued)

SR1.2.10

Information risk assessments should ensure that the results of assessments are documented and include:

a) a clear identification of key risks
b) an assessment of the level of potential business impact and likelihood of threats materialising
c) a list of risk treatment options (eg accepting risks, avoiding risks, transferring risks or mitigating risks by applying security controls).

SR1.2.11

The results of information risk assessments (including risk treatment options and any identified residual risk) should be:

a) communicated to the relevant owner
b) signed off by the relevant owner
c) compared with information risk assessments conducted in other areas of the organisation
d) presented in a format that is clear and understandable to the business (ie written in business language).

Related content	ISF resources
SR1.6 Information Risk Treatment	*Risk Convergence: Implications for Information Risk Management*
SI2.2 Information Risk Reporting	*Reporting Information Risk*
Appendix A: The ISF Business Impact Reference Table	*IRAM – Risk Analyst Workbench (RAW)*
Appendix B: The ISF Threat List	*Cyber Security Strategies: Achieving cyber resilience*

SECURITY REQUIREMENTS **FUNDAMENTAL**

SR1.3 Confidentiality Requirements

Principle The business impact of unauthorised disclosure of business information associated with target environments should be assessed.

Objective To document and agree the confidentiality requirements (the need for information to be kept secret or private within a predetermined group) for information associated with target environments (eg critical business environments, business processes, business applications (including those under development) and information systems).

SR1.3.1

Business requirements should take account of the need to protect the confidentiality of information.

SR1.3.2

The analysis of confidentiality requirements should determine how the disclosure of sensitive information could have a financial impact on the organisation in terms of:

a) loss of sales, orders or contracts (eg sales opportunities missed, orders not taken or contracts not signed)
b) loss of tangible assets (eg through fraud, theft of money or lost interest)
c) penalties / legal liabilities (eg through breach of legal, regulatory or contractual obligations)
d) unforeseen costs (eg recovery costs, uninsured losses or increased insurance)
e) depressed share price (eg sudden or prolonged loss of share value, or random share value fluctuation).

SR1.3.3

The analysis of confidentiality requirements should determine how the disclosure of sensitive information could have an operational impact on the organisation in terms of:

a) loss of management control (eg impaired decision-making, inability to monitor financial positions, or process management failure)
b) loss of competitiveness (eg repetitive production line failures, degraded customer service or introduction of new pricing policies)
c) new ventures held up (eg delayed new products, delayed entry into new markets or delayed mergers / acquisitions)
d) breach of operating standards (eg contravention of regulatory, quality or safety standards).

SR1.3.4

The analysis of confidentiality requirements should determine how the disclosure of sensitive information could have a customer-related impact on the organisation in terms of:

a) delayed deliveries to customers or clients (eg failure to meet product delivery deadlines or failure to complete contracts on time)
b) loss of customers or clients (eg customer / client defection to competitors or withdrawal of preferred supplier status by customer / client)
c) loss of confidence by key institutions (eg adverse criticism by investors, regulators, customers or suppliers)
d) damage to reputation (eg confidential financial information published in media or compromising internal memos broadcast by media).

SR1.3.5

The analysis of confidentiality requirements should determine how the disclosure of sensitive information could have an employee-related impact on the organisation in terms of:

a) reduction in staff morale / productivity (eg reduced efficiency, lost time or job losses)
b) injury or death.

FUNDAMENTAL

SECURITY REQUIREMENTS

SR1.3 Confidentiality Requirements (continued)

Related content

SR1.6 Information Risk Treatment

SI2.2 Information Risk Reporting

Appendix A: The ISF Business Impact Reference Table

ISF resources

Practical Approaches to Information Classification: Workshop Report

Information Risk Analysis Methodology (IRAM) - Business Impact Assessment

SECURITY REQUIREMENTS **FUNDAMENTAL**

SR1.4 Integrity Requirements

Principle The business impact of the accidental corruption or deliberate manipulation of business information associated with target environments should be assessed.

Objective To document and agree the integrity requirements (the need for information to be valid, accurate and complete) for information associated with target environments (eg critical business environments, business processes, business applications (including those under development) or information systems).

SR1.4.1

Business requirements should take account of the need to protect the integrity of information.

SR1.4.2

The analysis of integrity requirements should determine how the accidental corruption or deliberate manipulation of information could have a financial impact on the organisation in terms of:

a) loss of sales, orders or contracts (eg sales opportunities missed, orders not taken or contracts not signed)
b) loss of tangible assets (eg through fraud, theft of money or lost interest)
c) penalties / legal liabilities (eg through breach of legal, regulatory or contractual obligations)
d) unforeseen costs (eg recovery costs, uninsured losses or increased insurance)
e) depressed share price (eg sudden or prolonged loss of share value, or random share value fluctuation).

SR1.4.3

The analysis of integrity requirements should determine how the accidental corruption or deliberate manipulation of information could have an operational impact on the organisation in terms of:

a) loss of management control (eg impaired decision-making, inability to monitor financial positions, or process management failure)
b) loss of competitiveness (eg repetitive production line failures, degraded customer service or introduction of new pricing policies)
c) new ventures held up (eg delayed new products, delayed entry into new markets or delayed mergers / acquisitions)
d) breach of operating standards (eg contravention of regulatory, quality or safety standards).

SR1.4.4

The analysis of integrity requirements should determine how the accidental corruption or deliberate manipulation of information could have a customer-related impact on the organisation in terms of:

a) delayed deliveries to customers or clients (eg failure to meet product delivery deadlines or failure to complete contracts on time)
b) loss of customers or clients (eg customer / client defection to competitors or withdrawal of preferred supplier status by customer / client)
c) loss of confidence by key institutions (eg adverse criticism by investors, regulators, customers or suppliers)
d) damage to reputation (eg confidential financial information published in media or compromising internal memos broadcast by media).

SR1.4.5

The analysis of integrity requirements should determine how the accidental corruption or deliberate manipulation of information could have an employee-related impact on the organisation in terms of:

a) reduction in staff morale / productivity (eg reduced efficiency, lost time or job losses)
b) injury or death.

FUNDAMENTAL

SECURITY REQUIREMENTS

SR1.4 Integrity Requirements (continued)

Related content

SR1.6 Information Risk Treatment

SI2.2 Information Risk Reporting

Appendix A: The ISF Business Impact Reference Table

ISF resources

Information Risk Analysis Methodology (IRAM)
- Business Impact Assessment

SECURITY REQUIREMENTS **FUNDAMENTAL**

SR1.5 Availability Requirements

Principle The business impact of business information associated with target environments being unavailable for any length of time should be assessed.

Objective To document and agree the availability requirements (the need for information to be accessible when required) for information associated with target environments (eg critical business environments, business processes, business applications (including those under development) or information systems).

SR1.5.1

Business requirements should take account of the need to protect the availability of information.

SR1.5.2

The analysis of availability requirements should determine how a loss of availability of information could have a financial impact on the organisation in terms of:

a) loss of sales, orders or contracts (eg sales opportunities missed, orders not taken or contracts not signed)
b) loss of tangible assets (eg through fraud, theft of money or lost interest)
c) penalties / legal liabilities (eg through breach of legal, regulatory or contractual obligations)
d) unforeseen costs (eg recovery costs, uninsured losses or increased insurance)
e) depressed share price (eg sudden or prolonged loss of share value, or random share value fluctuation).

SR1.5.3

The analysis of availability requirements should determine how a loss of availability of information could have an operational impact on the organisation in terms of:

a) loss of management control (eg impaired decision-making, inability to monitor financial positions, or process management failure)
b) loss of competitiveness (eg repetitive production line failures, degraded customer service or introduction of new pricing policies)
c) new ventures held up (eg delayed new products, delayed entry into new markets or delayed mergers / acquisitions)
d) breach of operating standards (eg contravention of regulatory, quality or safety standards).

SR1.5.4

The analysis of availability requirements should determine how a loss of availability of information could have a customer-related impact on the organisation in terms of:

a) delayed deliveries to customers or clients (eg failure to meet product delivery deadlines or failure to complete contracts on time)
b) loss of customers or clients (eg customer / client defection to competitors or withdrawal of preferred supplier status by customer / client)
c) loss of confidence by key institutions (eg adverse criticism by investors, regulators, customers or suppliers)
d) damage to reputation (eg confidential financial information published in media or compromising internal memos broadcast by media).

SR1.5.5

The analysis of availability requirements should determine how a loss of availability of information could have an employee-related impact on the organisation in terms of:

a) reduction in staff morale / productivity (eg reduced efficiency, lost time or job losses)
b) injury or death.

FUNDAMENTAL

SECURITY REQUIREMENTS

SR1.5 Availability Requirements (continued)

SR1.5.6

Business requirements should take into account the critical timescale of the application (ie the timescale beyond which a loss of service would be unacceptable to the organisation).

Related content	ISF resources
SR1.6 Information Risk Treatment SI2.2 Information Risk Reporting Appendix A: The ISF Business Impact Reference Table	*Information Risk Analysis Methodology (IRAM)* *- Business Impact Assessment*

SECURITY REQUIREMENTS   **FUNDAMENTAL**

SR1.6   Information Risk Treatment

Principle   Information risks should be treated in accordance with business requirements and the approach taken approved by the relevant business owner.

Objective   To help ensure information risks are treated (eg accepted, avoided, transferred or mitigated) in a suitable manner.

SR1.6.1

Risks identified as part of an information risk assessment should be treated according to the organisation's security requirements (risk appetite), taking into account business circumstances and level of threat – and approved by executive management.

SR1.6.2

Options to treat information risk (risk treatment) should include:

a) accepting risks (eg business owners take responsibility for accepting the business consequences and signing off the risks)
b) avoiding risks (eg by cancelling a high risk project or deciding not to pursue a particular business initiative)
c) transferring risks (eg by sharing the risks with an external party or by taking out insurance)
d) mitigating the risk, typically by applying appropriate security controls (eg malware protection, digital rights management or data leakage protection (DLP)).

SR1.6.3

Accepting information risks (ie the business owner takes responsibility for accepting the business consequences) should include:

a) consideration of predefined limits for levels of risk (eg quantitative values such as financial thresholds or qualitative values such as a ratings scale of very low to very high)
b) approval and sign-off by a senior individual with authority, such as a representative of executive management (eg senior executive or equivalent)
c) acknowledging that risk is still present and management will accept the consequences if incidents occur
d) recording them in a central register (where they can be reviewed and compared with other risks and related treatment decisions).

SR1.6.4

Avoiding information risks should involve a decision by a senior individual to cancel or postpone a particular project or initiative that introduces the risk (eg adopting a particular technology, allowing external access, offering products in a new market (jurisdiction) or providing a new service to customers).

SR1.6.5

Transferring information risks should involve:

a) sharing the risks with external parties such as joint venture partners, outsource providers or cloud service providers (eg sharing financial investment and resources)
b) obtaining insurance against particular types of incident occurring for high risk activities.

FUNDAMENTAL

SECURITY REQUIREMENTS

SR1.6 Information Risk Treatment (continued)

SR1.6.6

Applying security controls to mitigate information risk should include:

a) applying (or mapping to) a reputable security control framework (eg ISO/IEC 27002, COBIT, NIST SP 800-53 and ITIL)
b) evaluating the strengths and weaknesses of security controls
c) selecting security controls that will reduce the likelihood of serious information security incidents occurring – and reducing their impact if they do occur
d) selecting security controls that will satisfy relevant compliance requirements (eg those outlined in the Sarbanes-Oxley Act, legislation associated with EU Directives 2006/43/EC and 2006/46/EC, the Payment Card Industry Data Security Standard (PCI DSS), Basel III, data privacy requirements and anti-money laundering requirements)
e) assessing the costs of implementing security controls (eg costs associated with: design, purchase, implementation and monitoring of the controls; hardware and software; training; overheads, such as facilities; and consultancy fees)
f) identifying specialised security controls required by particular business environments (eg data encryption or strong authentication)
g) identifying and obtaining sign-off for any residual risk (ie the proportion of risk that still remains after selected controls have been implemented).

SR1.6.7

Information risk treatment actions (including any residual risk) should be detailed in a risk treatment plan, which is:

a) communicated to the relevant owner
b) signed off by the relevant owner and at least one representative of executive management (eg senior executive, head of business unit / department or equivalent)
c) compared with information risk assessments conducted in other areas of the organisation.

Related content	ISF resources
SR1.1 Managing Information Risk Assessment	Reporting Information Risk
SR1.2 Information Risk Assessment Methodologies	Information Security Assurance: An overview for implementing an information security assurance programme
SI2.2 Information Risk Reporting	*Information Risk Analysis Methodology (IRAM) - Control Selection*

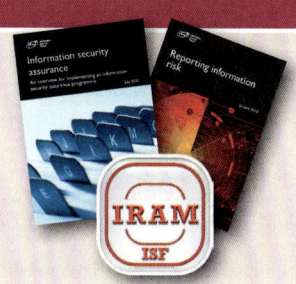

SECURITY REQUIREMENTS   **FUNDAMENTAL**

AREA SR2 – Compliance

List of Topics
SR2.1 Legal and Regulatory Compliance
SR2.2 Information Privacy

SR2.1 Legal and Regulatory Compliance

Principle A process should be established to identify and interpret the information security implications of relevant laws and regulations.

Objective To comply with laws and regulations affecting information security.

SR2.1.1

Legal and regulatory requirements affecting information security should be recognised by:

a) executive management
b) business owners
c) the head of information security (or equivalent)
d) representatives of other security-related functions (eg legal, operational risk, internal audit, insurance, human resources, and physical security).

SR2.1.2

A process should be established for ensuring compliance with relevant legal and regulatory requirements affecting information security across the organisation, which covers:

a) information security-specific legislation (eg computer crimes, encryption export, data breach notification and e-discovery)
b) general legislation which has security implications (eg data privacy, investigatory powers, intellectual property and human rights)
c) regulation (eg financial regulation, anti-money laundering, corporate governance, healthcare and industry-specific regulations such as the Payment Card Industry Data Security Standard (PCI DSS)).

SR2.1.3

The compliance process should enable decision-makers to:

a) discover laws and regulations that affect information security (eg by using the services of law firms and industry watchdog groups that provide updates on new regulations, changes to existing regulations and results of litigation (case law or precedent))
b) interpret the information security implications of discovered laws and regulations
c) identify potential legal / regulatory non-compliance (eg performing a risk assessment of compliance with laws and regulations)
d) address areas of potential legal / regulatory non-compliance.

SR2.1.4

The compliance process should be documented, signed off by executive management, and kept up-to-date.

FUNDAMENTAL

SR2.1 Legal and Regulatory Compliance (continued)

SR2.1.5

A review of compliance with legal and regulatory requirements that affect information security should:

a) be performed regularly or when new legislation or regulatory requirements come into effect
b) involve representatives from key areas of the organisation (eg executive management, business owners, legal department, IT management, and the information security function)
c) result in the update of information security standards / procedures to accommodate any necessary changes.

Related content	ISF resources
SI2.3 Monitoring Information Security Compliance	*Monitoring Compliance: Workshop Report*

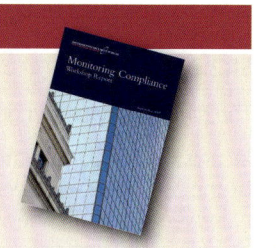

SECURITY REQUIREMENTS   FUNDAMENTAL

SR2.2 Information Privacy

Principle Responsibility for managing information privacy should be established and security controls for handling personally identifiable information (ie information that can be used to identify an individual person) applied.

Objective To prevent information about individuals being used in an inappropriate manner, and ensure compliance with legal and regulatory requirements for information privacy.

SR2.2.1

A high-level working group, committee or equivalent body should be established to be responsible for managing information privacy issues, and an individual appointed to co-ordinate information privacy activity (eg a Chief Privacy Officer or a Data Protection Manager).

SR2.2.2

The high-level working group should be aware of:

a) privacy-related legislation and regulation with which the organisation needs to comply
b) the location(s) of personally identifiable information held about individuals (eg application and database servers, computer devices, consumer devices and portable storage devices)
c) how and when personally identifiable information (ie information that can be used to identify an individual person) is used.

SR2.2.3

An information privacy programme should be established which includes:

a) identifying individuals (or a group of individuals) within the organisation who are responsible for implementing the programme
b) establishing an awareness programme to make staff and external parties (eg customers, clients and suppliers) aware of the importance of information privacy (or integrating into existing awareness campaigns)
c) performing privacy assessments against critical business processes and critical business applications across the organisation to identify privacy-related risks
d) undertaking privacy audits to determine the level of compliance with relevant legislation and internal policies.

SR2.2.4

There should be a documented information privacy policy that covers the:

a) acceptable use of personally identifiable information (ie information that can be used to identify an individual person)
b) rights of individuals about whom personally identifiable information is held
c) legal and regulatory requirements for privacy
d) need for privacy assessments, awareness and compliance programmes
e) technical controls (including privacy enhancing technologies (PETs)).

FUNDAMENTAL

SECURITY REQUIREMENTS

SR2.2 Information Privacy (continued)

SR2.2.5

The information privacy policy should require that where personally identifiable information is stored or processed, there should be a process to ensure that it is:

a) classified and labelled (eg as personal or personally identifiable information (PII))
b) adequate, relevant and not excessive for the purposes for which it is collected
c) accurate (ie recorded correctly and kept up-to-date)
d) kept confidential (ie protected against unauthorised disclosure)
e) processed fairly and legally, and used only for specified, explicit and legitimate purposes
f) held in a format that permits identification of individuals for no longer than is necessary
g) only provided to external parties that can demonstrate compliance with legal and regulatory requirements for handling personally identifiable information
h) retrievable in the event of a legitimate request for access (eg a subject access request under UK Data Protection law).

SR2.2.6

Individuals about whom personally identifiable information is held (eg the 'data subject' according to the EU Directive on Data Protection) should:

a) have their approval sought before this information is collected, stored, processed or disclosed to external parties
b) be informed of who is collecting this information, how this information will be used, allowed to check its accuracy and be able to have their records corrected or removed
c) have the ability to opt-out of the collection and disclosure of this information (eg to external parties)
d) have a method available to them to hold the organisation accountable for following information privacy principles (ie those common to the majority of privacy-related legislation).

SR2.2.7

Personally identifiable information should be:

a) handled in accordance with relevant legislation (eg the EU Directive on Data Protection and the US Health Insurance Portability and Accountability Act (HIPAA))
b) protected throughout its lifecycle (ie through creation, processing, storage, transmission and destruction).

SR2.2.8

Technical controls (often referred to as privacy enhancing technologies (PETs)) should be used to help protect privacy-related information, including:

a) encryption to prevent unauthorised disclosure
b) data masking (also known as data obfuscation, data de-identification, data depersonalisation, data scrubbing, and data scrambling), which involves concealing parts of information (eg names, addresses, social security numbers and credit card numbers) when being stored or transmitted
c) tokenisation, which substitutes valid information (eg database fields, records) with random information and provides authorised access to this information via the use of tokens
d) protecting privacy-related metadata (eg document attributes or descriptive information that may contain personal information such as the name of the person who last updated a file).

SR2.2.9

A method of dealing with data privacy breaches should be established, which includes:

a) identifying when a data privacy breach occurs (typically by monitoring event logs or using intrusion detection and information leakage protection tools)
b) responding to a data privacy breach (typically as part of the organisation's information security incident management process).

SECURITY REQUIREMENTS

FUNDAMENTAL

SR2.2 Information Privacy (continued)

Related content
CF3.1 Information Classification

ISF resources
Solving the Data Privacy Puzzle: Achieving Compliance

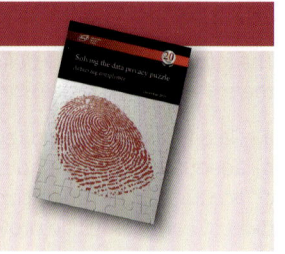

CONTROL FRAMEWORK

Contents

CF1 Security Policy and Organisation

CF1.1 Information Security Policy
CF1.2 Information Security Function

CF2 Human Resource Security

CF2.1 Staff Agreements
CF2.2 Security Awareness Programme
CF2.3 Security Awareness Messages
CF2.4 Security Education / Training
CF2.5 Roles and Responsibilities

CF3 Asset Management

CF3.1 Information Classification
CF3.2 Document Management
CF3.3 Sensitive Physical Information
CF3.4 Asset Register

CF4 Business Applications

CF4.1 Application Protection
CF4.2 Browser-based Application Protection
CF4.3 Information Validation

CF5 Customer Access

CF5.1 Customer Access Arrangements
CF5.2 Customer Contracts
CF5.3 Customer Connections

CF6 Access Management

CF6.1 Access Control
CF6.2 User Authorisation
CF6.3 Access Control Mechanisms
CF6.4 Access Control Mechanisms – Password
CF6.5 Access Control Mechanisms – Token
CF6.6 Access Control Mechanisms – Biometric
CF6.7 Sign-on Process

CF7 System Management

CF7.1 Computer and Network Installations
CF7.2 Server Configuration
CF7.3 Virtual Servers
CF7.4 Network Storage Systems
CF7.5 Back-up
CF7.6 Change Management
CF7.7 Service Level Agreements

Control Framework Contents (continued)

CF8 Technical Security Infrastructure

CF8.1	Security Architecture
CF8.2	Identity and Access Management
CF8.3	Critical Infrastructure
CF8.4	Cryptographic Solutions
CF8.5	Cryptographic Key Management
CF8.6	Public Key Infrastructure
CF8.7	Information Leakage Protection
CF8.8	Digital Rights Management

CF9 Network Management

CF9.1	Network Device Configuration
CF9.2	Physical Network Management
CF9.3	External Network Connections
CF9.4	Firewalls
CF9.5	Remote Maintenance
CF9.6	Wireless Access
CF9.7	Voice over IP (VoIP) Networks
CF9.8	Telephony and Conferencing

CF10 Threat and Vulnerability Management

CF10.1	Patch Management
CF10.2	Malware Awareness
CF10.3	Malware Protection Software
CF10.4	Security Event Logging
CF10.5	System / Network Monitoring
CF10.6	Intrusion Detection

CF11 Incident Management

CF11.1	Information Security Incident Management
CF11.2	Cybercrime Attacks
CF11.3	Emergency Fixes
CF11.4	Forensic Investigations

CF12 Local Environments

CF12.1	Local Environment Profile
CF12.2	Local Security Co-ordination
CF12.3	Office Equipment

CF13 Desktop Applications

CF13.1	Inventory of Desktop Applications
CF13.2	Protection of Spreadsheets
CF13.3	Protection of Databases
CF13.4	Desktop Application Development

CF14 Mobile Computing

CF14.1	Remote Environments
CF14.2	Mobile Device Configuration
CF14.3	Mobile Device Connectivity
CF14.4	Portable Storage Devices
CF14.5	Consumer Devices

CF15 Electronic Communications

CF15.1	Email
CF15.2	Instant Messaging

Control Framework Contents (continued)

CF16 External Supplier Management

CF16.1   External Supplier Management Process
CF16.2   Hardware / Software Acquisition
CF16.3   Outsourcing
CF16.4   Cloud Computing Policy
CF16.5   Cloud Service Contracts

CF17 System Development Management

CF17.1   System Development Methodology
CF17.2   System Development Environments
CF17.3   Quality Assurance

CF18 Systems Development Lifecycle

CF18.1   Specifications of Requirements
CF18.2   System Design
CF18.3   System Build
CF18.4   Systems Testing
CF18.5   Security Testing
CF18.6   System Promotion Criteria
CF18.7   Installation Process
CF18.8   Post-implementation Review

CF19 Physical and Environmental Security

CF19.1   Physical Protection
CF19.2   Power Supplies
CF19.3   Hazard Protection

CF20 Business Continuity

CF20.1   Business Continuity Strategy
CF20.2   Business Continuity Programme
CF20.3   Resilience
CF20.4   Crisis Management
CF20.5   Business Continuity Planning
CF20.6   Business Continuity Arrangements
CF20.7   Business Continuity Testing

CONTROL FRAMEWORK

FUNDAMENTAL

AREA CF1 – Security Policy and Organisation

List of Topics
CF1.1   Information Security Policy
CF1.2   Information Security Function

CF1.1   Information Security Policy

Principle   A comprehensive, documented information security policy should be produced and communicated to all individuals with access to the organisation's information and systems.

Objective   To document the governing body's direction on and commitment to information security, and communicate it to all relevant individuals.

CF1.1.1

There should be a documented information security policy, ratified at board level, that applies across the organisation. There should be an individual (or a group of individuals) responsible for maintaining the policy.

CF1.1.2

The information security policy should define information security, associated responsibilities and the information security principles to be followed by all staff.

CF1.1.3

The information security policy should require that:

a) information is classified in a way that indicates its importance to the organisation
b) owners (typically the people in charge of business processes that are dependent on information and systems) are appointed for all critical information and systems
c) important information and systems be subject to an information risk assessment on a regular basis or before a major change
d) staff are made aware of information security
e) compliance with software licenses and with other legal, regulatory and contractual obligations is met
f) breaches of the information security policy and suspected information security weaknesses are reported
g) tampering with evidence in the case of information security incidents that may require forensic investigation is prohibited
h) information is protected in terms of its requirements for confidentiality, integrity and availability.

CF1.1.4

The information security policy should be:

a) aligned with other high-level policies (eg those relating to human resources, health and safety, finance and information technology)
b) communicated to all staff and external individuals (eg consultants, contractors and employees of external parties) with access to the organisation's information or systems
c) reviewed regularly according to a defined review process
d) revised to take account of changing circumstances (eg new threats, vulnerabilities and risks, reorganisation of the organisation, changes to contractual, legal and regulatory requirements, or changes to the technical infrastructure).

FUNDAMENTAL

CONTROL FRAMEWORK

CF1.1 Information Security Policy (continued)

CF1.1.5

The organisation's information security policy should be supported by detailed acceptable usage policies (AUPs) that define the way in which individuals are expected to use technology within the organisation.

> An acceptable usage policy (AUP) typically defines the organisation's rules on how an individual (eg an employee or contractor) can use technology, including software, computer equipment and connectivity.

CF1.1.6

Acceptable usage policies should clearly state:

a) the ownership and purpose of technology provided to individuals
b) expected security-related behaviour of individuals (eg using strong passwords and encrypting files)
c) unacceptable behaviour (eg sending or copying sensitive information to unauthorised individuals or storing sensitive information on non-corporate devices)
d) permitted use of technology (eg Internet browsing for business purposes, VoIP, wireless networking and personal Internet browsing at predetermined times of the day)
e) prohibited use of technology (eg non-corporate web browsers, unauthorised connections to public VoIP services or connecting unapproved computers to the corporate network)
f) details of any monitoring activities to be performed (eg browsing of Internet websites or the use of VoIP) to detect malicious activity or accidental leakage of business information.

CF1.1.7

Acceptable usage policies should be:

a) documented and supported by guidelines for acceptable use, which provide additional information for users
b) approved by an appropriate business representative with authority
c) communicated to relevant individuals with access to the organisation's information, software, equipment and connectivity
d) easily accessible by individuals (eg by locating copies on business users' computers and displaying them on a dedicated area of the corporate intranet, portal or shared database)
e) kept up-to-date
f) signed off by executive management.

CF1.1.8

A method should be established to:

a) enable individuals to confirm their acceptance of and compliance with the information security policy and supporting policies when they are issued and updated (eg by displaying a confirmation dialogue box as part of the login process for their computer, when starting business applications and upon accessing the organisation's intranet)
b) assess compliance with the information security policy and supporting policies on a regular basis (eg in the form of audits).

CF1.1.9

A method should be established to ensure individuals understand that disciplinary actions may be taken against them if they violate the information security policy and supporting acceptable usage policies.

Related content	ISF resources
CF2.2 Security Awareness Programme	Information Security Policy: Overview
CF2.3 Security Awareness Messages	Protecting Information in the End User Environment
CF14.5 Consumer Devices	

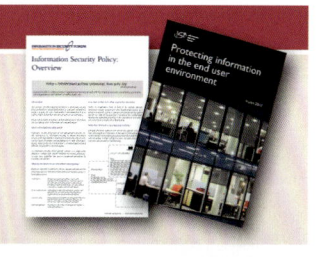

CONTROL FRAMEWORK **FUNDAMENTAL**

CF1.2 Information Security Function

Principle A specialist information security function should be established, which has responsibility for promoting information security throughout the organisation.

Objective To ensure good practice in information security is applied effectively and consistently throughout the organisation.

CF1.2.1

The organisation should be supported by an information security function (or equivalent), which has responsibility for promoting good practice in information security throughout the organisation.

CF1.2.2

The information security function should support the organisation's information security policy by:

a) assisting in the development and maintenance of an information security strategy
b) developing information security standards / procedures and guidelines
c) defining a set of security services (eg identity services, authentication services, cryptographic services), which provide a coherent range of security capabilities
d) co-ordinating information security across the organisation
e) monitoring the effectiveness of information security arrangements (eg using tools such as the ISF's *Return on Security Investment (RO$I)* and *Security Healthcheck*)
f) overseeing the investigation of information security incidents.

CF1.2.3

The information security function should represent a 'centre of excellence' for information security by:

a) providing expert advice on all aspects of information security (including information risk assessment, identity and access management, protecting information in the local environment, malware protection and information security incident management)
b) running an ongoing, continuous programme of information security awareness and developing security skills for staff throughout the organisation
c) incorporating information security requirements into documented agreements (eg contracts or service level agreements)
d) providing support for protecting the information associated with the organisation's critical infrastructure (eg equipment for operations, telecommunications, utilities and buildings)
e) evaluating the security implications of specialised business initiatives (eg outsourcing, electronic commerce initiatives and information exchange)
f) taking part in intelligence sharing activities and collaborating with 'cyber-partners' (eg ISPs, security analysts, government and industry regulators, law enforcement and intelligence agencies).

CF1.2.4

The information security function should provide proactive support for:

a) information risk assessment activities
b) classification of information and systems according to their importance to the organisation
c) the use of cryptography
d) important security-related projects
e) major IT projects with security requirements
f) the development of the organisation's business continuity programme
g) security audits.

FUNDAMENTAL

CONTROL FRAMEWORK

CF1.2   Information Security Function (continued)

CF1.2.5

The information security function should monitor current, new and emerging:

a) general business trends (eg prospects for growth, internationalisation, merger / acquisitions, joint ventures, divestitures, consumerisation, outsourcing and cloud computing)
b) technological developments (eg web-based technology, virtualisation, encryption standards, and IPv6)
c) information security solutions (eg federated identity and access management (FIAM), digital rights management (DRM) and intrusion prevention)
d) industry / international information security-related standards (eg ISO/IEC 27001 and 27002, COBIT, NIST SP 800-53 and ITIL)
e) legislation or regulations related to information security (eg those concerning data breach notification, data privacy, digital signatures and industry-specific standards such as Basel III and the Payment Card Industry Data Security Standard (PCI DSS)).

CF1.2.6

The information security function should gather and analyse internal and external intelligence information about:

a) emerging and changing threats (eg cybercrime, identity theft, spear phishing and cyber-espionage attacks)
b) known vulnerabilities and exploits associated with key operating systems, applications and other software (eg using vendor websites and mailing lists)
c) information security incidents affecting major organisations (including type of incidents, frequency of occurrence and preceding events)
d) impacts being experienced by major organisations (eg including those associated with brand, reputational, legal and financial impact).

> Intelligence information is typically obtained from a broad range of sources including: service providers (including Internet, outsource and cloud providers); government, cyber-intelligence and law enforcement agencies; industry groups and regulators; security analysts and experts in computer / software companies; and organisations in the supply chain.

CF1.2.7

The information security function should be adequately resourced in terms of:

a) the number of staff
b) their range and level of skills (eg by achieving professional security certifications, such as those provided by (ISC)^2, ISACA, IISP, ISSA and SANS)
c) tools or techniques (eg information risk assessment methodologies, forensic investigation software and an enterprise-wide security architecture).

CF1.2.8

The information security function should:

a) have sufficient impact on the organisation and strong support from executive management, other business managers and IT managers
b) maintain contact with counterparts in the commercial world, government and law enforcement agencies and with security experts in computer / software companies and service providers
c) be reviewed on a regular basis (eg to ensure it performs as expected).

CONTROL FRAMEWORK

FUNDAMENTAL

CF1.2   Information Security Function (continued)

Related content

SG1.1 Security Governance Framework

SG1.2 Security Direction

SG2.1 Information Security Strategy

ISF resources

Information Security Strategy: Workshop Report

Role of Information Security in the Enterprise (RISE): Workshop Report

ISF Digest: Managing a Security Function

Managing a Security Function Diagnostic Tool

ISF Briefing: The Insider View – the role of information security in the enterprise

ROSI – Return on Security Investment: Workshop Report

RO$I – Return on Security Investment Tool

Principles for Information Security Practitioners

Cyber Security Strategies: Achieving cyber resilience

FUNDAMENTAL   CONTROL FRAMEWORK

AREA CF2 – Human Resource Security

List of Topics

CF2.1   Staff Agreements
CF2.2   Security Awareness Programme
CF2.3   Security Awareness Messages
CF2.4   Security Education / Training
CF2.5   Roles and Responsibilities

CF2.1 Staff Agreements

Principle   Staff agreements should be established that specify information security responsibilities, are incorporated into staff contracts, and are taken into account when screening applicants for employment.

Objective   To ensure that staff behave in a manner that supports the organisation's information security policy and information security strategy.

CF2.1.1

Information security responsibilities for all staff throughout the organisation should be specified in job descriptions, terms and conditions of employment (eg in a contract or employee handbook) and performance objectives.

CF2.1.2

Terms and conditions of employment should:

a) state that information security responsibilities extend outside normal working hours and premises, and continue after employment has ended
b) explain the employee's legal responsibilities and rights (eg regarding copyright laws, data protection or privacy legislation)
c) require the employee to adhere to the organisation's information security policy and supporting policies (eg acceptable usage policies)
d) include a non-disclosure / confidentiality clause.

CF2.1.3

There should be a requirement for internal staff to accept terms and conditions of employment in writing, and external individuals (eg consultants, contractors, engineers and employees of external parties) to sign non-disclosure / confidentiality agreements.

CF2.1.4

There should be a documented requirement for access privileges to be revoked immediately when an authorised user no longer requires access to information or systems as part of their job, or when they leave the organisation.

CF2.1.5

Applicants for employment (including internal staff and external individuals such as consultants, contractors, engineers and employees of external parties) should be screened prior to commencing work (eg by taking up references, checking career history / qualifications and confirming identity, such as by inspecting a passport).

CF2.1.6

Key staff documents, such as policies or job descriptions, should be reviewed by an information security specialist, signed off by executive management (or equivalent) and kept up-to-date.

CF2.1 Staff Agreements (continued)

CF2.1.7

Upon termination of employment, staff and external individuals should be required to return assets (or equivalent) that belong to the organisation, including:

a) important documentation (eg about business processes, technical procedures and key contact details) stored on portable storage media or in paper form
b) equipment (eg mobile devices, laptops, ultrabooks, tablets, smartphones, portable storage devices and specialist equipment)
c) software (including media, documentation and licensing information)
d) authentication hardware (eg physical tokens, smartcards and biometric equipment).

CF2.1.8

Upon termination of employment, staff and external individuals should be required to:

a) confirm (in writing) that they have destroyed all copies of information owned by the organisation
b) document information related to processes (eg recently developed procedures, updated contact lists or reports of current activities).

Related content	ISF resources
CF1.1 Information Security Policy	*Protecting Information in the End User Environment*

FUNDAMENTAL

CONTROL FRAMEWORK

CF2.2   Security Awareness Programme

Principle   Specific activities should be undertaken, such as a security awareness programme, to promote security awareness to all individuals who have access to the information and systems of the organisation.

Objective   To create a security-positive culture where all relevant individuals apply security controls and prevent critical and sensitive information used throughout the organisation from being compromised.

CF2.2.1

A security awareness programme should be established to promote security awareness throughout the organisation and establish a security-positive culture. This programme should be:

a) endorsed by executive management
b) the responsibility of a particular individual, organisational unit, working group or committee
c) supported by a documented set of objectives
d) delivered as part of an on-going information security awareness programme
e) subject to project management disciplines
f) kept up-to-date with current practices and requirements
g) based on the results of one or more documented information risk assessments
h) aimed at reducing the frequency and magnitude of information security incidents.

> Security awareness is the extent to which staff understand the importance of information security, the level of security required by the organisation and their individual security responsibilities. A security-positive culture is typically established by changing user behaviour, which is typically driven by compulsory attendance at security awareness training, publicising security successes and failures throughout the organisation and linking security to personal performance objectives / appraisals.

CF2.2.2

Objectives for raising awareness of information security should be set, which are:

a) specific (ie the objective should be clear and define the problem that it will address)
b) measurable (ie the objective should be quantifiable)
c) action-oriented (ie the action should be clearly defined such that all activities can clearly relate to the objective)
d) realistic (ie if success is to be measured against the objective, then it should be realistic)
e) time-delimited (ie the objective should clearly state when it will be met).

CF2.2.3

The security awareness programme should be promoted:

a) to individuals throughout the organisation, including executive management, business representatives, IT staff and external individuals
b) by providing information security education / training (eg using techniques such as presentations, structured workshops, virtual environments, videos, computer-based training (CBT), e-learning and competitions)
c) by supplying specialised security awareness material, such as brochures, newsletters, booklets, posters and intranet-based electronic documents
d) using key messages, tone and approaches that are relevant and meaningful to each audience.

CF2.2.4

The security awareness programme should ensure particular attention is given to high-risk individuals likely to be targeted by cybercriminals, hactivists or malicious competitors (or equivalent), such as senior executives and individuals with access to highly sensitive information.

CF2.2 Security Awareness Programme (continued)

CF2.2.5

Security-positive behaviour should be encouraged by:

a) making attendance at security awareness training compulsory
b) publicising security successes and failures throughout the organisation
c) linking security to personal performance objectives / appraisals
d) incorporating information security into regular day-to-day activities (eg by considering security requirements in planning decisions and budgeting activities, and including the consideration of information risk in business decisions, meetings and audits)
e) making security awareness messages personal (eg by helping staff protect their computers at home, highlighting how threats can impact individuals as well as the organisation and emphasising how individuals can make a difference in managing information risk)
f) involving users in protecting important information (eg as part of a specific exercise or as part of meetings, asking them what the risks are to information, why they are considered to be risks and what suggestions they have to reduce the risks).

CF2.2.6

Staff should:

a) be updated regularly with information security messages using a broad range of communication methods (eg email, instant messaging, smartphones (texts), e-book readers, media players and intranets)
b) confirm their compliance with the information security policy (and other related policies) on a regular basis (eg by selecting a confirmation dialogue box as part of the login process for their computer, when starting business applications or upon accessing the organisation's intranet)
c) be tested on their knowledge of information security throughout the year (eg using questionnaires, computer-based training (CBT) and interviews).

CF2.2.7

The effectiveness of security awareness should be monitored by:

a) measuring the level of information security awareness of staff
b) reviewing the level of information security awareness regularly
c) measuring the benefits of security awareness activities (eg by measuring the amount of confidential waste produced, comparing the number of security-related calls to the information security helpdesk or equivalent, testing the strength of passwords or monitoring the frequency and magnitude of information security incidents experienced)
d) obtaining feedback from users (ie what worked well and what needs to be improved).

Related content	ISF resources
CF1.1 Information Security Policy CF2.3 Security Awareness Messages	Effective Security Awareness: Workshop Report The Evolution of Security Awareness: Overview Protecting Information in the End User Environment Beyond the Clear Desk Policy: Releasing untapped potential in your staff Cyber Citizenship in an Enterprise Environment (Briefing paper)

FUNDAMENTAL

CONTROL FRAMEWORK

CF2.3   Security Awareness Messages

Principle   Individuals who have access to the information and systems of the organisation should have tailored and appropriate security messages communicated to them on a regular basis.

Objective   To ensure individuals remain aware of the importance and need for information security on an ongoing basis, and maintain a security-positive culture throughout the organisation.

CF2.3.1

Individuals who have access to information and systems should be made aware of:

a) the meaning of information security (ie the protection of the confidentiality, integrity and availability of information)
b) why information security is needed to protect information and systems
c) the common types of threat the organisation faces (eg identity theft, mobile malware, hacking, information leakage and insider threat)
d) the importance of complying with information security policies and applying associated standards / procedures
e) their personal responsibilities for information security (eg protecting privacy-related information and reporting actual and suspected information security incidents).

CF2.3.2

Security awareness messages should cover details about information and related threats, including the:

a) definition of the information lifecycle (ie creation, processing, storage, transmission and destruction) and the risks of handling the different formats of information at different stages of its lifecycle (eg electronic files, emails and paper-based documents)
b) difference between critical information, which needs to be available and have integrity (eg product prices / exchange rates, manufacturing information and medical records) and sensitive information, which can only be disclosed to authorised individuals (eg product designs, merger and acquisition plans, medical records and business strategy information)
c) threats associated with users, the technology they use and the physical location(s) of the local environment (eg information leakage as a result of blogging, social engineering attacks and corruption of information in desktop applications).

CF2.3.3

Security awareness messages should cover details about required activity, including the:

a) actions and behaviour expected of users to help address these threats (including rules on the use of blogging and social networking websites and being aware of social engineering attacks)
b) steps to be taken to address control areas that have been assessed as weak
c) security arrangements requiring proactive steps by the user, such as when handling information beyond the control of the organisation (eg when working at home or travelling, and using the telephone and voice messaging services)
d) need to comply with policies such as those for 'clear desk' initiatives and logging off or locking systems when leaving a computing device unattended.

CF2.3.4

Individuals who have access to and use electronic communication technologies (eg email messages, instant messages, social network blogs (web logs) and messages posted on collaboration websites) should be made aware:

a) of appropriate behaviour (eg only attaching files to emails when necessary and avoiding the sharing of email threads)
b) of the security features provided with electronic communications (eg digitally signing emails and encrypting instant messages)
c) that the content of messages may be legally and contractually binding
d) that electronic communications may be intercepted and monitored.

CONTROL FRAMEWORK

FUNDAMENTAL

CF2.3 Security Awareness Messages (continued)

CF2.3.5

Individuals who use information systems to communicate should be made aware that they are prohibited from:

a) making sexual, racist or other statements that may be offensive (eg when using email, instant messaging, collaboration software, the Internet, or the telephone)
b) making obscene, discriminatory or harassing statements, which may be illegal (eg when using email, instant messaging, collaboration software, the Internet, or the telephone)
c) downloading illegal material (eg with obscene or discriminatory content or which breaches copyright)
d) opening attachments from unknown or untrusted sources
e) sending messages to unknown recipients.

CF2.3.6

Individuals who have access to information and systems should be made aware that they are prohibited from:

a) unauthorised use of the organisation's information or systems
b) using information and systems for purposes that are not work-related
c) using unauthorised information facilities or equipment (eg unauthorised external party software, USB sticks or modems)
d) unauthorised copying of information or software
e) disclosing sensitive information (eg customer records, product designs and pricing policies) to unauthorised individuals
f) compromising passwords (eg by writing them down or disclosing them to others)
g) using personally identifiable information (ie information that can be used to identify an individual person) unless explicitly authorised
h) moving information or equipment off-site without authorisation (or when unencrypted)
i) failing to protect computer equipment when using them in remote environments (eg when travelling or working from home).

CF2.3.7

Individuals who have access to information and systems should be made aware of the dangers of:

a) being overheard when discussing business information over the telephone or in public places (eg train carriages, airport lounges or bars)
b) including sensitive information in voice messages on landline and mobile voicemail messaging systems.

Related content

CF1.1 Information Security Policy

CF2.2 Security Awareness Programme

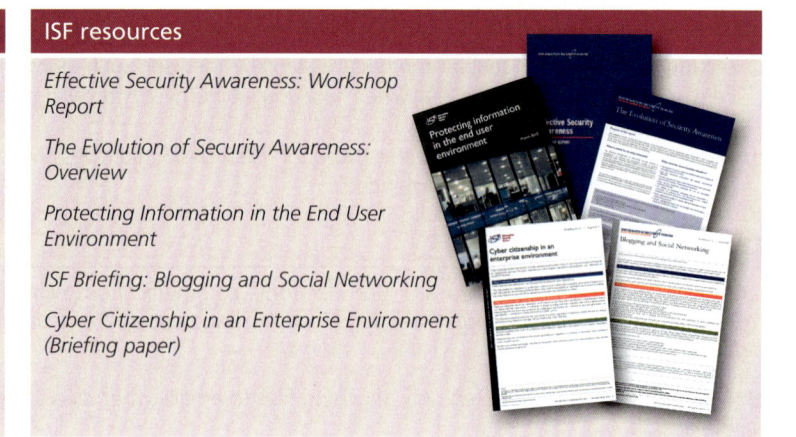

ISF resources

Effective Security Awareness: Workshop Report

The Evolution of Security Awareness: Overview

Protecting Information in the End User Environment

ISF Briefing: Blogging and Social Networking

Cyber Citizenship in an Enterprise Environment (Briefing paper)

FUNDAMENTAL

CONTROL FRAMEWORK

CF2.4   Security Education / Training

Principle   Staff should be educated / trained in how to run systems correctly and how to develop and apply information security controls.

Objective   To provide staff with the skills required to protect systems and fulfil their information security responsibilities.

CF2.4.1

Education / training should be given to provide staff with the skills they need to:

a) understand information risk (ie concepts of business impact, likelihood and how they relate to each other)
b) assess security requirements
c) propose information security controls
d) ensure that security controls function effectively in the business environments in which they are applied
e) support the organisation's information security incident management process (eg by taking the actions required when an incident occurs or is suspected).

CF2.4.2

Education / training should be given to provide business users with the skills they need to correctly use:

a) business applications (including enterprise software, commercial-off-the-shelf (COTS) software and desktop applications (eg those developed using spreadsheets))
b) computer equipment (including desktop computers, laptops, ultrabooks, tablets and smartphones)
c) specialist equipment (eg scanning devices, bar code readers, data capture appliances and monitoring equipment)
d) portable storage media (eg CDs, DVDs, magnetic tapes, computer disks and portable storage devices)
e) networking technologies such as local area networks (LANs), wireless local area networks (WLANs), Voice over IP (VoIP), Internet and Bluetooth
f) telephony and conferencing equipment, including teleconference and videoconference facilities (eg speakers, cameras and display screens) and online web-based collaboration
g) office equipment, including printers and photocopiers, facsimile machines and scanners and multifunction devices (MFDs)
h) access control mechanisms (eg passwords, tokens and biometrics).

CF2.4.3

Education / training given to business users should include guidance on how to protect information, and cover:

a) creating and protecting electronic files
b) classifying and labelling information
c) removing unnecessary metadata from electronic documents
d) deleting unwanted information once no longer required
e) separating business and personal information.

CF2.4 Security Education / Training (continued)

> Electronic documents, such as word processed files, spreadsheets and presentations, can often include confidential or inappropriate information, left unintentionally in electronic documents (often referred to as 'hidden data' or 'metadata').
>
> Types of information that could be accidentally disclosed to unauthorised parties in electronic documents include:
>
> - document properties (that might contain confidential comments, individuals' names and classification levels)
> - tracked changes (that might contain private comments or potentially controversial statements)
> - hidden rows, columns, sheets and database fields (that might contain customer or employee information, or credit card details)
> - embedded objects (that might contain financial charts, private pictures and populated spreadsheets)
> - header and footer information (that might contain project names and classification levels)
> - hyperlinks (that might reveal sensitive information)
> - ink annotations in electronic documents created using tablet PCs
> - hidden confidential text or figures (eg coloured white).
>
> File cleansing software can be used to help identify confidential information that may be hidden within electronic documents.

CF2.4.4

Education / training should be given to provide business users with the skills they need to apply information security controls associated with protecting:

a) business applications (eg using templates instead of existing documents to create new electronic documents or using validation routines when developing spreadsheet-based applications)
b) equipment (eg using file-based encryption to protect electronic files stored on mobile devices, portable storage media and in transit, and password-protecting consumer devices)
c) access control mechanisms (eg by physically removing smartcards from the reader when leaving computers unattended)
d) connectivity (eg disabling communication settings, encrypting wireless networks and using a virtual private network (VPN) when connecting to the corporate network)
e) locations in which they work (eg locking paper documents away overnight and logging off or locking desktop PCs and laptops when unattended).

CF2.4.5

Education / training should be given to provide IT and systems development staff with the skills they need to:

a) design systems and develop security controls in a disciplined manner (eg using an approved systems development lifecycle (SDLC))
b) implement information security controls effectively
c) configure and maintain computer installations, storage systems and networks correctly
d) apply required security controls effectively (eg preventing unauthorised or incorrect updates).

CF2.4.6

Education / training should be provided to enable information security specialists to:

a) understand the business environment
b) run security-related projects
c) communicate effectively (eg making presentations, facilitating meetings or influencing management)
d) perform specialist security activities (eg information risk assessment, forensic investigations and business continuity planning).

FUNDAMENTAL CONTROL FRAMEWORK

CF2.4 Security Education / Training (continued)

CF2.4.7

Information security staff should demonstrate their experience and knowledge of information security by obtaining industry-accepted, professional security certifications, such as those provided by (ISC)², ISACA, IISP, ISSA and SANS.

CF2.4.8

Education / training should include practical recommendations for users to follow, such as:

a) adhering to the organisation's policy on social networking
b) understanding the terms and conditions when signing up to social networking websites
c) withholding the elements of the user's personal life that don't need to be made public
d) taking control of personal information (eg by resisting the urge to make a blog entry when tired or upset and avoiding publication of work related information on websites)
e) being sceptical (eg questioning or doubting unusual messages to help detect social engineering attacks).

CF2.4.9

Business users should be instructed not to share, transfer, upload, store online or comment on business sensitive information in the public domain.

CF2.4.10

Business users should be instructed to:

a) lock away sensitive media or documentation when not in use (ie complying with a 'clear desk' policy)
b) collect sensitive printed material from printer output trays in a timely manner
c) log off or lock systems if leaving a terminal unattended (eg during a meeting, lunch break or overnight).

Related content	ISF resources
CF1.1 Information Security Policy	*Effective Security Awareness: Workshop Report*
	Protecting Information in the End User Environment
	ISF Briefing: Blogging and Social Networking
	Principles for Information Security Practitioners

CONTROL FRAMEWORK   **FUNDAMENTAL**

CF2.5   Roles and Responsibilities

Principle   Ownership of critical and sensitive target environments (eg critical business environments, critical processes, critical business applications, critical computer systems and networks) should be assigned to capable individuals, with responsibilities for key tasks to protect critical information clearly defined and accepted.

Objective   To achieve individual accountability for business applications, information systems and networks, provide a sound management structure for staff running or using them and give responsible individuals a vested interest in their protection.

CF2.5.1

Ownership of critical and sensitive information, business applications, information systems and networks should be assigned to individuals (eg business managers), and the responsibilities of owners documented. Responsibilities for protecting critical and sensitive information, business applications, information systems and networks should be communicated to and accepted by owners.

CF2.5.2

Responsibilities of owners should include:

a) understanding and identifying information risks
b) determining business (including information security) requirements and signing them off
c) ensuring information, business applications, information systems and networks are protected in line with their importance to the organisation
d) defining information interchange agreements (or equivalent)
e) developing service level agreements (SLAs)
f) authorising new or significantly changed business applications, information systems and networks
g) contributing to security audits.

CF2.5.3

The responsibilities of owners should involve:

a) participating in information risk assessment activities (eg by helping to identify threats, vulnerabilities and controls)
b) determining which users are authorised to access particular information, business applications, information systems and networks
c) signing off access privileges for each user or set of users
d) ensuring users are aware of their security responsibilities and are able to fulfil them.

CF2.5.4

A process should be established for:

a) providing owners with the necessary skills, tools, staff and authority to fulfil their responsibilities
b) assigning responsibilities for protecting information, business applications, information systems and networks when owners are unavailable
c) reassigning ownership when owners leave or change roles.

CF2.5.5

Individuals involved in implementing and maintaining business applications, information systems and networks should be:

a) assigned clear responsibilities
b) able to administer and use them correctly and deal with normal processing requirements
c) competent to deal with error, exception and emergency conditions
d) aware of information security principles and associated good practice
e) sufficient in number to handle required normal and peak workloads at all times.

FUNDAMENTAL

CONTROL FRAMEWORK

CF2.5   Roles and Responsibilities (continued)

CF2.5.6

Individuals should be supported by approved methods of:

a) administering users (eg adding new business users, updating access privileges, and revoking user access rights)
b) monitoring key security-related events (eg system crashes, unsuccessful login attempts of authorised users, and unsuccessful changes to access privileges)
c) validating processes / data
d) reviewing error / exception reports
e) identifying potential security weaknesses / breaches (eg as a result of analysing user behaviour or patterns of network traffic).

CF2.5.7

The risk of staff disrupting the running of business applications, information systems and networks either in error or by malicious intent should be reduced by:

a) separating the duties of staff running business applications, information systems and networks from the duties of staff designing, developing and testing them
b) minimising reliance on key individuals (eg by automating processes, ensuring supporting documentation is complete and accurate, arranging alternative cover, job rotation and deputies for key positions)
c) organising duties in such a way as to minimise the risk of theft, fraud, error and unauthorised changes to information (eg by supervising and recording activities, prohibiting lone working and the segregation of duties).

CF2.5.8

The activities of individuals running business applications, information systems or networks should be monitored (eg by providing supervision, recording activities and maintaining audit trails).

Related content

CF2.1 Staff Agreements

CF2.2 Security Awareness Programme

ISF resources

Protecting Information in the End User Environment

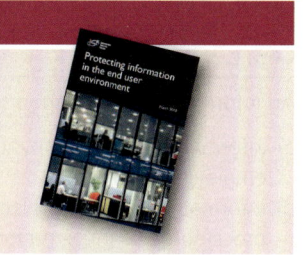

CONTROL FRAMEWORK

SPECIALISED

AREA CF3 – Asset Management

List of Topics

CF3.1 Information Classification
CF3.2 Document Management
CF3.3 Sensitive Physical Information
CF3.4 Asset Register

CF3.1 Information Classification

Principle An information classification scheme should be established that applies throughout the organisation, based on the confidentiality of each piece of information.

Objective To determine the level of protection that should be applied to particular types of information, thereby preventing unauthorised disclosure.

CF3.1.1

There should be an information classification scheme that applies across the organisation, which:

a) is used to determine varying levels of confidentiality of information (eg top secret, company-in-confidence and public)
b) provides a description of each level of confidentiality
c) takes into account the potential business impact from the loss of confidentiality of information
d) lists examples of information types for each specific classification level.

> Some organisations also take into account requirements for integrity (ie the need for information to be valid, accurate and complete) and availability (ie the need for information to be accessible when required) when classifying information.

CF3.1.2

An information classification scheme should be established to classify:

a) information stored in physical form (eg contracts, board meeting minutes, business plans, product designs and employment contracts)
b) information stored in electronic form (eg files created using spreadsheet and database programs, word processors and presentation packages)
c) electronic communications (eg messages sent via email, instant messaging and online collaboration systems).

CF3.1.3

The information classification scheme should require:

a) that information is protected in line with its assigned level of classification (eg top secret, company-in-confidence or public)
b) sign-off of the assigned classification applied to information by the relevant business owner
c) that information classifications are reviewed and updated regularly and when changes are made.

CF3.1.4

The information classification scheme should:

a) provide guidance on handling requirements for each level of classification at each stage of the information lifecycle (eg when creating, processing, copying, printing, storing and destroying information)
b) explain how to handle conflicting classifications.

SPECIALISED

CF3.1 Information Classification (continued)

CF3.1.5

The information classification scheme should take into account requirements for document retention (based on the organisation's document retention policy), including:

a) legal and regulatory obligations (eg the minimum and maximum statutory length of time that privacy-related and financial information must be retained)
b) business requirements (eg ensuring staff have access to intellectual capital and business intelligence or customers have access to transactional and customer-related records)
c) technical requirements (eg relating to key audit trails, index cross-references and configuration files).

CF3.1.6

There should be approved methods for labelling classified:

a) information stored in paper form (eg using rubber ink stamps, adhesive labels, hologram lamination)
b) information stored in electronic form (eg using electronic watermarking, labelling headers and footers, using filename conventions)
c) electronic communications (eg using digital signatures, clearly identifying the classification in the subject headers of emails and selecting the appropriate label from a menu).

CF3.1.7

Information classification details should be:

a) recorded in an inventory or equivalent (eg a database, specialised piece of software, or on paper)
b) included in agreements with customers, service providers and external suppliers
c) made widely available (eg as part of communications to and training of staff).

CF3.1.8

Information classification details recorded should include the:

a) type of information being classified (eg merger and acquisition contract, salary details or marketing forecasts)
b) level of classification of the information
c) date for reclassification
d) identity of the information owner.

Related content

CF3.2 Document Management

Appendix A: The ISF Business Impact Reference Table

ISF resources

Practical Approaches to Information Classification: Workshop Report

The Information Lifecycle: A new way of looking at information risk

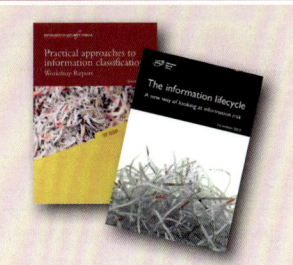

CF3.2 Document Management

Principle Documents should be managed in a systematic, structured manner, and information security requirements met throughout the document lifecycle.

Objective To protect information contained in documents in accordance with legal requirements, ensure critical information remains available when required, preserve the integrity of critical information and protect sensitive information from unauthorised disclosure.

CF3.2.1

Documents should be managed throughout the document lifecycle (ie creation, categorisation, storage, retrieval, modification and destruction).

CF3.2.2

The management of documents should be supported by a:

a) document retention policy
b) retention schedule
c) document management process.

CF3.2.3

A document retention policy should be developed, which:

a) is supported by executive management
b) specifies employee obligations for document management and the consequences of non-compliance
c) covers the different formats of information that are subject to the policy (including paper-based and electronic documents)
d) defines important terms (eg what constitutes a document and a record, and their respective lifecycles)
e) explains how to back-up and archive information.

> In many organisations documents that have been officially assessed by the organisation to have a significant business value (eg a set of company board minutes or product designs), or are within the scope of specific laws or regulations (eg financial files, trade secrets or medical documents), are often categorised as records and subject to more rigorous record management.

CF3.2.4

A document retention policy should detail requirements for legal and regulatory compliance, including:

a) any relevant standards relating to retention that are to be used
b) mechanisms for handling conflicting requirements (eg retention periods in different jurisdictions)
c) a process for dealing with legal discovery (eg requests for information held in a document management system).

CF3.2.5

A document retention policy should be supported by a comprehensive document retention schedule, which contains the retention period for each type of document used by the organisation (eg payroll records, legal correspondence, insurance policies, financial statements or tax returns).

SPECIALISED

CF3.2 Document Management (continued)

CF3.2.6

There should be a process in place for managing the organisation's documents throughout the complete document lifecycle, including:

a) creation (eg by a business user or by an automated business process)
b) categorisation of important documents as records
c) storage (eg locally on a business user's computing device or centrally on a network folder)
d) retrieval (by one or more business users)
e) modification (eg adding to, changing or deleting content)
f) destruction (eg securely destroying documents when no longer required).

CF3.2.7

Records should be subjected to a more rigorous management process to meet business, legal and regulatory requirements. This process should include:

a) storing only one instance of each record (ie all other originals or copies are destroyed)
b) monitoring each record to ensure it complies with the organisation's document retention policy and schedule (eg providing a notification when the retention period has ended)
c) providing a copy of a record when retrieved (ie the original record remains in the document management system)
d) ensuring secure destruction of the original and all copies of a record (eg when the retention period has ended).

CF3.2.8

The document management process should be supported by an automated document management system (or equivalent) to:

a) improve the management of documents (eg by storing documents centrally and prompting users to classify and label them)
b) maintain the confidentiality, integrity and availability of each document during its lifecycle (eg by automatically encrypting, digitally signing, time-stamping or backing up documents).

Related content	ISF resources
CF3.1 Information Classification	*Practical Approaches to Information Classification: Workshop Report*
	ISF Digest: Document Retention and Record Management
	The Information Lifecycle: A new way of looking at information risk

CONTROL FRAMEWORK

FUNDAMENTAL

CF3.3   Sensitive Physical Information

Principle   Sensitive information held in physical form (sensitive physical information) should be protected against corruption, loss or disclosure.

Objective   To protect sensitive physical information in accordance with information security and regulatory requirements, preserve the integrity of sensitive physical information and protect it from unauthorised disclosure.

CF3.3.1

There should be documented standards / procedures for the protection of sensitive physical information (eg blank cheques, bonds or print-outs of documents such as personal information, financial projections, business plans or product designs), which cover:

a) identification and labelling of sensitive physical information
b) storage of sensitive physical information
c) protection against unauthorised disclosure of sensitive physical information
d) secure transportation of sensitive physical information
e) handling and disposing of sensitive physical information.

CF3.3.2

Sensitive physical information should be:

a) identified and documented
b) classified according to the organisation's information classification scheme (eg top secret, company-in-confidence or sensitive)
c) monitored by recording its issue, use and return.

CF3.3.3

Sensitive physical information should be protected against theft or copying by:

a) storing important papers and printed material in a physically secure location (eg a locked, document fireproof safe, cabinet or container) when not in use
b) restricting physical access to important post / facsimile points, office equipment (eg network printers, photocopiers, facsimile machines, scanners and multifunction devices (MFDs)) and local environments
c) locating equipment used for sensitive printed material in secure physical areas.

CF3.3.4

Sensitive physical information should be protected from unauthorised disclosure (eg by concealing classified documents in sealed folders or keeping relevant printers / photocopiers in locked areas).

CF3.3.5

Sensitive physical information should be protected in transit by:

a) minimising distribution
b) using double-packaging (ie one package inside another)
c) recording authorised recipients
d) clearly marking all packaging with the identity of the authorised recipient
e) confirming receipt of transmitted information (eg documents via post or courier)
f) reviewing records of authorised recipients regularly.

FUNDAMENTAL

CONTROL FRAMEWORK

CF3.3   Sensitive Physical Information (continued)

Double-packaging is a technique often used to conceal the level of sensitivity and classification of information when using postal or courier services. The labelling is only applied to the inner package, thereby concealing it from individuals who handle the outer package, which only contains the details of the recipient.

CF3.3.6

Sensitive physical information should be destroyed using a secure means of disposal (eg incineration or cross-cut shredding) when no longer required.

CF3.3.7

A method should be established for verifying the secure destruction of sensitive physical information, which includes:

a) approval of the destruction by the business owner
b) observation of the destruction by a business representative, ensuring all items have been destroyed and in an effective manner
c) recording details of the destruction and sign-off by the business representative.

Related content	ISF resources
CF16.2 Hardware / Software Acquisition CF19.1 Physical Protection	*Protecting Information in the End User Environment*

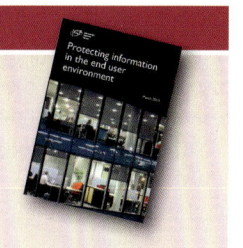

CONTROL FRAMEWORK **FUNDAMENTAL**

CF3.4 Asset Register

Principle All hardware / software should be recorded in an accurate and up-to-date asset register.

Objective To help support risk-based decisions regarding hardware / software, reduce the risk of information security being compromised by weaknesses in hardware / software, protect assets against loss, support development of contracts and meet compliance requirements for licensing.

CF3.4.1

There should be documented standards / procedures for asset management, which cover:

a) recording of hardware / software in an asset register (or equivalent)
b) protecting the asset register and keeping it up-to-date
c) maintaining the accuracy of details in the register.

CF3.4.2

Types of hardware to be recorded in an asset register should include:

a) computer equipment (including servers, desktop computers, ultrabooks, laptops and netbooks)
b) consumer devices (including tablets and smartphones)
c) virtual systems (eg virtual servers and virtual desktops)
d) network storage systems (including Storage Area Network (SAN) and Network-Attached Storage (NAS))
e) network equipment (eg routers, switches, wireless access points and firewalls)
f) telephony (including VoIP) and conferencing equipment
g) portable storage media (eg external hard disk drives and USB memory sticks)
h) authentication hardware (eg physical tokens, smartcards and biometric equipment)
i) office equipment (eg network printers, photocopiers, facsimile machines, scanners and multifunction devices (MFDs))
j) specialist equipment (eg equipment that is used to support or enable the organisation's critical infrastructure).

CF3.4.3

Types of software (including licensing details) to be recorded in an asset register should include:

a) operating system and virtualisation software
b) enterprise software (eg enterprise resource planning (ERP) and customer relationship management (CRM) applications)
c) commercial-off-the-shelf (COTS) software
d) security software (eg data leakage protection (DLP), digital rights management (DRM) and intrusion detection software (IDS)).

CF3.4.4

Asset registers should specify important information about each asset, including:

a) a unique description of hardware and software in use (eg using a serial number)
b) versions of hardware and software in use
c) the location of hardware and software in use
d) licensing details (eg license keys and proof of ownership).

CF3.4.5

The asset register should be checked regularly to identify any discrepancy with physical assets or software licenses. Any discrepancies identified (eg unlicensed software, unused mobile devices or missing portable storage media) should be investigated and resolved (eg by purchasing new licenses, removing unlicensed software, locating missing hardware or securely destroying equipment).

FUNDAMENTAL

CF3.4 Asset Register (continued)

CF3.4.6

The accuracy of details about hardware / software recorded in the asset register should be supported by the use of automated discovery / mapping tools to:

a) identify discrepancies in the register
b) detect the illegal use of software (eg no license)
c) highlight the possible theft of equipment (eg hard disk drives or computer memory).

CF3.4.7

Asset registers should be:

a) signed off by an appropriate business representative
b) protected against unauthorised change
c) kept up-to-date
d) reviewed independently.

Related content	ISF resources
CF10.1 Patch Management CF16.2 Hardware / Software Acquisition	*Protecting Information in the End User Environment*

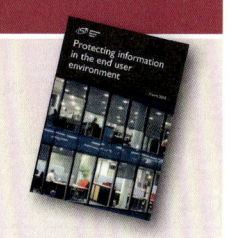

AREA CF4 – Business Applications

List of Topics
CF4.1   Application Protection
CF4.2   Browser-based Application Protection
CF4.3   Information Validation

CF4.1   Application Protection

Principle   Business applications should be protected by using sound security architecture principles.

Objective   To help ensure business applications use consistent security functionality, align with the organisation's technical security infrastructure and protect the information they process.

CF4.1.1

Business applications should be protected against invalid connections by:

a) assuming input from external systems (eg Web Services, SOA components and other applications) is insecure by default
b) checking access permissions when a request is made to access an object (eg a database record, file or equivalent)
c) repeating any client validation upon connection to the server, to defend against 'man-in-the-middle' attacks.

CF4.1.2

Business applications should be protected against unauthorised access to information by:

a) hardening the operating system (eg ensuring that all unnecessary software, network services and applications have been disabled / removed)
b) providing 'defence in depth' (ie using multiple layers of different types of protection) to avoid reliance on one type or method of security control
c) employing secure defaults (eg requiring authentication and recording user activity in an event log as a preselected option)
d) ensuring key components 'fail securely' (ie in the event of a system failure, information is not accessible to unauthorised individuals, and cannot be tampered with or modified).

CF4.1.3

Business applications should protect against unauthorised disclosure of sensitive information by ensuring that they:

a) run with 'least privilege' (ie only the minimum possible access privileges are granted to a user or a process when accessing the system, and not high-level privileges such as 'root' in UNIX systems or 'Administrator' in Windows systems)
b) enforce separation of privilege (eg by dividing application functions and splitting cryptographic keys)
c) are prevented from initiating network connections to the Internet (eg through server configuration or by rules on a firewall)
d) prevent information about the internal workings of applications (eg in application responses or error messages) from being disclosed.

CF4.1.4

Business applications should incorporate security controls to protect the integrity of information by:

a) minimising manual intervention (eg by automating processes)
b) preventing unauthorised changes to software (eg malware protection, change management disciplines)
c) producing error and exception reports.

SPECIALISED

CONTROL FRAMEWORK

CF4.1　Application Protection (continued)

CF4.1.5

Business applications should incorporate security controls to help ensure availability of information by:

a) providing adequate capacity to cope with normal / peak volumes of work
b) performing load-balancing and load-monitoring
c) reducing or eliminating single-points-of-failure.

CF4.1.6

Servers that support critical business applications should be:

a) segregated from internal networks and untrusted networks (eg by locating them in a 'Demilitarised Zone' (DMZ))
b) run on one or more dedicated computers (ie they do not provide other services such as file and print, database, email or other business applications).

CF4.1.7

Connections between servers (eg web servers) and back-office systems (eg application and database servers) should be:

a) protected by firewalls
b) restricted to only the services that are required by business applications
c) restricted to those originating from web server applications (ie rather than originating from client applications)
d) based on documented, tested and approved application programming interfaces (APIs)
e) encrypted (eg using IPSec).

Related content	ISF resources
CF7.1 Computer and Network Installations	Security Architecture: Workshop Report
CF8.1 Security Architecture	Securing Business Applications
CF18 Systems Development Lifecycle	ISF Briefing: Security of Service Oriented Architecture (SOA) and Web Services

CONTROL FRAMEWORK

SPECIALISED

CF4.2 Browser-based Application Protection

Principle Specialised procedural and technical controls should be applied to internal and 'Internet-facing' browser-based applications and the servers on which they run.

Objective To ensure that the increased risks associated with browser-based applications are minimised.

CF4.2.1

Additional security controls should be employed when deploying browser-based applications and supporting systems to protect against increased risks associated with being accessible from unprotected networks (eg the Internet).

CF4.2.2

Information used by browser-based applications (eg configuration files) should be protected against corruption or unauthorised disclosure by:

a) locating them on partitions inaccessible to web servers (or other connected servers)
b) restricting file permissions.

CF4.2.3

Website content (eg web pages, articles, images) should be protected against corruption or unauthorised disclosure by:

a) storing it separately from the operating system (eg on a separate partition / disk)
b) setting strict file permissions
c) restricting updates to authorised individuals and using approved methods (eg via removable media at the web server console or transferring files using secure shell (SSH) or secure FTP from a predefined IP address)
d) reviewing content to ensure that it is accurate, that hyperlinks are valid and functional, and that vulnerabilities have not been introduced by scripts or 'hidden' form fields
e) performing regular checks to ensure that website content is not defamatory, offensive or in breach of legal and regulatory requirements.

CF4.2.4

Sensitive information in transit should be protected against unauthorised disclosure by using:

a) encryption (eg using Secure Sockets Layer (SSL), Transport Layer Security (TLS) or equivalent)
b) Secure Sockets Layer (SSL) certificates and Transport Layer Security (TLS) certificates that have been obtained from a reputable, approved internal or external (ie public) Certification Authority.

CF4.2.5

The unauthorised disclosure of information about system configuration (that could be useful to hackers) should be prevented by:

a) suppressing or modifying the server field in HTTP headers that identify the web server's brand and version
b) verifying that directories of files on web servers are not indexable
c) preventing source code of server-side executables and scripts from being viewed by a web browser
d) ensuring that the source of HTML, JavaScript and other client-side scripting languages does not contain unnecessary information (eg comments and details of functions).

CF4.2.6

Web application sessions should be protected against being hijacked or cloned by:

a) ensuring SessionIDs cannot be easily predicted (eg by using randomly generated SessionIDs)
b) configuring the security parameters in 'cookies' used to hold session information
c) encrypting network traffic between the web browser and the web server.

SPECIALISED

CONTROL FRAMEWORK

CF4.2 Browser-based Application Protection (continued)

CF4.2.7

'Internet-facing' web servers that support business applications should be configured to:

a) record actions performed (eg those associated with server-side executables and scripts)
b) log security-related events generated by the website.

CF4.2.8

There should be a process to ensure that:

a) important domain name registrations are renewed (eg every two years)
b) details of 'Internet-facing' web servers are recorded in a register (or equivalent), which includes details about hosting location, IP address(es), domain name(s) and digital certificates used
c) domain names that could be used to masquerade as the organisation are registered by the organisation
d) websites that may have been set up using domain names similar to those used by the organisation are monitored (eg by using external party monitoring services)
e) illegitimate websites (eg those used for phishing attacks) are closed down as quickly as possible
f) relationships with internet service providers (ISPs or equivalent) are covered by a service level agreement (SLA).

Related content	ISF resources
CF8.1 Security Architecture CF18 Systems Development Lifecycle	*Securing a Web Server Environment Security Guide*

CF4.3 Information validation

Principle Business applications should incorporate security controls that protect the confidentiality and integrity of information when it is input into, processed by and output from these applications.

Objective To protect the integrity (validity, accuracy, completeness and timeliness) of critical information, stored in or processed by business applications.

CF4.3.1

Information entered into business applications should be checked to ensure its validity (eg by using range, consistency and 'hash total' checks) and completeness (eg comparison with control balances or original documentation).

CF4.3.2

The integrity of information processed by business applications should be maintained by ensuring that:

a) information cannot be overwritten accidentally (eg by write-protecting key fields or files)
b) the processing of information is validated (eg by record counts, and hash, session, batch or balancing totals)
c) changes to key 'static' business information such as customer master files or currency exchange rates are reviewed (eg by inspecting the contents of records before and after they have been changed)
d) unauthorised or incorrect changes to information are detected (eg by inspecting change logs, using automated 'checksum' tools or reconciling data back to its original source).

CF4.3.3

The integrity (validity, accuracy, completeness and timeliness) of information processed and output by business applications should be confirmed by checking against external sources (eg by reconciling bank statements, comparing against order processing logs, customer / supplier records or physical stock, or by performing plausibility checks to ensure output is reasonable).

Related content	ISF resources
CF18 Systems Development Lifecycle	Securing Business Applications
	Protecting Information in the End User Environment

FUNDAMENTAL   CONTROL FRAMEWORK

AREA CF5 – Customer Access

List of Topics
CF5.1   Customer Access Arrangements
CF5.2   Customer Contracts
CF5.3   Customer Connections

CF5.1   Customer Access Arrangements

Principle   Access to business applications by customers should be established according to business requirements, subject to an information risk assessment and approved by application owners.

Objective   To ensure that all aspects of customer access to the organisation's business applications meet security requirements.

CF5.1.1

There should be documented standards / procedures for the provision of access to the organisation's business applications by customers.

> This topic focuses on access to business applications by individuals (eg a purchaser placing orders for goods on a website, users of online banking or representatives of an organisation gaining access on behalf of a corporation). As a result, customer access arrangements for business applications should take into account each individual connection and not the collective connections of external parties such as suppliers and supply chain partners.

CF5.1.2

Standards / procedures should cover:

a) actions to be performed before granting customer access
b) recording of customer connections
c) access control requirements
d) customer access arrangements
e) legal and regulatory requirements
f) security awareness required for customers
g) reviewing customer access arrangements.

CF5.1.3

Prior to providing customers with access to business applications (eg for a goods ordering, travel booking or online banking system):

a) business risks associated with customer access should be assessed and required controls identified
b) the criticality and sensitivity of information being accessed should be evaluated
c) responsibility for authorising customer access should be assigned to sufficiently senior and knowledgeable staff
d) testing of connections should be performed
e) a single point of contact for dealing with security issues (eg a helpdesk or call centre) should be identified and agreed
f) agreed contracts should be in place, which are signed off by an appropriate business owner (eg the individual in charge of the business application being accessed).

CF5.1 Customer Access Arrangements (continued)

CF5.1.4

All customers accessing the organisation's business applications should be:

a) uniquely identified (typically by business owners)
b) approved by the respective business owner (eg the individual in charge of the business application being accessed).

CF5.1.5

A record of customer connections should be maintained (eg in a log or equivalent), which includes:

a) details of authorised customers
b) customer access rights for target business applications
c) types of information accessed by the customer
d) authentication details (eg protocols used for identity and access management (IAM) or federated identity and access management (FIAM), and types of access control mechanism used such as password, token or biometric).

CF5.1.6

Customer access arrangements should take into account relevant business aspects, including the:

a) relationship with customers to be granted access (from well-known, established customers to new, unknown organisations)
b) types of business process to be performed by customers (eg information retrieval, order submission or funds transfer)
c) restrictions imposed by legal or regulatory requirements (eg Basel III, Sarbanes-Oxley Act or the Payment Card Industry Data Security Standard (PCI DSS))
d) controls required to protect personally identifiable information (PII)
e) need for information classification definitions and protection levels to be compatible and consistent
f) information security implications of providing services to customers in different legal jurisdictions
g) lack of direct control over individuals or system components used by customers
h) obligations to customers (eg to provide a reliable service and supply timely, accurate information).

CF5.1.7

Customer access arrangements should take into account relevant technical aspects, including the:

a) devices permitted to connect to business applications
b) types of connection to business applications (eg leased line, Internet, MPLS or ISDN)
c) need for user provisioning and access control (eg by implementing federated identity and access management (FIAM) arrangements)
d) effectiveness of the technical infrastructure in restricting individuals to agreed capabilities.

CF5.1.8

Customers should be provided with security awareness training and education regarding the:

a) threats associated with customer access (eg phishing, man-in-the-middle attacks and fraud)
b) vulnerabilities associated with customer access (eg weak and poorly protected passwords, lack of malware protection software, a personal firewall, and out-of-date web browser software)
c) likely consequences in the event customer access is compromised (eg financial loss and identity theft)
d) actions to be taken in the event of an information security incident.

FUNDAMENTAL

CONTROL FRAMEWORK

CF5.1 Customer Access Arrangements (continued)

CF5.1.9

The organisation's information security incident management process should comprise additional activities relating to customers, which include:

a) providing agreed points of contact within the organisation, who are sufficiently senior and competent to deal with security incidents
b) agreeing predetermined times (eg 24 hours a day, 365 days a year) that support will be available
c) a method of minimising business disruption of security incidents (eg by blocking the connection (ie disconnection of the session) and / or disabling the originating user account)
d) contacting the customer when a security incident occurs, via a pre-agreed mechanism (eg individually by telephone or in writing).

CF5.1.10

Customer access arrangements, related standards / procedures and contracts should be:

a) signed off by executive management (or equivalent)
b) kept up-to-date
c) reviewed regularly (eg by an information security specialist) to ensure that risks remain within an agreed, acceptable limit.

Related content	ISF resources
CF6 Access Management	*Identity and Access Management (IAM): Workshop Report*
CF8.2 Identity and Access Management	
CF9.3 External Network Connections	*Federated Identity and Access Management: Creating a connected world*
CF11 Incident Management	

CF5.2 Customer Contracts

Principle All customer access to the organisation's business applications should be supported by agreed, approved contracts, which cover security arrangements.

Objective To ensure customers are legally and contractually bound to protect the organisation's information, business applications and systems, and the organisation's security obligations are met.

CF5.2.1

Customer access to the organisation's business applications should be supported by documented contracts (customer contracts), which are:

a) assessed by an information security specialist
b) signed off by executive management (or equivalent)
c) reviewed on a regular basis (eg annually)
d) retained by an appropriate business function (eg the procurement or legal department).

CF5.2.2

Customer contracts should be signed by an authorised person representing the customer to demonstrate their acceptance of security responsibilities.

CF5.2.3

Customer contracts should clearly specify:

a) who is in charge of delivering the required service (eg an internal specialised department or external service provider)
b) dates / times when the service is required
c) maximum permissible down-time
d) critical timescales (ie the timescale beyond which a loss of service would be unacceptable to the customer)
e) timeframes for completion of transactions (eg processing sales order requests, changing inventory levels, and transferring funds).

CF5.2.4

Customer contracts should clearly define the:

a) obligations, responsibilities and liabilities of both parties
b) access control and management procedures (eg covering revocation of physical and logical access, and network connectivity, and any procedures associated with managing federated identity and access management (FIAM))
c) ownership of information and systems (eg retaining copyright of information, licensing software and maintaining ownership of physical resources supplied to customers)
d) details about ownership of the information covered by the agreement (including intellectual property rights, copyright assignment and collaborative work)
e) actions to be taken in the event of a breach of the contract (eg revoke customer access).

SPECIALISED

CF5.2 Customer Contracts (continued)

CF5.2.5

Customer contracts should cover information security activities to be performed by the organisation, which include:

a) protecting the personally identifiable information (PII) of individuals associated with the customer (and other external parties)
b) limiting access to customer information to a minimum number of authorised staff
c) meeting legal and regulatory requirements (eg data protection legislation and the Payment Card Industry Data Security Standard (PCI DSS))
d) defining the way in which the organisation is permitted to outsource to external parties
e) providing dedicated support (eg identified support staff and method of contacting them directly)
f) notifying the customer about security management activities, such as managing changes to information systems and business applications
g) dealing with security issues effectively via agreed points of contact within the organisation, who are available at predetermined times (eg 24 hours a day, 365 days a year).

CF5.2.6

Customer contracts should cover information security activities to be performed by the customer, which include:

a) performing account management procedures (eg for connections using federated identity and access management (FIAM))
b) applying agreed security controls (eg access control mechanisms and malware protection software)
c) preventing unauthorised disclosure of information (eg by encrypting sensitive information or ensuring sensitive paper documents are stored in physically secure locations)
d) protecting information when processing, storing and exchanging information with external parties
e) safeguarding important information, software and hardware (eg cryptographic keys, application code and authentication devices)
f) returning or destroying information, software or equipment on an agreed date, or upon request
g) providing information about actual or suspected security incidents.

CF5.2.7

Customer contracts should cover a method for securely handling the termination of the relationship (ie exit arrangements) between both parties.

Related content	ISF resources
CF9.3 External Network Connections	No recent ISF material

CONTROL FRAMEWORK

FUNDAMENTAL

CF5.3 Customer Connections

Principle Access to business applications by customers should be uniquely identified, recorded in an inventory of connections, protected using access control mechanisms and monitored.

Objective To protect the confidentiality, integrity and availability of sensitive or critical information relating to either the organisation or the customer.

CF5.3.1

There should be documented standards / procedures for establishing the technical security arrangements for customer connections, which cover:

a) providing access control mechanisms for customer access
b) protecting the integrity of critical information
c) managing customer connections.

CF5.3.2

Access control requirements for customers should be defined to protect critical and sensitive information, and include:

a) authorisation of individuals before they are granted access to business applications
b) access privileges required to access business applications or particular functionality in a business application
c) access control mechanisms (eg passwords, tokens or biometrics).

CF5.3.3

Customers should be required to use access control mechanisms (eg passwords, tokens, digital certificates or biometrics) to gain access to business applications, which comprise:

a) a unique identifier, such as a UserID (eg johndoe001), a serial number of a token (eg 800123) or a digital representation of a physical characteristic (eg the user's face or fingerprint)
b) an authenticator, such as a password (eg P4sw@rD), digital certificate (eg an x509 certificate) or an action (eg speech or writing on a pressure pad).

CF5.3.4

Access controls for critical business applications or sensitive business applications should be strengthened by requiring:

a) multi-factor authentication (ie a combination of password, token and / or biometric)
b) the use of authentication hardware, such as physical smartcard readers, physical tokens or smartphones
c) additional information to verify the origin of access (eg by location-based authentication that uses IP address geo-location, GPS or GSM Cell-ID positioning).

CF5.3.5

The integrity of critical information should be protected by:

a) encrypting information when in transit
b) using 'digital signatures' so that transactions and communications cannot be repudiated (ie non-repudiation)
c) providing additional authentication for sensitive transactions or procedures (eg when making payments or performing high-value funds transfer) to prevent attacks, such as man-in-the-middle attacks.

FUNDAMENTAL

CF5.3 Customer Connections (continued)

CF5.3.6

Customer access should be subject to a sign-on process before access to business applications is granted. This process should include:

a) performing integrity checks to ensure connecting devices have not been compromised by malware (including computer viruses, worms, trojan horses, spyware, rootkits, keystroke loggers and botnet software)
b) displaying contractual conditions that limit the liabilities of the organisation to customers (eg through the use of using on-screen warnings).

CF5.3.7

Customer access to business applications should be protected (based on the principle of 'least access') by:

a) restricting methods of connection (eg to defined remote access connection devices or entry points and only through firewalls)
b) configuring information systems and networks to restrict access (eg to specific IP addresses or an IP range)
c) restricting the type of access granted (ie in terms of information, application capabilities and access privileges)
d) terminating customer connections on a timely basis (eg when a security breach occurs or when they are no longer required).

Related content	ISF resources
CF6 Access Management	No recent ISF material
CF9.3 External Network Connections	

CONTROL FRAMEWORK

FUNDAMENTAL

AREA CF6 – Access Management

List of Topics
CF6.1   Access Control
CF6.2   User Authorisation
CF6.3   Access Control Mechanisms
CF6.4   Access Control Mechanisms – Password
CF6.5   Access Control Mechanisms – Token
CF6.6   Access Control Mechanisms – Biometric
CF6.7   Sign-on Process

CF6.1   Access Control

Principle   Access control arrangements should be established to restrict access to business applications, information systems, networks and computing devices by all types of user, who should be assigned specific privileges to restrict them to particular information or systems.

Objective   To ensure that only authorised individuals gain access to business applications, information systems, networks and computing devices, that individual accountability is assured and to provide authorised users with access privileges that are sufficient to enable them to perform their duties but do not permit them to exceed their authority.

CF6.1.1

Arrangements should be made to restrict access to business applications, information systems, networks and computing devices, and the information stored on and processed by them.

CF6.1.2

Access control arrangements should be supported by documented standards / procedures, which take account of:

a) an information security policy, information classifications, agreements with application owners, requirements set by the owner of systems and legal, regulatory and contractual obligations
b) the need to achieve individual accountability, apply additional control for users with special access privileges and provide segregation of duties.

CF6.1.3

Access control arrangements should cover access:

a) by all types of individual (eg business users, individuals running systems, IT specialists, such as technical support staff and individuals from external parties)
b) to all types of information and software (eg live business information, application and system software, access control data, back-up files, and system documentation).

CF6.1.4

Access control arrangements should:

a) limit access in line with access policies set by owners of business applications and information systems
b) restrict the system capabilities that can be accessed (eg by providing menus that enable access only to the particular capabilities needed to fulfil a defined role)
c) identify the location of computing devices in use
d) supplement passwords (eg by using strong authentication, such as smartcards, biometrics or tokens), when necessary
e) minimise the need for special access privileges (eg UserIDs that have additional capabilities, such as 'Administrator' in Windows systems, or special capabilities, such as UserIDs that can be used to authorise payments).

FUNDAMENTAL

CONTROL FRAMEWORK

CF6.1 Access Control (continued)

CF6.1.5

Access privileges for both business users and computer staff (eg computer operators and system administrators) should be approved by an appropriate business representative.

CF6.1.6

Before access privileges come into effect:

a) authorisations should be checked to confirm access privileges are appropriate
b) details of users should be recorded, including their true identity, associated identifier (eg UserID) and access privileges to be granted
c) users should be advised of – and be required to confirm understanding of – their access privileges and associated conditions of use.

CF6.1.7

Access privileges should not be assigned collectively (eg using identifiers such as UserIDs or authenticators such as passwords shared in a group) unless special circumstances apply. Whenever they need to be assigned collectively, this should be documented, approved by an appropriate business representative and subject to additional controls (eg restricted access privileges and contractual conditions).

CF6.1.8

Additional controls should be applied to special access privileges, including high-level privileges (eg 'root' in UNIX or 'Administrator' in Windows systems, powerful utilities and privileges that can be used to authorise payments or perform financial transactions), which include:

a) specifying the purpose of special access privileges
b) restricting the use of special access privileges to narrowly-defined circumstances
c) requiring individual approval for the use of special access privileges
d) requiring users with special access privileges to sign-on using identification codes or tokens that differ from those used in normal circumstances
e) logging and reviewing the use of special access privileges.

CF6.1.9

A process for terminating the access privileges of users should be established to ensure that:

a) authentication details and access rights are revoked promptly on all systems to which the user had access
b) access profiles / accounts are deleted
c) components dedicated to providing access, such as tokens, modems or virtual private networks (VPNs) are disabled or removed.

CF6.1.10

Access control arrangements should be:

a) reviewed on a regular basis
b) upgraded in response to new threats, capabilities, business requirements or experience of information security incidents.

Related content

CF8.2 Identity and Access Management

ISF resources

Identity and Access Management (IAM): Workshop Report

Federated Identity and Access Management: Creating a connected world

CONTROL FRAMEWORK

FUNDAMENTAL

CF6.2 User Authorisation

Principle All individuals with access to business applications, information systems, networks and computing devices should be authorised before they are granted access privileges.

Objective To restrict access to business applications, information systems, networks and computing devices to authorised users.

CF6.2.1

The processes for authorising users should:

a) be defined in writing, approved by the relevant owner and applied to all users
b) associate access privileges with defined users (eg using unique identifiers such as UserIDs)
c) assign users with default access based on the principle of least privilege (eg 'none' rather than 'read')
d) ensure redundant identifiers (eg UserIDs) are not reissued for use.

CF6.2.2

A file or database containing details of all authorised users for each system should be established, which should be maintained by designated individuals, such as particular system administrators, and protected against unauthorised change or unauthorised disclosure.

CF6.2.3

Details of authorised users should be reviewed:

a) to ensure that access privileges remain appropriate
b) to check that redundant authorisations have been deleted (eg for individuals who have changed roles or left the organisation)
c) on a regular basis (eg at least every six months)
d) on a more regular basis for users with special access privileges (eg every three months).

Related content	ISF resources
CF8.2 Identity and Access Management	Identity and Access Management (IAM): Workshop Report
	Federated Identity and Access Management: Creating a connected world
	Managing access in a changing world: Digest Report

FUNDAMENTAL

CONTROL FRAMEWORK

CF6.3   Access Control Mechanisms

Principle   Access to business applications, information systems, networks and computing devices should be restricted to authorised individuals by the use of access control mechanisms.

Objective   To limit access to only authorised individuals.

CF6.3.1

Access to business applications, information systems, networks and computing devices should be restricted by using access control mechanisms, such as passwords, tokens or biometrics.

> Access control mechanisms typically involve the submission of two pieces of information to prove an identity: a unique identifier (eg UserID or a user's email address) and a corresponding authenticator (eg a password, digital certificate or fingerprint scan).
>
> Access control mechanisms are often classified in terms of the factors that are used to authenticate users, and are based upon something the user:
>
> - knows (eg a password)
> - has (eg physical token, smartcard or digital certificate)
> - is or does (eg biometrics such as fingerprint, iris pattern, hand geometry, voice characteristic or writing style).

CF6.3.2

The implementation of access control mechanisms should be based on:

a) the results of a risk assessment
b) an assessment of the criticality of information being accessed
c) determining the access control requirements (eg usability, resistance to attack and budgetary constraints)
d) evaluating access control mechanism functionality
e) considering additional selection factors (eg vendor preference or integration with a physical security system)
f) selecting the most suitable access control mechanism (eg following a comparison of assessed access control mechanisms).

> Organisations often choose to combine more than one access control mechanism (eg passwords and tokens or passwords and biometrics) to provide stronger authentication.

CF6.3.3

The use of access control mechanisms should be based on:

a) usability (eg simplicity, reliability, speed of use and ease of user administration)
b) resistance to attack (eg brute force, social engineering, malware and theft of authentication equipment)
c) budgetary constraints (eg licensing, integration, provisioning and training, and maintenance).

CF6.3.4

The functionality of potential access control mechanisms should be subject to an evaluation to determine the degree to which they will meet access requirements. The evaluation should take into account:

a) the strength of existing controls that influence the suitability of access control mechanisms (eg identity and access management, physical security or system hardening)
b) special factors that may influence the choice of access control mechanism (eg vendor preference, integration with physical security or regulatory pressures).

CF6.3 Access Control Mechanisms (continued)

CF6.3.5

Access control mechanisms should be provided using approved hardware / software (eg 'pictures and patterns' software, physical tokens, fingerprint readers and iris scanners).

Related content	ISF resources
CF5.3 Customer Connections	*Identity and Access Management (IAM): Workshop Report* *Managing access in a changing world: Digest Report*

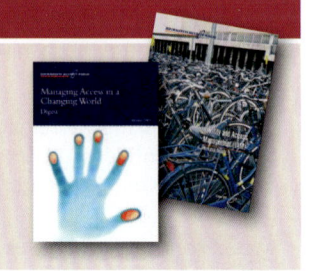

SPECIALISED

CONTROL FRAMEWORK

CF6.4   Access Control Mechanisms – Password

Principle   Target environments (eg business applications, information systems or network devices) that are configured with access control mechanisms based on passwords, should require users to provide a valid UserID and password before they can gain access to them.

Objective   To prevent unauthorised users from gaining access to password-protected critical or sensitive information, business applications, information systems, networks or computing devices.

CF6.4.1

All users should be authenticated by using an identifier (eg a UserID) and an authenticator (eg a password (sometimes referred to as a passphrase, passcode and PIN code)) before they can gain access to any critical or sensitive business information, business applications, operating systems, computing devices or networks.

> Organisations often enhance password authentication to resist attacks (eg from key loggers and malicious browser plug-ins) by using 'obscured passwords' or 'pictures and pattern' recognition techniques. These techniques typically resist attack by requiring the user to use a combination of information displayed on the screen (eg determining the corresponding password using a translation grid), selections made using the mouse (eg clicking on images) and entering information via keyboards (eg a translated password). This method reduces the likelihood of malware detecting complete password characters being typed in at the keyboard.

CF6.4.2

Users of access control mechanisms based on passwords should be advised to:

a) keep passwords confidential (ie to avoid making them visible to others by writing them down or disclosing them to others)
b) change passwords that may have been compromised
c) report if passwords have been or are suspected of being compromised.

CF6.4.3

Access control mechanisms based on passwords should be enforced by automated means that:

a) ensure UserIDs are unique
b) ensure passwords are not displayed on screen or on print-outs
c) issue temporary passwords to users that must be changed on first use
d) force new passwords to be verified before the change is accepted
e) ensure users set their own passwords
f) restrict the re-use of passwords (eg so that they cannot be used again within a set period or set number of changes).

CF6.4.4

Access control mechanisms based on passwords should be enforced by automated means that ensures passwords:

a) are a minimum number of characters in length (eg eight characters)
b) differ from their associated UserIDs
c) contain no more than two identical characters in a row
d) are not dictionary words
e) are not made up of all numeric or alpha characters
f) are changed regularly (eg every 30 days) and more frequently for users with special access privileges.

CONTROL FRAMEWORK

SPECIALISED

CF6.4 Access Control Mechanisms – Password (continued)

The frequency with which a password is changed is often dependent on the complexity of the password and the likelihood of attack (eg by brute-force or dictionary password attack). To provide a balance that minimises inconvenience for the user, organisations often choose to increase the minimum number of characters (eg to 10 characters) in order to reduce the frequency of password change (eg between 60-180 days). This approach is often seen as an acceptable compromise that improves the chances of the user accepting a complex password.

CF6.4.5

There should be a process for issuing new or changed passwords that:

a) ensures that passwords are not sent in the form of clear text (eg in email or text messages)
b) directly involves the person to whom the password uniquely applies (eg face-to-face registration in a secure location or via registered delivery requiring the person's proof of identification and their signature)
c) verifies the identity of the user, such as via a special code or through independent confirmation
d) includes notification to users when passwords are due to expire in a short time (eg 10 days).

Related content	ISF resources
CF6.3 Access Control Mechanisms	*Managing access in a changing world: Digest Report*

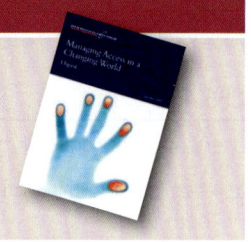

SPECIALISED

CONTROL FRAMEWORK

CF6.5 Access Control Mechanisms – Token

Principle Target environments (eg business applications, information systems or network devices) that are configured with access control mechanisms based on tokens, should require users to provide a valid token (eg physical token, soft token or smartcard) and any related authentication information before they can gain access to them.

Objective To prevent unauthorised users from gaining access to token-protected critical or sensitive information, business applications, information systems, networks or computing devices.

CF6.5.1

Users should be authenticated by using token authentication (eg physical tokens, soft tokens or smartcards) before they can gain access to critical or sensitive business information, business applications, operating systems, computing devices or networks.

> Token authentication is a form of authentication that typically involves the use of either physical tokens, software tokens or smartcards. Token authentication is often used by administrators, privileged users such as individuals that authorise payments, traders, individuals that require remote access to the corporate network via a virtual private network, external individuals (eg those from customers, business partners and suppliers) and authorised individuals connecting from non-corporate equipment.

CF6.5.2

Token authentication should be provided using approved hardware (eg smartcard readers or physical tokens).

CF6.5.3

There should be a process for registering new token users and issuing them with tokens that:

a) ensures that passwords relating to tokens are not sent in the form of clear text (eg in email or text messages)
b) directly involves the person to whom the token uniquely applies (eg face-to-face registration in a secure location)
c) verifies the identity of the user, such as via a special code or through independent confirmation.

CF6.5.4

Users of token authentication should be advised to:

a) keep passwords for access to tokens confidential (ie to avoid making them visible to others by writing them down or disclosing them to others)
b) protect tokens against loss, theft and misuse (eg avoid sharing with unauthorised individuals)
c) report if the tokens have been or are suspected of being compromised (eg tampered with).

CF6.5.5

There should be a secure process to enable users to authenticate when the token authentication fails (eg issuing temporary or one-time passwords).

CF6.5.6

Where passwords are used to supplement token authentication (eg to access a physical token or for fall-back purposes) good password practices should be applied, such as preventing the use of weak passwords, changing passwords regularly and restricting the re-use of passwords.

CF6.5 Access Control Mechanisms – Token (continued)

Related content

CF6.3 Access Control Mechanisms

CF8.4 Cryptographic Solutions

CF8.5 Cryptographic Key Management

CF8.6 Public Key Infrastructure

ISF resources

Managing access in a changing world: Digest Report

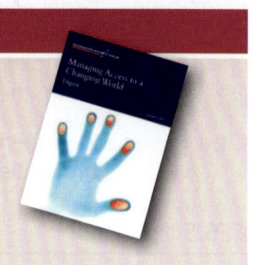

SPECIALISED

CF6.6 Access Control Mechanisms – Biometric

Principle Target environments (eg business applications, information systems or network devices) that are configured with access control mechanisms based on biometrics, should require users to provide a valid biometric (eg fingerprint / vein recognition, iris / retina patterns or voice characteristics) and any related authentication information before they can gain access to them.

Objective To prevent unauthorised users from gaining access to biometric-protected critical or sensitive information, business applications, information systems, networks or computing devices.

CF6.6.1

Users should be authenticated by using biometric access control mechanisms (eg fingerprint / vein recognition, iris / retina patterns or voice characteristics) before they can gain access to critical or sensitive business information, business applications, operating systems, computing devices or networks.

> Biometric authentication is a form of authentication that uses specialised physical readers to measure a physical characteristic of a user such as their fingerprint, voice or iris pattern. Biometric authentication is often used by administrators, privileged users such as individuals that authorise payments, traders, individuals who require remote access to the corporate network via a virtual private network, external individuals (eg those from customers, business partners and suppliers) and authorised individuals connecting from non-corporate equipment.

CF6.6.2

There should be a process for registering users' biometrics that:

a) directly involves the person to whom the biometric uniquely applies (ie face-to-face registration in a secure location)
b) verifies the identity of the user, such as via face-to-face confirmation and inspecting official identity documentation (eg a passport, national ID card or driving license)
c) ensures that biometric information (ie the digital template stored in an authentication database, repository or equivalent) is not made available to unauthorised individuals.

CF6.6.3

Users of biometric authentication should be advised to:

a) keep passwords for access to biometric equipment confidential (ie to avoid making them visible to others by writing them down or disclosing them to others)
b) protect equipment used for biometric authentication against loss, theft and misuse (eg sharing with unauthorised individuals)
c) report if the biometric equipment has been or is suspected of being compromised (eg tampered with).

CF6.6.4

Biometric authentication should include a method of confirming the user is alive (eg by monitoring for a pulse, or waiting for the user to blink).

CF6.6.5

There should be a secure process to enable users to authenticate when the biometric authentication fails (eg issuing temporary or one-time passwords).

CF6.6.6

Where passwords are used to supplement biometric authentication (eg to access a physical token or for fall-back purposes) good password practices should be applied, such as preventing the use of weak passwords, changing passwords regularly and restricting the re-use of passwords.

CONTROL FRAMEWORK

SPECIALISED

CF6.6 Access Control Mechanisms – Biometric (continued)

CF6.6.7

Biometric authentication should be configured (often referred to as tuning) to reduce the likelihood of false positives and false negatives.

> Tuning is the process of balancing the accuracy required for authentication against the speed of operation. Tuning aims to balance the numbers of false positives (when the user is wrongly granted access) and false negatives (where the user is wrongly rejected) to a level that is acceptable to the organisation.

Related content	ISF resources
CF6.3 Access Control Mechanisms	*Managing access in a changing world: Digest Report*

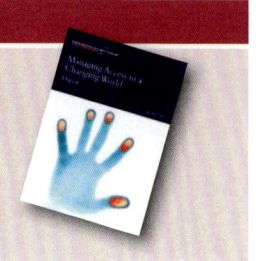

FUNDAMENTAL

CF6.7 Sign-on Process

Principle — Users should be subject to a rigorous sign-on process before being provided with access to business applications, information systems, networks and computing devices.

Objective — To ensure that only authorised users can gain access to business applications, information systems, networks and computing devices.

CF6.7.1

There should be a sign-on process that users need to follow before they are provided with access to information systems, which should enable individual users to be identified (eg using unique UserIDs).

CF6.7.2

Sign-on mechanisms should be configured so that they:

a) validate sign-on information only when it has all been entered
b) limit the number of unsuccessful sign-on attempts which are permitted (eg a re-try limit of three)
c) restrict additional sign-on attempts
d) limit the duration of any one sign-on session
e) are re-enabled automatically after interruption (eg following a disconnection from the application).

CF6.7.3

Sign-on mechanisms should be configured to provide information so that they:

a) display no identifying details until after sign-on is completed successfully
b) warn that only authorised users are permitted access
c) record all successful and unsuccessful sign-on attempts
d) advise users (on successful sign-on) of the date / time of their last successful sign-on and all unsuccessful sign-on attempts since their most recent successful sign-on.

CF6.7.4

Sign-on mechanisms should be configured so that they do not store authentication details as clear text in automated routines (eg in scripts, macros or cache memory).

CF6.7.5

The approval of an appropriate business representative should be obtained before any important features of the sign-on process are bypassed, disabled or changed.

Related content

CF8.2 Identity and Access Management

ISF resources

Identity and Access Management (IAM): Workshop Report

Federated Identity and Access Management: Creating a connected world

Managing access in a changing world: Digest Report

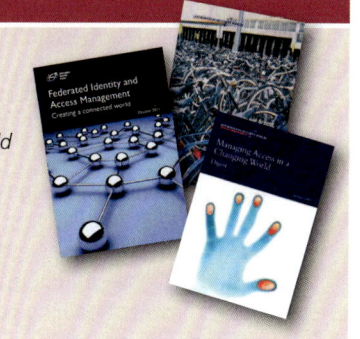

CONTROL FRAMEWORK

FUNDAMENTAL

AREA CF7 – System Management

List of Topics
CF7.1   Computer and Network Installations
CF7.2   Server Configuration
CF7.3   Virtual Servers
CF7.4   Network Storage Systems
CF7.5   Back-up
CF7.6   Change Management
CF7.7   Service Level Agreements

CF7.1   Computer and Network Installations

Principle   Computer system, network and telecommunication installations (eg data centres) should be designed to cope with current and predicted information processing requirements, and be protected using a range of in-built security controls.

Objective   To ensure computer system, network and telecommunication installations can meet the security requirements of the critical business applications they support (ie protect against the compromise of confidentiality, integrity and availability of information they process).

CF7.1.1

There should be documented standards / procedures for information system, network and telecommunication installation designs, which require:

a) designs to take account of security architecture principles, business and security requirements
b) compatibility to be maintained with other information systems, networks and telecommunication installations used by the organisation
c) information system, network and telecommunication installations to be designed to cope with foreseeable developments in the organisation's use of IT (eg growth projections or adoption of open / proprietary standards).

CF7.1.2

Information system, network and telecommunication installations should:

a) be managed from a central point (eg a computer or network operations centre)
b) minimise the need for manual intervention (eg by incorporating high-reliability or fault-tolerant computers and automating common operations such as patch management and back-up)
c) be set up so that they can be configured remotely, and automatically monitored against predefined thresholds
d) encrypt administrative access to information systems, network devices and telecommunications equipment (eg by using secure management consoles or secure remote login shells such as ssh).

CF7.1.3

Information system, network and telecommunication installations should be designed to incorporate security architecture principles by:

a) building security into the design of installations (ie 'security by design')
b) using multiple layers of different types of protection (ie 'defence in depth')
c) granting users the minimum level of access (ie 'least privilege')
d) incorporating a coherent, integrated set of technical standards
e) supporting consistent naming conventions (eg computer / server addresses, network device names, terminal locations and user identifiers)
f) minimising single points of failure (eg by providing load balancing, duplicate or alternative system components and network devices)
g) providing fail secure systems where in the event of a system failure, information is not accessible to unauthorised individuals, and cannot be tampered with or modified.

FUNDAMENTAL

CONTROL FRAMEWORK

CF7.1 Computer and Network Installations (continued)

CF7.1.4

Computer, network and telecommunications equipment (including network routers and switches, and in-house telephone exchanges) should have:

a) sufficient capacity to cope with peak workloads
b) expansion / upgrade capabilities to cope with projected demand
c) a control and monitoring facility capable of providing management reports.

CF7.1.5

Information systems should be designed to:

a) include the installation of malware protection software on key servers
b) enable a standard predetermined server configuration to be built (often referred to as a 'server image' or standard build), which can be automated
c) enable authorised users to access multiple systems and resources via reduced (or single) sign-on
d) be administered from a central point (eg via an identity and access management (IAM) system).

CF7.1.6

Networks should be designed to:

a) incorporate the use of security domains (including 'Demilitarised Zones' (DMZs)) to segregate systems with specific security requirements
b) employ firewalls in a manner that prevents them from being bypassed
c) isolate particular types of network traffic (eg VoIP data or Storage Area Network (SAN) storage data) using a dedicated network, to prevent impact on other network traffic
d) perform network traffic prioritisation and 'class of service' to reduce network latency
e) restrict the number of entry points into networks
f) allow access only to 'trusted' devices by preventing unauthorised devices from connecting to networks (eg by forcing authentication at the network level).

CF7.1.7

Key components of computer and network installations should be protected by:

a) segregating critical business applications from all other business applications and information, as agreed with their business owners
b) storing source code (or equivalent) in a secure location away from the live environment and restricting access to this code to authorised individuals
c) segregating different types of software and information (eg by storing them in separate directories)
d) permitting only execute access to executable software (eg run-time code, stored procedures or Common Gateway Interface (CGI) scripts).

CF7.1.8

Live environments should be segregated from development and acceptance testing activity by

a) using different computer rooms, processors, virtual servers, domains and partitions
b) by storing system utilities away from the live environment when not in use.

Related content	ISF resources
CF4.1 Application Protection	ISF Briefing: Network convergence
CF8.1 Security Architecture	Architectural Responses to the Disappearing Network Boundary

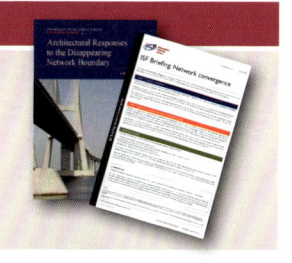

CF7.2 Server Configuration

Principle Servers should be configured to function as required, and to prevent unauthorised or incorrect updates.

Objective To ensure servers operate as intended and do not compromise the security of computer installations or other environments.

CF7.2.1

Servers should be configured in accordance with documented standards / procedures, which should cover:

a) providing standard firmware configurations
b) disabling or restricting unnecessary functions or services
c) restricting access to powerful system utilities and host parameter settings (eg Windows 'Registry Editor')
d) protection against unauthorised access
e) performing standard security management practices.

CF7.2.2

Servers should be provided with standard firmware configurations that include:

a) pre-configured BIOS settings (eg disabling the boot menu and USB / DVD boot option)
b) restricting access to the BIOS functions only to authorised administrators (eg by using password protection).

CF7.2.3

Servers should be configured to disable or restrict:

a) non-essential or redundant services (eg X Windows, Open Windows, fingerd and web browsers)
b) communication services that are inherently susceptible to abuse (eg tftp, RPC, rlogin, rsh or rexec)
c) communication protocols that are prone to abuse (eg HTTP, HTTPS, SSH, FTP, SMTP, Telnet and UUCP)
d) execute permissions on sensitive commands or scripts (eg rlogin, rcp, rsh, remsh, tstp and trtp)
e) powerful utilities (eg Windows 'Registry Editor') or 'control panels'
f) run commands or command processors (eg Perl or Tcl).

CF7.2.4

Access to powerful system utilities and server parameter settings should be:

a) restricted to a limited number of trusted individuals
b) restricted to narrowly-defined circumstances (eg for the duration of an authorised change)
c) subject to authorisation (eg by the person in charge of computer installations).

CF7.2.5

Servers should be protected against unauthorised access by:

a) disabling unnecessary or insecure user accounts (eg the 'Guest' account (or equivalent) for Microsoft Windows and UNIX systems)
b) changing important security-related parameters (eg passwords) to be different from the defaults set by suppliers
c) invoking time-out facilities that automatically log off computer devices (that connect to the server) after a set period of inactivity, clear screens and require users to sign-on again before restoring screens.

FUNDAMENTAL

CF7.2 Server Configuration (continued)

CF7.2.6

Servers should be subject to standard security management practices, which include:

a) restricting physical access to servers to authorised staff (eg by locating them in protected data centres or dedicated, locked storage rooms)
b) keeping them up-to-date (eg by applying approved change management and patch management processes)
c) deploying malware protection software to prevent infection by malicious software (eg computer viruses, worms, trojan horses, spyware, rootkits, keystroke loggers, and botnet software)
d) applying a comprehensive set of management tools (eg maintenance utilities, remote support, enterprise management tools and back-up software)
e) monitoring them (eg using Simple Network Management Protocol (SNMP)) so that events such as hardware failure and attacks against them can be detected and responded to effectively
f) reviewing them on a regular basis to verify configuration settings, evaluate password strengths and to assess activities performed on the server (eg by inspecting logs).

Related content	ISF resources
CF8 Technical Security Infrastructure	No recent ISF material
CF10.1 Patch Management	
CF16.2 Hardware / Software Acquisition	
CF19 Physical and Environmental Security	

CONTROL FRAMEWORK

SPECIALISED

CF7.3 Virtual Servers

Principle Virtual servers should be subject to approval, deployed on robust, secure physical servers and configured to segregate sensitive information.

Objective To prevent business disruption as a result of system overload or disclosure of sensitive information to unauthorised individuals.

CF7.3.1

Virtual servers should be deployed, configured and maintained in accordance with documented standards / procedures.

> Server virtualisation enables organisations to create one or more discrete environments on a single physical server. Virtualisation involves three main components: a physical server; a hypervisor; and one or more virtual servers. The hypervisor allocates the physical server's resources to each virtual server (including CPU, memory, hard disk or network) allowing them to operate simultaneously and in isolation from each other.

CF7.3.2

Standards / procedures should cover the protection of:

a) physical servers that are used to host virtual servers
b) hypervisors associated with virtual servers
c) virtual servers that run on a physical server.

CF7.3.3

Physical servers that are used to host virtual servers should be protected by:

a) locating them in physically secure environments (eg data centres or equivalent)
b) restricting physical and logical access to authorised individuals (eg administrators)
c) requiring authorisation when any access is needed (eg by the administrator(s), owner(s) or business user(s) of the physical or virtual servers).

CF7.3.4

Physical servers that are used to host virtual servers should be protected against:

a) unmanaged and *ad hoc* deployment (often referred to as 'virtual server sprawl')
b) resource overload (eg excessive use of the CPU, memory, hard disk and network) by restricting the maximum number of virtual servers that can be created on each physical server.

CF7.3.5

Hypervisors should be configured to:

a) segregate virtual servers according to the confidentiality requirements of information they process
b) logically separate each virtual server to prevent information being transferred between discrete environments
c) restrict access to a limited number of authorised individuals (eg hypervisor administrators) who are capable of creating virtual servers and making changes to them correctly and securely
d) encrypt communications between virtual servers (eg using Secure Sockets Layer (SSL) or IPSec)
e) segregate the roles of hypervisor administrators (for multiple virtual servers).

SPECIALISED

CF7.3 Virtual Servers (continued)

CF7.3.6

Virtual servers should be protected by applying standard security management practices to hypervisors, which include:

a) applying a strict change management process (eg changes are validated, tested and deployed within a critical timeframe) to help ensure the hypervisor remains up-to-date
b) monitoring, reporting and reviewing administrator activities to help ensure actions and privileges that they are allowed to perform are specifically aligned to their duties
c) restricting access to the virtual server management console (or equivalent)
d) monitoring network traffic between different virtual servers and between virtual servers and physical servers to detect malicious or unexpected behaviour.

CF7.3.7

Each virtual server should be protected by applying standard security management practices (including restricting physical access, system hardening, applying change management and malware protection, monitoring and performing regular reviews, and applying network-based security controls (eg firewalls, intrusion detection and data leakage protection)).

Related content	ISF resources
CF7.2 Server Configuration	ISF Briefing: Server Virtualisation
CF19 Physical and Environmental Security	

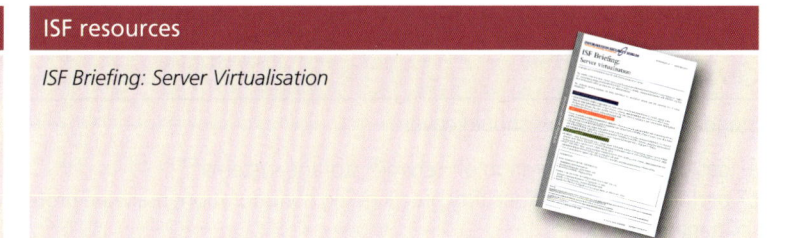

CF7.4 Network Storage Systems

Principle Network storage systems should be protected using system and network controls.

Objective To ensure network storage systems operate as intended, are available when required and do not compromise the security of information they store.

CF7.4.1

Network storage systems, such as Storage Area Network (SAN) and Network-Attached Storage (NAS) should be deployed, configured and maintained in accordance with documented standards / procedures.

> Traditional data storage involves connecting an array of hard disks directly to individual servers (referred to as Direct-Attached Storage (DAS)). Alternative storage systems are now often provided over the network (network storage) in the form of:
>
> - Network-Attached Storage (NAS) – a self-contained intelligent storage device (often referred to as a NAS device or a NAS filer), which is attached to a network and is typically used by computing devices on that network to store files
> - Storage Area Network (SAN) – a dedicated network that comprises a variety of disparate storage technologies (eg disk arrays, storage systems, mainframe disks and tape libraries), which are accessible by servers as a unified network of storage.

CF7.4.2

Standards / procedures should cover:

a) design and configuration of network storage systems
b) performing standard security practices (eg configuration, malware protection, change management and patch management)
c) protection of network storage management consoles and administration interfaces
d) encryption of information stored on network storage systems
e) security arrangements specific to NAS and SAN.

CF7.4.3

Network storage systems should be designed and configured to:

a) use standardised components (eg avoid mixing hardware from different vendors)
b) be managed from a central point (eg a computer or network operations centre) using a minimum number of management consoles
c) restrict access to particular areas of storage (eg by implementing zoning where logical partitions on disks are allocated to particular servers, or masking which restricts access to areas of hard disk drives authorised servers) to prevent unauthorised or unauthenticated access
d) enable authorised users to access multiple systems and resources via single sign-on.

CF7.4.4

Network storage systems should be subject to standard security management practices (eg restricting physical access, performing system 'hardening', applying change management and malware protection, monitoring them and performing regular reviews).

CF7.4.5

Sensitive information stored on network storage systems should be protected according to its security requirements by:

a) restricting access to NAS devices to authorised network devices (eg using a VLAN or dedicated IP network)
b) enabling 'file-locking' (eg in conjunction with operating systems or LDAP directories).

SPECIALISED

CF7.4 Network Storage Systems (continued)

CF7.4.6

Network storage system components (including operating systems, SAN switches and management consoles and NAS device operating systems and utilities) should be protected by:

a) restricting administration access (eg to SAN management consoles and NAS device utilities) to a limited number of authorised staff (eg storage administrators)
b) using access controls that support individual accountability, and protected from unauthorised access
c) restricting management functions (eg in SAN management consoles and NAS device utilities)
d) using secure web protocols and secure services such as SSL and TLS for access to the management console and SSH for running terminal sessions.

Related content	ISF resources
CF6 Access Management	ISF Briefing: Securing Data Storage (NAS and SAN)
CF19.1 Physical Protection	
CF20.3 Resilience	

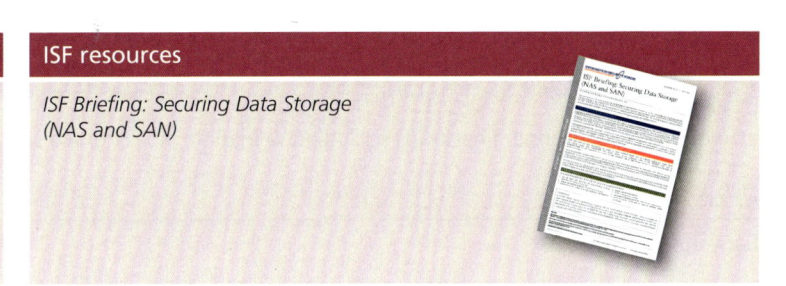

CONTROL FRAMEWORK

FUNDAMENTAL

CF7.5 Back-up

Principle Back-ups of essential information and software should be performed on a regular basis, according to a defined cycle.

Objective To ensure that, in the event of an emergency, essential information or software can be restored within critical timescales.

CF7.5.1

Back-ups of essential information and software (eg business information, systems information and application information) should be performed frequently enough to meet business requirements.

CF7.5.2

There should be documented standards / procedures for performing back-ups, which cover:

a) the types of information to be backed up
b) back-up cycles
c) methods for performing back-ups (including validation, labelling and storage).

CF7.5.3

Back-ups should be:

a) performed using specially designed back-up management software to strengthen the security of information backed up
b) encrypted to protect important information (eg in the event back-up media is stolen or is lost in transit to an alternative location, such as an off-site storage facility)
c) recorded in a log (or equivalent), which includes details about data backed up, the date and time of the back-up, the back-up media used and its physical location
d) verified to ensure that backed up software and information can be restored successfully
e) related to control points in live processes (eg by using time-stamps)
f) reconciled to the live version when copies are taken (eg by checking of file size, hash totalling or other methods of verification)
g) clearly and accurately labelled
h) protected from accidental overwriting, and be subject to the same level of protection as live information.

CF7.5.4

Critical timescales for data to be backed up should be identified (eg based on the availability requirements of information).

CF7.5.5

Back-up arrangements should enable software and information to be restored within a critical timescale (ie the timescale beyond which a loss of service would be unacceptable to the organisation) by using one or more:

a) online storage (which often involves backing up information to Direct-Attached Storage (DAS), Storage Area Network (SAN) or Network-Attached Storage (NAS)) that typically provides access to back-ups of information almost instantaneously
b) near-line storage (which often involves backing up information to an automated tape library) that enables the restore of information within minutes
c) off-line storage, which often involves IT staff who perform the back-up and restore activities manually and results in longer restore times.

> Many organisations will implement a back-up solution that combines online, near-line and off-line storage, and periodically moves backed up information from online storage to near-line storage and then to off-line storage, as requirements for access to the information change.

FUNDAMENTAL

CF7.5 Back-up (continued)

CF7.5.6

Back-ups should be protected from loss, damage and unauthorised access, by:

a) storing back-up media (eg DVDs, magnetic tapes, computer disks) in accordance with manufacturer specifications
b) locating them in a locked, computer media fireproof safe on-site, to enable important information to be restored quickly
c) keeping copies in secure facilities off-site, to enable systems or networks to be restored using alternative facilities in the event of a disaster
d) restricting access to authorised staff (eg through the use of access control software, physical locks and keys).

Related content	ISF resources
No direct references	No recent ISF material

CONTROL FRAMEWORK **FUNDAMENTAL**

CF7.6 Change Management

Principle Changes to business applications, computer systems and networks should be tested, reviewed and applied using a change management process.

Objective To ensure that changes are applied correctly and do not compromise the security of business applications, computer systems or networks.

CF7.6.1

A change management process should be established, which covers all types of change (eg upgrades and modifications to application and software, modifications to business information, emergency 'fixes', and changes to information systems and networks).

CF7.6.2

The change management process should be documented, and include approving and testing changes to ensure that:

a) they are made correctly and securely
b) they do not compromise security controls
c) no unauthorised changes have been made.

CF7.6.3

Prior to changes being applied to the live environment:

a) change requests should be documented (eg on a change request form) and accepted only from authorised individuals
b) changes should be approved by an appropriate business representative
c) the potential business impacts of changes should be assessed (eg in terms of overall risk and impact on other components of information systems and networks)
d) changes should be tested to help determine the expected results (eg the results of deploying a patch into the live environment)
e) changes should be reviewed to ensure that they do not compromise security controls (eg by checking software to ensure it does not contain malicious code, such as a computer virus, trojan horse or back door)
f) back-out positions should be established so that information systems and networks can recover from failed changes or unexpected results.

CF7.6.4

Changes to information systems and networks should be:

a) performed by skilled and competent individuals who are capable of making changes correctly and securely
b) supervised by an IT specialist
c) signed off by an appropriate business representative.

CF7.6.5

Arrangements should be made to ensure that once changes have been applied:

a) version control is maintained (eg using configuration management)
b) a record is maintained, showing what was changed, when, and by whom (eg using automated helpdesk / service desk software)
c) details of changes are communicated to relevant individuals (eg associated users, business managers and relevant external parties)
d) checks are performed to confirm that only intended changes have been made (eg by comparing code against a control version or checking 'before and after' contents of key records, such as within customer master files)
e) documents associated with information systems and networks are updated (eg design information, system configuration, implementation details, and records of all changes to information systems and networks)
f) the classification of information associated with information systems and networks is reviewed.

FUNDAMENTAL

CF7.6 Change Management (continued)

CF7.6.6

Checks should be performed on a regular basis to confirm that only intended changes have been made (eg by using code comparison programs or checking 'before and after' contents of key records such as customer master files).

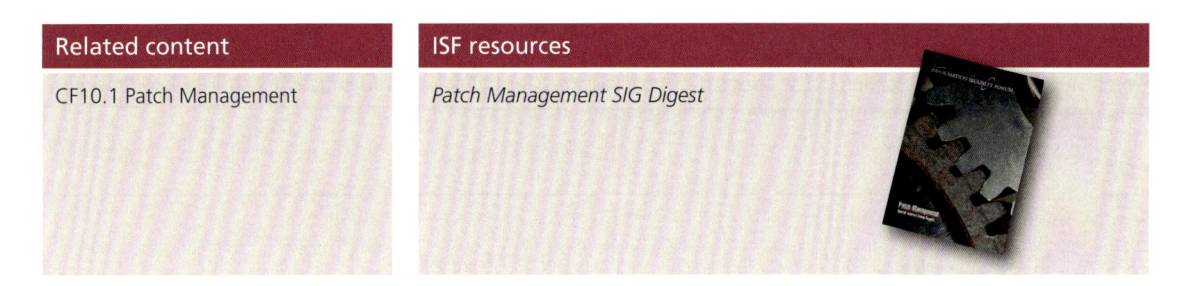

Related content	ISF resources
CF10.1 Patch Management	*Patch Management SIG Digest*

CONTROL FRAMEWORK **FUNDAMENTAL**

CF7.7 Service Level Agreements

Principle Computer and network services that support critical business processes and applications should only be obtained from service providers capable of providing required security controls, and be supported by documented contracts or service level agreements.

Objective To define the business requirements for providers of any computer or network services, including those for information security, and to ensure they are met.

CF7.7.1

Computer and network services that support critical business applications and processes should be defined in documented service agreements (eg contracts or service level agreements).

CF7.7.2

Service agreements should specify:

a) who is in charge of the computer and network services being provided
b) who is in charge of delivering the required service (eg an internal specialised department or external service provider, such as an ISP)
c) the level of criticality of the service
d) dates / times when the service is required
e) the capacity requirements of systems and networks (eg the projected number of users, normal and peak volumes of work to be handled, response times and transmission rates)
f) maximum permissible down-time
g) critical timescales (ie the timescale beyond which a loss of service would be unacceptable to the organisation)
h) the penalties to be imposed in the event the service provider fails to deliver the pre-agreed level of service.

CF7.7.3

Service agreements should specify access control requirements, including:

a) access restrictions (eg restricting business users and support staff; permissible / disallowed methods of connection; and access points)
b) authentication methods
c) restrictions on methods of connection (eg Internet, ISDN or dial-up) and access to particular services (eg public Internet services)
d) segregating computer and network components, such as dedicated lines for sensitive network traffic.

CF7.7.4

Service agreements should specify requirements for:

a) segregation of duties and facilities
b) protection against malware (eg computer viruses, worms, trojan horses, spyware, rootkits, botnet software, keystroke loggers, adware and malicious mobile code)
c) protecting confidential information in transit (eg by using encryption)
d) installation and maintenance activity relating to hardware and software
e) change management and patch management
f) information security incident management (including details of key contacts and escalation procedures)
g) detecting service interruptions and recovering from them
h) ensuring business and system continuity of service.

FUNDAMENTAL

CF7.7 Service Level Agreements (continued)

CF7.7.5

Arrangements should be made to:

a) restrict the use of services to those provided by approved suppliers
b) obtain independent confirmation of the security controls applied by the service provider
c) deal with security issues via a single point of contact and through an individual who is sufficiently senior and competent to deal with security issues effectively.

CF7.7.6

Service agreements should be:

a) assessed by an information security specialist
b) signed off by an appropriate business representative (eg the individual in charge of a business process or activity) and the service provider
c) enforced according to the agreed, documented conditions
d) reviewed on a regular basis to ensure service targets are being achieved and security requirements are being met.

Related content	ISF resources
CF5.2 Customer Contracts	No recent ISF material

CONTROL FRAMEWORK   **SPECIALISED**

AREA CF8 – Technical Security Infrastructure

List of Topics

CF8.1 Security Architecture	CF8.5 Cryptographic Key Management
CF8.2 Identity and Access Management	CF8.6 Public Key Infrastructure
CF8.3 Critical Infrastructure	CF8.7 Information Leakage Protection
CF8.4 Cryptographic Solutions	CF8.8 Digital Rights Management

CF8.1 Security Architecture

Principle A security architecture should be established, which provides a framework for the application of standard information security controls throughout the organisation.

Objective To enable system developers and administrators to implement consistent, simple-to-use security functionality across multiple business applications and computer systems throughout the organisation.

CF8.1.1

A security architecture should be established and be incorporated into the organisation's enterprise architecture (or equivalent).

CF8.1.2

Development of the security architecture should involve:

a) an assessment of business security requirements
b) the use of a layered security architecture model (eg consisting of conceptual, logical and physical layers)
c) the definition of security architecture principles
d) the identification of security components that may be included in the security architecture (eg security controls, security services and security technologies)
e) the development of tools and resources that will be used to help manage the security architecture (eg repositories of solutions, design patterns, code samples and application programming interfaces (APIs)).

> Security architecture principles (sometimes referred to as guiding principles or design principles) represent fundamental security rules that should be followed during the development of a security architecture, and applied via the implementation of corresponding security controls.

CF8.1.3

Development of the security architecture should include:

a) input from relevant internal specialists (eg a technical architect or information security specialist)
b) use of a security architecture specialist (eg a security architect)
c) education of individuals who need to use the security architecture (eg information security specialists, software developers and IT implementers).

CF8.1 Security Architecture (continued)

CF8.1.4

Security architecture principles should be applied when developing and implementing security controls, and include:

a) secure by design (ie considering the security requirements of a business application or information system as part of its overall requirements, to protect itself and the information it processes, and to resist attacks)
b) defence in depth (ie using multiple layers of different types of protection) to avoid reliance on one type or method of security control
c) secure by default (ie setting preselected options to limit the level of inherent vulnerability, such as providing least privilege (eg only granting the minimum possible access privileges to software and users) or making only necessary services and features available)
d) default deny (ie denying access to information systems by default to prevent unauthorised access)
e) fail secure (ie in the event of a system failure, information is not accessible to unauthorised individuals, remains available to authorised individuals and cannot be tampered with or modified)
f) secure in deployment (eg by providing complementary tools and guidance to help support system administrators and users, ensuring configuration is not difficult and software updates are simple to deploy)
g) usability and manageability (ie security controls should not obstruct users in performing their work and should not be difficult to manage).

CF8.1.5

The security architecture should support an enterprise-wide process for implementing coherent and consistent security services (eg identity services, authentication services and cryptographic services) and establishing common user and application programming interfaces (APIs).

CF8.1.6

The security architecture should be used throughout the organisation to help:

a) minimise the diversity of hardware / software in use
b) provide consistent security functionality across different hardware / software platforms
c) standardise user provisioning and access control to internal business applications (eg using identity and access management (IAM)) and external business applications (eg using federated identity and access management (FIAM))
d) integrate security controls at application, computer and network level
e) apply consistent cryptographic techniques
f) implement common naming conventions
g) segregate environments with different security requirements (eg by creating 'trusted' and 'untrusted' security domains)
h) control the flow of information between different environments.

CF8.1.7

The security architecture should be applied to:

a) the development of business applications (eg to help manage complexity and scale, make effective design decisions, and improve the quality and security of business applications)
b) help manage the technical infrastructure (eg to help in the development of a secure technical infrastructure, and assist in the review and analysis of the existing technical infrastructure)
c) major IT projects (eg to help deal with complexity, new information risks and large scale environments).

CONTROL FRAMEWORK

SPECIALISED

CF8.1   Security Architecture (continued)

CF8.1.8

The security architecture should be:

a) documented (eg in the form of blueprints, designs, diagrams, tables or models)
b) approved by business, IT and information security managers
c) assigned to an owner (eg a chief architect or a high-level working group, such as an architecture board, or equivalent)
d) maintained (eg involving reviews, exception handling and change management).

Related content	ISF resources
CF4.1 Application Protection	*Security Architecture: Workshop Report*
CF17 System Development Management	*Architectural Responses to the Disappearing Network Boundary*
CF18 Systems Development Lifecycle	*Federated Identity and Access Management: Creating a connected world*

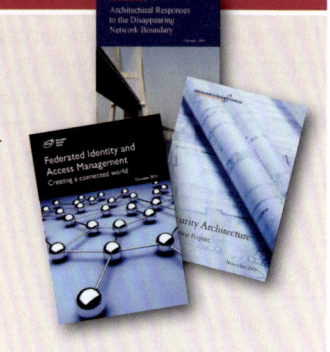

SPECIALISED

CF8.2 Identity and Access Management

Principle Identity and access management arrangements should be established to provide effective and consistent user administration, identification, authentication and access control mechanisms throughout the organisation.

Objective To restrict system access to authorised users and ensure the integrity of important user information.

CF8.2.1

Identity and access management arrangements should be established to provide enterprise-wide user provisioning and access control.

> Identity and access management (IAM) typically consists of a number of discrete activities that follow the stages of a user's lifecycle within the organisation. These activities fall into two categories, which are the:
>
> - provisioning process, which provides users with the user accounts and access rights they require to access systems and applications
> - user access process, which manages the actions performed each time a user attempts to access a new system, such as authentication and sign-on.

CF8.2.2

Identity and access management arrangements should be incorporated into an enterprise-wide solution, and applied to new business applications when they are introduced into the organisation.

CF8.2.3

Identity and access management arrangements should:

a) include a method for validating user identities prior to enabling user accounts
b) keep the number of sign-ons required by users to a minimum.

CF8.2.4

Identity and access management arrangements should provide a consistent set of methods for:

a) identifying users (eg using unique UserIDs)
b) authenticating users (eg using passwords, tokens or biometrics)
c) the user sign-on process
d) authorising user access privileges
e) administering user access privileges.

CF8.2.5

Identity and access management arrangements should be developed to improve the integrity of user information by:

a) making this information readily available for users to validate (eg by using an electronic information database or directory, such as white pages)
b) allowing users to correct their own user information (eg by providing users with a self-service application)
c) maintaining a limited number of identity stores (ie the location where UserID and authentication information is stored, such as a database, X500 / Lightweight Directory Access Protocol (LDAP) directory service, or commercial IAM product)
d) using an automated provisioning system (whereby user accounts are created for all target systems, following the creation of an initial entry for a user in a central IAM application)
e) using a centralised change management system.

CF8.2 Identity and Access Management (continued)

CF8.2.6

Identity and access management arrangements should:

a) enable access rights to be quickly and easily granted, changed or removed for a large number of users (eg by deploying role-based access rights)
b) enable management of user access privileges to be performed by relevant system owners (ie rather than by system administrators / IT staff).

CF8.2.7

Where federated identity and access management (FIAM) is used, arrangements should be made to ensure it:

a) builds upon the organisation's existing identity and access management (IAM) arrangements
b) is subject to separate governance, planning, risk assessment, review and monitoring
c) takes into account the needs of FIAM partners (ie those organisations to which FIAM connections will be established)
d) makes use of only agreed FIAM protocols (eg SAML, OpenID, WS-Trust and WS-Federation)
e) uses approved FIAM connection software.

> Federated Identity and Access Management (FIAM) is an extension of identity and access management (IAM) that delivers Single-Sign-On to applications delivered by external suppliers. It allows users in one organisation to be granted access to multiple business applications provided by external providers using a single set of user credentials (eg username and password) from their own organisation.

CF8.2.8

A process for managing FIAM connections should be established, which covers:

a) gaining approval for each FIAM connection, by both the identity provider and service provider (eg for user provisioning, FIAM protocols and connection software to be used)
b) designing each FIAM connection (eg determining how user access rights are managed, agreeing the structure of identifiers and attributes for users and the approach for provisioning user accounts, and updating contractual requirements)
c) implementing each FIAM connection (eg configuring agreed settings in FIAM software, updating IAM system and administration processes to support the FIAM connection, modifying the corresponding business application(s) to support the FIAM connection and subjecting the FIAM connection to standard IT management processes)
d) operating each FIAM connection (eg managing users' accounts and access rights, monitoring who has access to business applications, reporting user activity in FIAM business applications and monitoring the connection for actual or suspected security incidents)
e) reviewing each FIAM connection, for planned and unplanned changes to connections, on a regular basis.

Related content	ISF resources
CF6 Access Management	Identity and Access Management (IAM): Workshop Report
	Federated Identity and Access Management: Creating a connected world

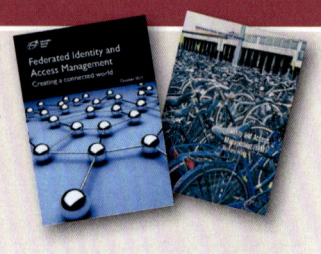

SPECIALISED

CONTROL FRAMEWORK

CF8.3 Critical Infrastructure

Principle Information systems that support or enable critical infrastructure should be protected by comprehensive security arrangements, which include security planning, information risk assessment and control selection, deployment, and monitoring.

Objective To enable an organisation's critical infrastructure to withstand a compromise of information processed or stored on supporting systems (ie disclosure to unauthorised individuals, corruption or unavailability).

CF8.3.1

There should be documented standards / procedures for the protection of information associated with the organisation's critical infrastructure.

> Organisations typically rely on infrastructure (eg operational equipment, telecommunications, utilities and buildings) to support business operations, such as manufacturing and assembling products, providing energy and water, delivering goods to customers, maintaining and supporting service equipment, and communicating information.
>
> In many cases this infrastructure, and the underlying technical infrastructure that supports it, can be identified as critical because it:
>
> - is used to support critical business operations (eg manufacturing and assembling products, delivering goods to customers, maintaining and supporting service equipment, and communicating information)
> - introduces a significant health and safety risk (eg production line machinery, industrial equipment, and transportation)
> - is subject to legal, regulatory and contractual obligations (eg network, telephone and mobile communications equipment and cabling)
> - supports or is considered part of the country's national infrastructure (eg water processing equipment, supply pipelines, electricity supply equipment, telecommunications and power cabling).

CF8.3.2

Standards / procedures should cover:

a) identifying the organisation's critical infrastructure
b) determining the information systems that support or enable the critical infrastructure
c) performing a risk assessment of information systems that support or enable critical infrastructure
d) establishing a framework of controls to help secure the critical infrastructure
e) monitoring the security controls that protect the critical infrastructure.

CF8.3.3

A review should be performed to identify the:

a) organisation's critical infrastructure (eg by liaising with senior executives, the business continuity management team and specialist business functions such as operational risk and internal audit)
b) information systems that support or enable critical infrastructure (eg SCADA systems, process control PCs and embedded systems).

CF8.3.4

Details about information systems that support or enable critical infrastructure should be recorded in an inventory (eg a configuration management database (CMDB) or equivalent).

CONTROL FRAMEWORK

SPECIALISED

CF8.3 Critical Infrastructure (continued)

CF8.3.5

Details recorded about information systems that support or enable critical infrastructure should include the:

a) types and classification of information processed by each critical information system
b) owner(s) of each critical information system
c) location and function of each critical information system
d) level of criticality of each information system
e) interrelationship (and any dependencies) with other information systems.

CF8.3.6

Information systems that support or enable critical infrastructure should be subject to a rigorous information risk assessment (eg using the ISF's *Information Risk Analysis Methodology (IRAM)*) to determine the security requirements for the supporting information systems.

> The level of risk to information systems that support or enable critical infrastructure is influenced by a broad range of threats that can be deliberate (eg cybercrime, hactivism, carrying out denial of service attacks and malware), accidental (eg making mistakes in data input, inadvertently deleting database records, information leakage when sending emails and exchanging electronic documents and sharing paper-based documents), internal individuals or external parties, man-made disasters (eg loss of power, system or software malfunctions, fire or explosions) and natural disasters (eg hurricane, volcanic eruption, storm or flood damage).

CF8.3.7

A framework of security controls to protect information systems that support or enable critical infrastructure should be established, which includes methods of:

a) monitoring and tracking critical infrastructure components and dependencies on information systems
b) sharing information about information risks (eg threats and vulnerabilities) with selected internal staff and appropriate external parties (eg suppliers, service providers and government agencies)
c) reviewing critical infrastructure and supporting information systems on a regular basis (eg every six months) to identify if and when it is no longer critical
d) storing spares on-site for critical components (often referred to as critical spares) or obtaining such spares at short notice
e) decommissioning aging / costly information systems and replacing them with up-to-date and cost effective technology.

CF8.3.8

Security controls applied to information systems that support or enable critical infrastructure should incorporate security architecture principles (eg 'secure by design', 'defence in depth', 'secure by default', 'default deny', 'fail secure', 'secure in deployment' and 'usability and manageability').

Related content	ISF resources
No direct references	*Securing Critical Infrastructure: Workshop Report* *Protecting Information in the End User Environment* *Hacktivism (Briefing paper)*

SPECIALISED CONTROL FRAMEWORK

CF8.4 Cryptographic Solutions

Principle Cryptographic solutions should be approved, documented and applied throughout the organisation.

Objective To protect the confidentiality of sensitive information, preserve the integrity of critical information and confirm the identity of the originator of transactions or communications.

CF8.4.1

Cryptography should be used across the organisation to:

a) protect the confidentiality of sensitive information or information that is subject to legal and regulatory-related encryption requirements (eg Payment Card Industry Data Security Standard (PCI DSS), US Health Insurance Portability and Accountability Act (HIPAA) and European Commission Directive 95/46/EC)
b) determine if critical information has been altered (eg by performing hash functions or digitally signing)
c) provide strong authentication for users of applications and systems (eg by using digital certificates and smartcards)
d) enable the identity of the originator of critical transactions or communications to be proven (eg by using digital signatures for non-repudiation).

CF8.4.2

There should be documented guidelines for the use of cryptography across the organisation, which cover the:

a) definition of circumstances where cryptography should be used (eg for high-value transactions involving external bodies or transmitting sensitive information across open networks such as the Internet)
b) restrictions on the export / use of cryptographic solutions
c) selection of approved cryptographic algorithms (eg Advanced Encryption Standard (AES) for confidentiality, and Secure Hash Algorithm (SHA) for integrity)
d) suitability of cryptographic solutions employed (including cryptographic key lengths and the cryptographic strength of both symmetric and asymmetric algorithms).

CF8.4.3

The selection and implementation of a cryptographic solution should take into account the legal aspects of using encryption, and include:

a) identifying legal obligations (for relevant jurisdictions)
b) assessing the risks (including legal risks) associated with using cryptographic solutions (including encryption algorithms)
c) selecting a suitable cryptographic solution (eg that meets legal, regulatory and industry standards).

CF8.4.4

Arrangements to manage cryptographic solutions should be established that include:

a) approving the use of cryptographic solutions (eg by executive management)
b) assigning responsibilities for cryptographic solutions
c) handling conflicting laws and regulations (including dealing with license issues) relating to the use of cryptographic solutions in different jurisdictions (eg by obtaining advice from the legal function)
d) keeping cryptographic solutions up-to-date.

CONTROL FRAMEWORK

SPECIALISED

CF8.4 Cryptographic Solutions (continued)

CF8.4.5

Relevant business managers should have access to:

a) expert technical and legal advice on the use of cryptography
b) a list of approved cryptographic solutions
c) an up-to-date register of cryptographic solutions.

CF8.4.6

A register of approved cryptographic solutions should be maintained, which:

a) specifies the intended use of encryption within the organisation
b) details the locations (including jurisdictions) where cryptographic solutions are applied
c) contains information relating to the licensing requirements for using cryptographic solutions
d) is made available to authorised external parties (eg regulatory authorities and law enforcement).

Related content	ISF resources
CF8.5 Cryptographic Key Management	ISF Briefing: Legal Aspects of Encryption
CF8.6 Public Key Infrastructure	

SPECIALISED

CONTROL FRAMEWORK

CF8.5 Cryptographic Key Management

Principle   Cryptographic keys should be managed tightly, in accordance with documented standards / procedures, and protected against unauthorised access or destruction.

Objective   To ensure that cryptographic keys are not compromised (eg through loss, corruption or disclosure), thereby exposing critical or sensitive information to attack.

CF8.5.1

There should be documented standards / procedures for managing cryptographic keys, which cover:

a) the lifecycle of cryptographic keys
b) responsibilities of cryptographic key owners
c) protection of cryptographic keys
d) mandatory key disclosure.

CF8.5.2

A documented process for managing cryptographic keys should be established, which covers:

a) generation of cryptographic keys, using approved key lengths
b) secure distribution, activation and storage, recovery and replacement / update of cryptographic keys
c) immediate revocation (deactivation) of cryptographic keys (eg if a key is compromised, or a key owner changes job or leaves the organisation)
d) recovery of cryptographic keys that are lost, corrupted or have expired
e) management of cryptographic keys that may have been compromised, such as by disclosure to an external party
f) back-up / archive of cryptographic keys and the maintenance of cryptographic key history (eg to access backed up or archived information)
g) allocation of defined activation / de-activation dates
h) restriction of access to cryptographic keys to authorised individuals
i) sharing of cryptographic keys (eg using split key generation) required for protecting sensitive information and critical systems.

CF8.5.3

Ownership of cryptographic keys should be assigned to individuals, who are:

a) made aware of their responsibilities for using and protecting keys (and where necessary disclosing keys) assigned to them
b) required to confirm they clearly understand their responsibilities for using and protecting cryptographic keys.

CF8.5.4

Cryptographic keys should be protected against:

a) access by unauthorised individuals or applications
b) accidental or malicious destruction.

CF8.5 Cryptographic Key Management (continued)

CF8.5.5

A method of handling 'mandatory cryptographic key disclosure' should be established, which includes:

a) managing cryptographic keys centrally and at an enterprise-wide level (eg so that a corporate copy of a user's cryptographic key can be disclosed)
b) establishing a cryptographic key escrow scheme (ie where copies of cryptographic keys are held by an authorised external party such as a legal representative, lawyer or equivalent)
c) providing users, that may cross international borders with computer equipment, with advice on disclosing cryptographic keys to the authorities (eg at international border control)
d) maintaining procedures for responding to e-discovery orders that relate to encrypted information.

Mandatory cryptographic key disclosure typically involves the right of governmental authorities to lawfully obtain cryptographic keys in order to access encrypted information (typically for the purposes of national security or crime prevention).

Related content	ISF resources
CF8.4 Cryptographic Solutions	*ISF Briefing: Legal Aspects of Encryption*
CF8.6 Public Key Infrastructure	

SPECIALISED

CF8.6 Public Key Infrastructure

Principle Where a public key infrastructure (PKI) is used, one or more Certification Authorities (CAs) and Registration Authorities (RAs) should be established and protected.

Objective To ensure that the PKI operates as intended, is available when required, provides adequate protection of related cryptographic keys and can be recovered in the event of an emergency.

CF8.6.1

A public key infrastructure (PKI) should be supported by documented standards / procedures, which cover the:

a) establishment of a root Certification Authority (CA) and one or more subsidiary CAs (sub-CAs)
b) methods of protecting important internal Certification Authorities (and related sub-CAs)
c) integration of the public key infrastructure with business applications and technical infrastructure that will use it
d) establishment of one or more Registration Authorities (RAs)
e) actions to be taken in the event of loss or compromise of the public key infrastructure.

> A Certification Authority (CA) comprises the people, processes and tools that are responsible for the creation, issue and management of public key certificates that are used within a PKI.

CF8.6.2

A PKI should be supported by establishing a root Certification Authority to:

a) generate public key certificates (digital certificates)
b) revoke public key certificates
c) publish public key certificates and certificate revocation lists (CRLs) in directories (or equivalent)
d) archive public key certificates and certificate revocation lists in an archive database (or equivalent).

> A root Certification Authority is positioned at the highest level in a hierarchical CA model. The root CA is a superior CA that provides trust for and certifies (ie issues certificates to) the next lower set of sub-CAs.

CF8.6.3

Important internal Certification Authorities (and related sub-CAs) should be protected by:

a) restricting access to a limited number of authorised individuals (eg by using strict access control mechanisms and strong authentication)
b) 'hardening' the operating system(s) that support them (eg by patching all known vulnerabilities, disabling unnecessary services and changing vendor supplied default parameters such as passwords and SNMP community strings)
c) employing other general security controls (eg change management, back-up and security event logging) in a particularly disciplined manner.

CF8.6.4

The private keys of important internal Certification Authorities (and related sub-CAs) should be protected by:

a) storing them on approved hardware (eg a hardware storage module (HSM)), which is subject to strong logical and physical controls
b) sharing them across two or more authorised individuals (often referred to as secret splitting or key sharing) to avoid misuse of the CA (and related sub-CAs).

CF8.6 Public Key Infrastructure (continued)

CF8.6.5

The public key infrastructure should:

a) be integrated with the organisation's user identity store (eg a database, X500 / Lightweight Directory Access Protocol (LDAP) directory service or equivalent) so that digital certificates are available to all authorised users and applications
b) use a consistent, trusted date and time source (eg using global positioning system (GPS), atomic clocks or time-server on the Internet) to ensure the CA provides accurate timestamps.

CF8.6.6

The public key infrastructure should be supported by:

a) a Certification Practice Statement (CPS) that defines the practices employed by the certification authority in issuing digital certificates
b) Certificate Policies (CP) for each type of digital certificate issued by the CA, which indicate the applicability of the certificates issued (eg for secure email or e-commerce transactions).

CF8.6.7

A Registration Authority (RA) should be established to:

a) verify the identity of individuals requiring the use of the PKI
b) issue authentication hardware (eg hardware tokens and smartcards) relating to the PKI
c) oversee cryptographic key generation
d) generate and submit requests for the issuance of PKI certificates.

> A Registration Authority (RA) typically represents the interface between a CA and users of the PKI. The RA is often a combination of technology and people responsible for functions such as verifying the identity of PKI users, registering users, providing status information about certificates, handling digital certificate requests and revoking certificates.

CF8.6.8

Users of the public key infrastructure should be made aware of:

a) the purpose and function of the PKI
b) their responsibilities (eg to protect their private keys)
c) how to use the PKI (eg using encryption and digital signatures).

CF8.6.9

Comprehensive continuity and contingency plans should be developed to deal with the possible:

a) loss of the public key infrastructure (eg as a result of a disaster)
b) compromise or suspected compromise of the public key infrastructure (eg invalidate the Root CA and any sub-CAs, and revoke all corresponding digital certificates).

SPECIALISED

CF8.6 Public Key Infrastructure (continued)

CF8.6.10

Certification Authorities should be configured to restrict the use of cryptographic key pairs generated for users by issuing separate key pairs for:

a) encrypting and decrypting information
b) producing and validating digital signatures.

> Separating the cryptographic key pairs for encryption and digital signatures allows one pair to be deactivated or replaced while the other key pair remains valid. For example, a user who replaces their cryptographic keys for encryption (eg due to being compromised) can continue to authenticate themselves using their original key pairs for producing digital signatures.

Related content	ISF resources
CF8.4 Cryptographic Solutions	No recent ISF material
CF8.5 Cryptographic Key Management	

CF8.7 Information Leakage Protection

Principle Information leakage protection mechanisms should be applied to systems and networks that process, store or transmit sensitive information.

Objective To identify sensitive information that may be at risk of unauthorised disclosure and detect if sensitive information is disclosed to unauthorised individuals or systems.

CF8.7.1

Information leakage protection mechanisms should be employed for systems and networks that process, store and transmit sensitive information (eg highly classified information, privacy-related information or information that is subject to regulatory requirements such as local data privacy legislation, Payment Card Industry Data Security Standard (PCI DSS), Sarbanes-Oxley Act or HIPAA).

> Information leakage protection (often referred to as data leakage protection (DLP)) typically involves the implementation of technical solutions that scan / monitor systems and networks in order to prevent and detect the (often accidentally) leakage (ie unintended disclosure) of sensitive information. Sensitive information that is at risk of leakage or is actually leaked often includes shared and unencrypted content such as word processed documents, presentation files and spreadsheets that could leave an organisation via many different points or channels (eg via email, instant messaging, Internet browsing or on portable storage devices).

CF8.7.2

Information leakage protection mechanisms should be supported by documented standards / procedures, which cover:

a) registering the types of sensitive information to be monitored (eg employee ID numbers, project names, customer names, medical records and credit card numbers)
b) methods of discovering sensitive information at risk of unauthorised disclosure (eg in unstructured electronic files on a user's computing device)
c) techniques for detecting sensitive information when disclosed during processing or transmission (eg when electronic files are emailed externally or uploaded to a website or FTP server)
d) methods of blocking user actions or network transmissions that expose sensitive information (eg preventing the copying of database entries into a spreadsheet or the saving of particular electronic files on a portable storage device)
e) the management of information leakage protection software
f) reporting of confidentiality breaches (or equivalent).

CF8.7.3

Information leakage protection mechanisms should be:

a) managed via a central management console (eg in a network operations centre (NOC) or security operations centre (SOC))
b) configured to include a register of the specific types of sensitive information (sometimes referred to as pre-registration) that need to be protected from unauthorised disclosure (eg employee ID numbers, product schematics, application source code, customer names, medical details and credit card numbers)
c) capable of taking into account the context of information (eg factors such as time, sender, receiver, subject heading, message content and file attachments) before identifying information as being at risk of disclosure or detected as being disclosed to unauthorised parties
d) updated on a regular basis and continuously refined to ensure their configuration (eg the rules) reflect the sensitive information that needs to be protected
e) reviewed to help minimise false positives and false negatives.

SPECIALISED

CF8.7 Information Leakage Protection (continued)

CF8.7.4

Information leakage protection mechanisms should:

a) identify pre-registered sensitive information at risk of unauthorised disclosure when being stored (eg by scanning databases, collaboration spaces, network folders and users' local hard disk drives, and monitoring the printing of electronic documents)
b) detect when pre-registered sensitive information is actually disclosed (eg by monitoring the use of business applications, such as the copying-pasting of customer credit card numbers between applications, email and instant messaging, web browsers and portable storage media).

CF8.7.5

Information leakage protection mechanisms should be configured to perform 'enforcement' actions to protect sensitive information that is at risk of disclosure or is being disclosed to unauthorised parties, including:

a) removing sensitive information from a particular location (eg a users laptop) if it is inadequately protected
b) warning users of potential unauthorised disclosure of pre-registered sensitive information
c) blocking unauthorised user actions (eg the use of unapproved business applications)
d) preventing the transmission of pre-registered sensitive information (eg via email or web browser)
e) quarantining information (ie placing the information in a secure location) for further analysis, for example to determine if the disclosure is a legitimate business action.

CF8.7.6

Information leakage protection mechanisms should be configured to:

a) provide an alert when unauthorised disclosure activity is detected (eg via a management console, email messages or SMS text messages to mobile telephones)
b) aggregate the results of discovery and detection to help determine the potential business impact as a result of multiple unauthorised disclosures over a period of time.

CF8.7.7

Actual or suspected unauthorised disclosure of sensitive information to unauthorised parties should be reported to a particular individual or team responsible for handling confidentiality breaches (eg legal, compliance or risk management).

Related content	ISF resources
CF10.5 System / Network Monitoring	*ISF Briefing: DLP Tools*

SPECIALISED

CF8.8 Digital Rights Management

Principle High-value sensitive information or software that is accessed and used outside of the control of the organisation should be protected by the use of digital rights management (DRM).

Objective To ensure that the access to and processing of highly sensitive information is restricted to specific functions by a limited number of authorised individuals.

CF8.8.1

High-value sensitive information or software that is used outside of the control of the organisation should be protected by using a digital rights management system (or equivalent).

> Digital Rights Management (DRM) is a technical security solution that is used to protect high-value sensitive information or software (eg high-value intellectual property or trade secrets) that often falls outside existing security protection is provided by the organisation (eg when stored on employees consumer devices or when shared with external parties). A DRM system typically comprises three main elements, which are:
>
> - a central DRM server, which manages requests (from DRM clients) to access and process information in the DRM system
> - DRM clients (which may use special DRM software (DRM 'agents') or 'DRM-enabled' applications) that communicate with the DRM server to determine how information can be used
> - DRM objects (sometimes referred to as DRM wrappers or containers), which contain information (typically in an encrypted form) together with access and usage rules that determine who can access the information and what functions they can perform on the information.

CF8.8.2

There should be documented standards / procedures for the provision and management of digital rights management across the organisation, which cover:

a) establishing a robust, recoverable technical infrastructure required to support digital rights management (eg information classification, identity and access management, public key infrastructure and cryptography)
b) the protection of sensitive information
c) technical requirements for digital rights management
d) the functions provided by the DRM system to protect information (including authentication, access control, electronic marking and encryption)
e) methods to limit circumvention of DRM controls.

CF8.8.3

Digital rights management should be built upon a robust, recoverable technical infrastructure that is supported by:

a) an information classification scheme that enables information and documents to be classified and labelled according to their security requirements
b) identity and access management arrangements to enable access privileges to be configured correctly and consistently
c) a public key infrastructure to help provide effective authentication, access control, data encryption, digital signatures, hashing and management of cryptographic keys
d) cryptography (using approved cryptographic algorithms and keys).

CF8.8.4

The digital rights management system should protect sensitive information by:

a) restricting access to the information
b) protecting the information against unauthorised changes, copying and distribution (including printing)
c) monitoring the use of the information
d) recording any changes that take place in case a future investigation is required.

SPECIALISED

CF8.8 Digital Rights Management (continued)

CF8.8.5

The digital rights management system should:

a) be compatible with the organisation's security architecture and technical infrastructure
b) meet the technical requirements of the individuals who will use the DRM system (eg staff using consumer devices, business partners or customers)
c) provide protection over the full lifecycle of information in each DRM object (eg creation, processing, storage, transmission and destruction)
d) be accessible in 'offline mode' (ie DRM clients can function as required when access to the central DRM server is not accessible, such as when Internet access is not available).

CF8.8.6

The digital rights management server should be subject to standard security management practices (eg restricting physical access, performing system 'hardening', applying change management and malware protection, monitoring them and performing regular reviews).

CF8.8.7

The digital rights management system should protect information within each DRM object by:

a) requiring authentication, a license key and / or a certificate to access information
b) restricting access to a specified timeframe (eg after a given date or until a particular date)
c) electronically marking the information as 'no changes permitted'
d) using encryption to protect information from being copied
e) defining the printing permissions for the information
f) recording who accesses the information and how the information is used
g) maintaining usage logs centrally for analysis (eg on a dedicated server)
h) raising alerts if attempts to misuse the information are detected.

CF8.8.8

The digital rights management system should reduce the likelihood of users circumventing DRM controls by:

a) providing DRM users with security education / training
b) informing DRM users of their obligation not to circumvent the DRM features (eg by printing screenshots or using a camera to perform unauthorised copies of information)
c) imposing strict contractual obligations on DRM users that specify the consequences of compromising information in the DRM system
d) applying strong encryption (ie strong cryptographic algorithms and strong cryptographic minimum key lengths)
e) clearly marking information with details of ownership and classification
f) tracking information handled within the DRM system (eg using digital watermarking or information hiding techniques).

Related content	ISF resources
CF3.1 Information Classification CF8.1 Security Architecture CF8.6 Public Key Infrastructure	ISF Briefing: Digital Rights Management

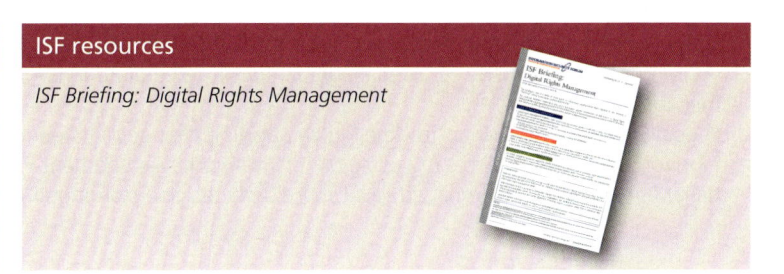

CONTROL FRAMEWORK

FUNDAMENTAL

AREA CF9 – Network Management

List of Topics

CF9.1	Network Device Configuration	CF9.5	Remote Maintenance
CF9.2	Physical Network Management	CF9.6	Wireless Access
CF9.3	External Network Connections	CF9.7	Voice over IP (VoIP) Networks
CF9.4	Firewalls	CF9.8	Telephony and Conferencing

CF9.1 Network Device Configuration

Principle Network devices (including routers, switches and firewalls) should be configured to function as required, and to prevent unauthorised or incorrect updates.

Objective To ensure that the configuration of network devices is accurate and does not compromise the security of the network.

CF9.1.1

There should be documented standards / procedures for configuring network devices (eg routers, hubs, bridges, concentrators, switches and firewalls), which cover:

a) security architecture principles
b) standard security management practices
c) device configuration
d) restricting access to network devices
e) vulnerability and patch management
f) changes to routing tables and settings in network devices
g) regular review of network device configuration and set-up.

CF9.1.2

Security controls applied to network devices should incorporate security architecture principles (eg 'secure by design', 'defence in depth', 'secure by default', 'default deny', 'fail secure', 'secure in deployment' and 'usability and manageability').

CF9.1.3

Network devices should be subject to standard security management practices, which include:

a) restricting physical access to network devices to authorised staff (eg by locating them in protected data centres or dedicated, locked storage rooms)
b) 'hardening' the operating system(s) that support them (eg by patching all known vulnerabilities, disabling unnecessary services, removing unnecessary scripts, drivers, features and sub-systems, and changing vendor-supplied default parameters such as passwords and SNMP community strings)
c) applying a comprehensive set of management tools (eg maintenance utilities, remote support and enterprise management tools)
d) keeping network devices up-to-date (eg by applying change management and patch management)
e) monitoring network devices (eg using Simple Network Management Protocol (SNMP)) so that events such as hardware failure and external attacks can be detected and responded to effectively.

FUNDAMENTAL

CONTROL FRAMEWORK

CF9.1 Network Device Configuration (continued)

CF9.1.4

Network devices should be configured to:

a) highlight overload or exception conditions when they occur
b) log events in a form suitable for review, and record them on a separate system
c) copy control information (eg event logs and tables) to authorised portable storage media
d) integrate with access control mechanisms in other devices (eg to provide strong authentication)
e) use a predefined secure set-up upon boot
f) ensure that passwords are not sent in clear text form
g) disable source routing (to retain control within the packet-forwarding device).

CF9.1.5

Network devices should be restricted to authorised network staff, using access controls that support individual accountability, and protected from unauthorised access.

CF9.1.6

There should be a process for dealing with vulnerabilities in network devices, which includes:

a) monitoring them for vulnerabilities (eg by tracking CERT alerts, vendor websites and mailing lists, subscribing to a vulnerability notification service or running vulnerability checking software)
b) issuing instructions to network staff on the action to be taken if a network device fails
c) automatically re-routing network traffic to an alternative network device
d) testing patches for network devices and applying them in a timely manner.

CF9.1.7

Network devices that perform routing (eg routers and switches) should be configured to prevent unauthorised or incorrect updates by:

a) verifying the source of routing updates (eg by using techniques such as Open Shortest Path First (OSPF) or Routed Internet Protocol (RIP))
b) verifying the destination of routing updates (eg by transmitting updates only to specific routers)
c) protecting the exchange of routing information (eg by using passwords)
d) encrypting the routing information being exchanged.

CF9.1.8

Network devices should be reviewed on a regular basis to verify configuration settings (eg routing tables and parameters), evaluate password strengths and to assess activities performed on the network device (eg by inspecting logs).

Related content	ISF resources
CF9.4 Firewalls	*ISF Briefing: Network convergence*
	Architectural Responses to the Disappearing Network Boundary

CONTROL FRAMEWORK

FUNDAMENTAL

CF9.2 Physical Network Management

Principle Networks (including voice networks) should be protected by physical controls and supported by accurate, up-to-date documentation and labelling of essential components.

Objective To ensure that networks (including voice networks) are configured accurately and securely and provide employees with a clear statement of the security disciplines they are expected to follow.

CF9.2.1

Telecommunications cables (ie network and telephone cables) should be protected by:

a) attaching identification labels to communications equipment and cables
b) concealing the installation of cabling
c) using armoured conduit
d) locking inspection / termination points
e) providing alternative feeds or routing
f) avoiding routes through publicly accessible areas.

CF9.2.2

Network access points should be protected by:

a) locating them in secure environments (eg locked rooms or cabinets)
b) disabling them on the network device (eg a network switch) until required.

CF9.2.3

Networks should be supported by documentation, which includes:

a) network configuration diagrams, showing nodes and connections
b) an inventory of communications equipment, software, links and services provided by external parties
c) one or more diagrams of in-house cable runs for each physical location
d) configurations and settings for in-house telephone exchanges
e) details about telephones and associated wiring / cables.

CF9.2.4

Network documentation (eg diagrams, inventories and schedules) should be:

a) kept up-to-date
b) readily accessible to authorised individuals
c) subject to supervisory review
d) generated automatically, using software tools.

Related content	ISF resources
CF19.1 Physical Protection	No recent ISF material

FUNDAMENTAL

CONTROL FRAMEWORK

CF9.3   External Network Connections

Principle   All external network connections to computer systems and networks should be individually identified, verified, recorded, and approved by the information systems or network owner.

Objective   To prevent unauthorised external users from gaining access to information systems and networks.

CF9.3.1

There should be documented standards / procedures for managing external network access to the organisation's information systems and networks, which specify that:

a) external connections should be identified
b) information systems and networks should be configured to restrict access
c) only authorised types of remote access device are permitted
d) details of external connections should be documented
e) external connections should be removed when no longer required.

> While external network connections are typically established over IP-based networks, such as the Internet, many organisations still support dial-up access via modem (often to enable service providers and support staff to login remotely to perform maintenance or troubleshooting activities). Modem access can provide an opportunity for attackers to gain unauthorised access to computer systems and networks. As a result, dial-up connections should be subject to a similar level of protection as that provided for IP-based external network connections.

CF9.3.2

Information systems and networks accessible by external connections should be designed to:

a) achieve technical compatibility (eg using standards for information formats and communications protocols)
b) conceal computer or network names and topologies from external parties (eg by using dual or split network directories / name servers)
c) protect sensitive information stored on information systems and transmitted to external party locations (eg using encryption).

CF9.3.3

Information systems and networks accessible by external connections should:

a) restrict external network traffic to only specified parts of information systems and networks
b) restrict connections to defined entry points (eg specific network gateways)
c) verify the source of external connections (eg by checking the source IP address or using Calling Line Identification (CLI))
d) log activity (eg to help track individual transactions and enforce accountability).

CF9.3.4

Access to the network should be restricted to devices that meet minimum security configuration requirements, which includes verifying that devices:

a) have been authorised
b) are running up-to-date malware protection
c) have the latest systems and software patches installed
d) are connecting over an encrypted network (eg a virtual private network (VPN))
e) have a correctly configured personal firewall.

CF9.3 External Network Connections (continued)

CF9.3.5

Devices that do not meet the minimum security configuration requirements (ie fail a system integrity check) should be connected to a protected network (eg a quarantine area or a 'Demilitarised Zone' (DMZ)) where their configuration can be updated, or access denied.

CF9.3.6

External access to information systems and networks (eg via Internet connections) should be restricted by:

a) establishing 'Demilitarised Zones' (DMZs) between untrusted networks, such as the Internet and internal networks
b) routing network traffic through firewalls (eg stateful inspection firewalls (typically located in the perimeter of a network) or proxy firewalls (typically located between internal networks))
c) limiting the methods of connection (eg via Internet, ISDN or dial-up)
d) granting access only to specific business applications, computer systems or specified parts of the network (eg domains).

CF9.3.7

External access should be provided using a dedicated remote access server, which:

a) provides reliable and complete authentication for external connections (eg by running an authentication system such as Radius or TACACS+)
b) provides information for troubleshooting (eg router and firewall logs)
c) logs all connections and sessions, including details of call start / stop time, call duration and user tracking
d) helps identify possible information security breaches (eg by logging events such as connections and terminations in a database and collating them centrally).

CF9.3.8

External access to information systems and networks should be subject to strong authentication (eg challenge / response devices featuring one-time passwords, smartcards, tokens or biometrics).

CF9.3.9

Unauthorised external connections should be identified (eg for investigation or possible removal) by:

a) performing manual audits of network equipment and documentation to identify discrepancies with records of known external connections
b) employing computer and network management and diagnostic tools (eg port probes and network discovery / mapping tools)
c) checking accounting records of bills paid to telecommunications suppliers and reconciling them against known connections.

CF9.3.10

External access should be prevented if unauthorised (or when no longer required) by removing or disabling:

a) computer and network connections (eg by physically removing a network connection, modifying firewall rules, updating access control lists and configuring routing tables on network routers)
b) equipment (eg redundant modems and communications lines)
c) control settings (eg software configuration settings).

Related content	ISF resources
No direct references	No recent ISF material

FUNDAMENTAL

CONTROL FRAMEWORK

CF9.4   Firewalls

Principle   Network traffic should be routed through a well-configured firewall prior to being allowed access to networks, or before leaving networks.

Objective   To prevent unauthorised network traffic from gaining access to networks, or leaving networks.

CF9.4.1

Networks should be protected from malicious traffic on other networks or sub-networks (internal or external) by one or more firewalls.

> Organisations often use a combination of firewalls to protect critical business applications from applications and systems on other (wired and wireless) networks, including:
>
> - stateful inspection firewalls, which are typically located in the perimeter of a network
> - application proxy firewalls, which are typically located between different internal networks
> - web application firewalls, which are typically located between web applications and the network.
>
> Some network routers provide firewall capabilities, such as network traffic filtering, inspection and blocking. As a result, this topic also applies to these types of network router.

CF9.4.2

There should be documented standards / procedures for managing firewalls (including switches and routers), which cover:

a) filtering of specific types or sources of network traffic (eg IP addresses, TCP ports or information about the state of communications and users)
b) blocking or otherwise restricting particular types or sources of network traffic
c) the development of predefined rules (or tables) for filtering network traffic
d) protecting firewalls against attack or failure (eg by restricting access to authorised individuals)
e) limiting the disclosure of information about networks and network devices.

CF9.4.3

Firewalls should be used to check:

a) destination addresses (eg IP addresses) and ports (eg TCP ports)
b) information about the state of associated communications (eg saving the outgoing port command of an FTP session so that an associated, incoming FTP communication can be checked against it)
c) information about the state of users (eg permitting access to users only where they have been authenticated in a previous communication)
d) the validity of a network service (eg by using an application proxy firewall).

CF9.4.4

Firewall configuration should incorporate security architecture principles (eg 'secure by design', 'defence in depth', 'secure by default', 'default deny', 'fail secure', 'secure in deployment' and 'usability and manageability').

CF9.4 Firewalls (continued)

CF9.4.5

Firewalls should be configured to:

a) protect communication protocols that are prone to abuse (eg HTTP, HTTPS, SSH, FTP, SMTP, Telnet and UUCP)
b) block network packets typically used to execute 'denial of service' attacks (eg ICMP Echo, UDP and TCP Echo, Chargen and Discard)
c) deny incoming traffic where the source address is known to have been 'spoofed' (eg where the source address claims to be from the destination network)
d) deny outgoing traffic where the source address is known to have been 'spoofed' (eg where the source address does not reflect the network from which it originates)
e) limit the disclosure of information about networks at the network level by using 'IP masquerading' (ie network address translation (NAT) or port address translation (PAT)).

CF9.4.6

Firewalls should be configured to block or otherwise restrict communications based on specified source / destination:

a) addresses (eg a particular IP address)
b) ports (eg ports 20 and 21 for FTP and port 23 for Telnet).

CF9.4.7

Filtering of network traffic should be based on predefined rules (or tables) that:

a) have been developed by trusted individuals, and are subjected to supervisory review
b) are based on the principle of 'least access'
c) use clear, consistent naming conventions (eg host_name_IP_address or network_IP_range)
d) are grouped into sets (eg 20 rules) to help manage and understand long rule sections
e) are documented (with version control) and kept up-to-date
f) take account of an information security policy, network standards / procedures and user requirements.

CF9.4.8

Before new or changed rules are applied to firewalls, their strength and correctness should be tested and verified, and they should be signed off by the network owner.

CF9.4.9

Firewall configurations should be documented and include justification for network traffic that is permitted to pass through the firewall (eg standard services and protocols such as VPN, HTTP, SSL and SSH, and non-standard services and protocols that may introduce additional information risk).

CF9.4.10

Firewall configurations should be reviewed on a regular basis to ensure that:

a) each firewall rule is approved and signed off by a business owner
b) expired or unnecessary rules are removed
c) conflicting rules are resolved
d) unused / duplicate objects (eg networks or information systems) are removed.

Related content	ISF resources
CF9.1 Network Device Configuration	No recent ISF material

SPECIALISED

CF9.5 Remote Maintenance

Principle Remote maintenance of critical systems and networks should be restricted to authorised individuals, confined to individual sessions, and subject to review.

Objective To prevent unauthorised access to critical systems and networks through the misuse of remote maintenance facilities.

CF9.5.1

Access to critical systems and networks by external individuals for remote maintenance purposes (eg remote diagnosis / testing, software maintenance) should be managed by:

a) defining and agreeing the objectives and scope of planned work
b) authorising sessions individually
c) restricting access rights so that they do not exceed those required to meet the objectives and scope of planned work
d) logging all activity undertaken
e) revoking access rights and changing passwords immediately after agreed maintenance is complete
f) performing an independent review of remote maintenance activity.

CF9.5.2

Diagnostic ports on network equipment should be protected by access controls (eg passwords and physical locks).

CF9.5.3

Non-Disclosure Agreement(s) / confidentiality clause(s) should be signed by external suppliers' IT and information security staff or incorporated into their employment contracts prior to being granted access to the organisation's applications, systems or networks.

CF9.5.4

Dial-up connections should be protected by using dial-back security (to verify the source of dial-up connection), which is implemented by:

a) configuring mandatory dial-back for all accounts authorised to connect through an access point
b) disconnecting the line at the host, rather than at the client
c) disabling call-forwarding for the dial-back line.

Related content	ISF resources
CF6 Access Management	No recent ISF material

CF9.6 Wireless Access

Principle Wireless access should be authorised, users and computing devices authenticated, and wireless traffic encrypted.

Objective To ensure that only authorised individuals and computing devices gain wireless access to networks and minimise the risk of wireless transmissions being monitored, intercepted or modified.

CF9.6.1

Wireless access to the network should be subject to an information risk assessment and signed off by an appropriate business representative (eg the network owner), prior to its implementation.

CF9.6.2

There should be documented standards / procedures for controlling wireless access to the network, which cover:

a) placement and configuration of wireless access points (hardware devices that provide interfaces between the wireless network and a wired network)
b) methods of limiting access to authorised users
c) use of encryption (eg Wi-Fi Protected Access II (WPA2)) for protecting information in transit
d) detection of unauthorised wireless access points and wireless devices.

CF9.6.3

Wireless access points should be:

a) configured for low power to limit range
b) placed in locations that minimise the risk of interference (eg away from radio transmitters, microwave equipment and cordless telephones)
c) configured and managed centrally (eg in a network operations centre (NOC) or security operations centre (SOC))
d) assigned a unique Service Set Identifier (SSID).

CF9.6.4

Networks should be protected against unauthorised wireless access by using a security 'filtering' device (eg a firewall or edge server).

CF9.6.5

Wireless access should be protected using layers of access control, including:

a) network access control (eg IEEE 802.1X)
b) device authentication (eg EAP-TLS)
c) user authentication.

CF9.6.6

Wireless access should be protected by:

a) using encryption (eg Wi-Fi Protected Access II (WPA2)) between computing devices and wireless access points
b) using one or more dedicated wireless networks for access by non-corporate devices (eg devices used by visitors and contractors or consumer devices used by employees) by segregating them using a virtual local area network (VLAN) and a firewall
c) changing encryption keys regularly
d) scanning the wireless network for unauthorised (rogue) wireless access points and wireless devices (eg by roaming buildings with a wireless network detector).

FUNDAMENTAL

CF9.6 Wireless Access (continued)

CF9.6.7

Critical wireless access connections should be subject to additional security controls, such as virtual private networks (VPNs).

Related content	ISF resources
CF9.1 Network Device Configuration	*Wireless LAN Security* *Security in Wireless LAN Update* *Security in Wireless LAN Case Studies*

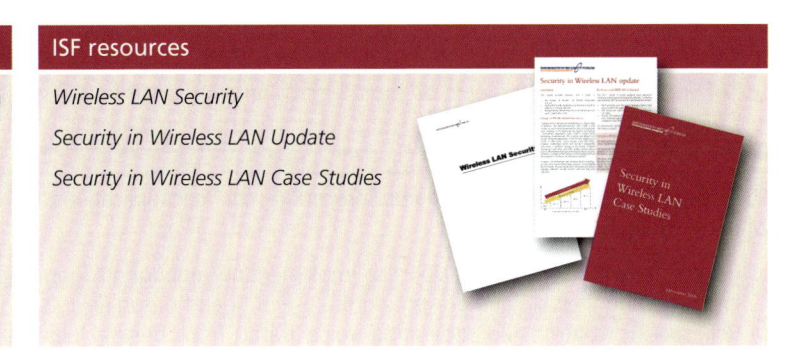

SPECIALISED

CF9.7 Voice over IP (VoIP) Networks

Principle VoIP networks should be approved and protected by a combination of general network and VoIP specific controls.

Objective To ensure the availability of VoIP networks, and protect the confidentiality and integrity of sensitive information (eg the content of telephone calls) in transit.

CF9.7.1

Use of Voice over IP (VoIP) should be signed off by an appropriate business representative.

CF9.7.2

There should be documented standards / procedures for VoIP applications and underlying technical infrastructure, which include:

a) general network controls for VoIP (eg implementing monitoring tools, providing resilience and redundancy, implementing firewalls and preventing the use of unauthorised devices)
b) VoIP-specific controls (eg separating voice traffic from general network traffic, hardening VoIP devices, identifying vulnerabilities, encrypting sensitive VoIP traffic, and monitoring VoIP-related event logs).

CF9.7.3

General network security controls for VoIP should be applied, which include:

a) monitoring bandwidth using tools that are capable of recognising VoIP traffic
b) deploying network components to provide resilience and redundancy
c) implementing firewalls that can filter VoIP traffic
d) restricting access to VoIP networks to authorised devices.

CF9.7.4

VoIP-specific controls should be applied, which include:

a) separating voice traffic using virtual local area networks (VLANs)
b) hardening VoIP devices (eg IP phones, routers and IP PBXs)
c) scanning VoIP networks for vulnerabilities
d) encrypting sensitive VoIP traffic
e) monitoring VoIP-related event log files.

Related content	ISF resources
No direct references	No recent ISF material

SPECIALISED CONTROL FRAMEWORK

CF9.8 Telephony and Conferencing

Principle Telephony and conferencing facilities should be protected with a combination of physical and logical controls, monitored regularly and access to them restricted.

Objective To prevent and detect unauthorised use or misuse of telephony and conferencing facilities.

CF9.8.1

There should be documented standards / procedures for telephony and conferencing, which cover:

a) use of the organisation's telephones
b) moves and changes of telephone users
c) registration and authentication of users with access to voice-mail
d) protection of voice-mail systems against unauthorised access (eg by use of password protection)
e) the use and set-up of web-based conferencing facilities (including teleconferencing, videoconferencing and online web-based collaboration).

CF9.8.2

Access to operator consoles associated with in-house telephone exchanges should be restricted by the use of passwords (or equivalent), which are:

a) changed on installation, to ensure standard passwords set by the supplier cannot be exploited by unauthorised individuals
b) applied to the access ports used for remote diagnosis.

CF9.8.3

Changes to the configuration of settings for in-house telephone exchanges (including extension numbers) should be performed by authorised, skilled individuals.

CF9.8.4

A method of reviewing telephone services should be established, which includes:

a) monitoring patterns of telephone use to determine adequate capacity of in-house telephone exchanges and operator workloads / staffing requirements
b) inspecting voice network bills / invoices to identify unusual patterns of use which may indicate fraud or improper behaviour.

CF9.8.5

Access to voice-mail should be restricted to authorised users by using a password (or equivalent).

CF9.8.6

Conferencing facilities (including teleconferencing, videoconferencing and online web-based conferencing) should be protected against unauthorised access by:

a) requiring authentication before users are granted access to a conference
b) providing a unique password for each new conference (ie not repeating the same password for consecutive conferences)
c) maintaining a record of who joins and leaves a conference
d) ensuring conferencing hardware (eg screens and cameras), software (eg presentation, screen sharing and remote takeover applications) and any network connections are disabled or closed once a conference has ended.

Related content	ISF resources
No direct references	No recent ISF material

CONTROL FRAMEWORK

FUNDAMENTAL

AREA CF10 – Threat and Vulnerability Management

List of Topics

CF10.1 Patch Management
CF10.2 Malware Awareness
CF10.3 Malware Protection Software
CF10.4 Security Event Logging
CF10.5 System / Network Monitoring
CF10.6 Intrusion Detection

CF10.1 Patch Management

Principle A process should be established for the deployment of system and software patches.

Objective To address technical system and software vulnerabilities quickly and effectively in order to reduce the likelihood of vulnerabilities being exploited and serious business impact arising.

CF10.1.1

There should be documented standards / procedures for patch management which specify the:

a) requirement to patch a range of business applications, information systems and network devices
b) organisation's approach to patching (eg what is to be patched)
c) testing requirements (eg provision of a test environment)
d) methods of patch distribution (eg automated deployment).

CF10.1.2

A patch management process should be established to govern the application of patches to:

a) business applications, operating system software and firmware (eg on servers, mobile devices and consumer devices)
b) computer equipment (including servers, desktop computers, ultrabooks, laptops and netbooks)
c) consumer devices (including tablets and smartphones)
d) virtual systems (eg virtual servers and virtual desktops)
e) network storage systems (including Storage Area Network (SAN) and Network-Attached Storage (NAS))
f) network equipment (eg routers, switches, wireless access points and firewalls)
g) VoIP telephony software and conferencing equipment
h) office equipment (eg network printers, photocopiers, facsimile machines, scanners and multifunction devices (MFDs))
i) specialist equipment (eg information systems that support or enable the organisation's critical infrastructure such as SCADA systems, process control PCs and embedded systems).

CF10.1.3

A method should be established for:

a) defining roles and responsibilities for patch management
b) determining the importance of information systems (eg based on the information handled, the business processes supported and the environments in which they are used) to help identify the extent of patching, timescales for deploying patches and the order in which patches need to be deployed
c) recording patches that have been applied (eg using an asset register, configuration management database (CMDB) or equivalent).

FUNDAMENTAL

CONTROL FRAMEWORK

CF10.1 Patch Management (continued)

CF10.1.4

The patch management process should be:

a) documented
b) approved by relevant management
c) assigned an owner
d) applied on a continuous basis (at least daily).

CF10.1.5

The patch management process should help relevant managers to:

a) discover software vulnerabilities as soon as they become known (eg by working with software vendors and monitoring announcements by security research organisations or equivalent)
b) determine whether software code that can exploit a new vulnerability (often referred to as a 'zero day exploit') is publicly available, either as a 'proof of concept' or as actual malicious code
c) identify and obtain patches when they are available to address discovered vulnerabilities (eg by tracking CERT alerts, vendor websites and mailing lists)
d) decide when to deploy patches (eg by assessing potential post-deployment impact to the organisation, determining the criticality of patches (using the Common Vulnerability Scoring System (CVSS) or equivalent) and analysing the results of testing patches).

CF10.1.6

The patch management process should:

a) specify methods of validating patches (eg ensuring that the patch is from an authorised source)
b) assess the business impact of implementing patches (or not implementing a particular patch)
c) ensure patches are tested against known criteria
d) describe methods of deploying patches in a timely manner (eg grouping multiple patches and using software distribution tools)
e) provide methods of deploying patches to systems that are not connected to the network (eg standalone computers) or devices that connect to the network infrequently (eg travelling staff)
f) report on the status of patch deployment across the organisation
g) include methods of dealing with the failed deployment of a patch (eg redeployment of the patch).

CF10.1.7

Methods should be established to protect information, business applications and technical infrastructure if no patch is available for an identified vulnerability (eg by disabling services, adding additional access controls and performing detailed monitoring).

Related content	ISF resources
CF11.3 Emergency Fixes	*Patch Management SIG Digest*

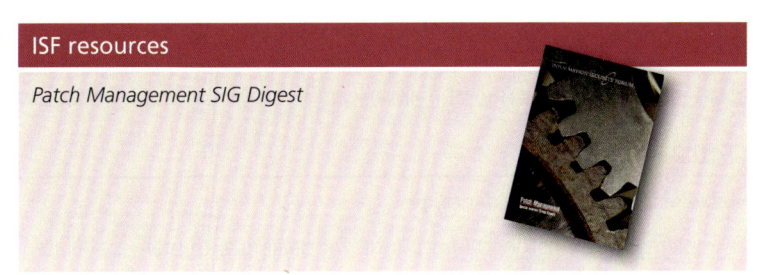

CONTROL FRAMEWORK   **FUNDAMENTAL**

CF10.2 Malware Awareness

Principle All individuals who have access to information and systems of the organisation should be made aware of the risks from malware, and the actions required to minimise those risks.

Objective To ensure all relevant individuals understand the key elements of malware protection, why it is needed, and help to keep the impact of malware to a minimum.

CF10.2.1

There should be documented standards / procedures covering protection against malware, which:

a) provide users with information about malware
b) warn users how to reduce the risk of malware infection.

> Malware typically includes computer viruses, worms, trojan horses, spyware, rootkits, botnet software, adware and malicious mobile code (eg malicious executable code, often in the form of Java applets, ActiveX, JavaScript or VBScript, that has been written deliberately to perform unauthorised functions).

CF10.2.2

Users should be informed about the:

a) prevalence of malware and associated risks (eg unauthorised access to critical business applications, corruption of critical business information or leakage of sensitive information)
b) ways in which malware can install itself on computing devices
c) common symptoms of malware (eg poor system performance, unexpected application behaviour, sudden termination of an application).

CF10.2.3

Users should be:

a) advised to manually scan (often referred to as on-demand scanning) files when attaching portable storage devices or when receiving unknown or questionable files
b) notified quickly of significant new malware-related risks (eg by email, freeware or suspicious websites)
c) instructed to report suspected or actual malware to a single point of contact for support (eg a helpdesk or telephone hot line)
d) supported by specialist technical support at required times (eg 24 hours a day, 365 days a year).

CF10.2.4

The risk of malware infection should be reduced by warning users not to:

a) install software from untrusted sources
b) open untrusted attachments
c) click on suspicious or unknown hyperlinks within emails or documents
d) attempt to manually resolve malware problems (without specialist assistance such as a helpdesk).

CF10.2.5

Malware protection should include:

a) implementing emergency procedures for dealing with malware-related information security incidents
b) monitoring external intelligence sources (eg media and security vendors) about new malware threats
c) informing external parties of the organisation's malware protection standards / procedures.

Related content	ISF resources
CF10.3 Malware Protection Software	No recent ISF material

FUNDAMENTAL

CONTROL FRAMEWORK

CF10.3 Malware Protection Software

Principle Effective malware protection software should be installed, configured, and maintained throughout the organisation.

Objective To protect the organisation against malware attacks and ensure malware infections can be addressed within defined timescales.

CF10.3.1

There should be documented standards / procedures related to malware protection software, which specify:

a) methods for installing and configuring malware protection software (eg anti-virus protection software, anti-spyware software)
b) update mechanisms for malware protection software (including automatic updates)
c) the processes required to review the effectiveness of malware protection software
d) steps required to reduce the risk of malware being downloaded.

CF10.3.2

Malware protection software should be installed on systems that are exposed to malware (eg those that are connected to networks or the Internet, or are accessed by multiple external suppliers), including:

a) relevant servers (eg servers that are at risk from malware, such as file and print servers, application servers, web servers and database servers)
b) messaging gateways (eg those that scan network traffic and electronic messages in real time)
c) computing devices (eg desktop computers, laptops and netbooks)
d) consumer devices (eg tablets and smartphones)
e) office equipment (eg network printers, photocopiers, facsimile machines, scanners and multifunction devices (MFDs))
f) information systems that support or enable the organisation's critical infrastructure (eg SCADA systems, process control PCs and embedded systems).

CF10.3.3

Malware protection software should protect against all forms of malware (eg computer viruses, worms, trojan horses, spyware, rootkits, botnet software, keystroke loggers, adware and malicious mobile code).

CF10.3.4

Malware protection software should be distributed automatically, and within defined timescales to reduce the risk of systems being exposed to the most recent malware (including those that are associated with 'zero-day' attacks).

CF10.3.5

Malware protection software should be configured to scan:

a) computer firmware (ie the basic input / output system (BIOS) and memory)
b) the master boot record (MBR) of hard disk drives (a popular target for boot sector-infecting viruses)
c) targeted files (including executables, image files such as JPEG, document formats such as Adobe PDF and macro files in desktop software)
d) protected files (eg compressed or password-protected files)
e) portable storage media (eg CDs, DVDs and USB storage devices)
f) network traffic entering the corporate network (including email and downloads from the Internet)
g) network traffic leaving the corporate network (including email attachments and shared documents).

CF10.3 Malware Protection Software (continued)

CF10.3.6

Malware protection software should be configured to:

a) be active at all times (ie scanning files as they are accessed to provide real-time protection)
b) perform scheduled scanning at predetermined times
c) provide a notification when suspected malware is identified (eg by producing an event log entry and providing an alert)
d) quarantine files suspected to contain malware (eg for further investigation)
e) remove discovered malware and any associated files
f) ensure that important settings cannot be disabled or functionality minimised.

CF10.3.7

Regular reviews of servers, desktop computers, mobile devices and consumer devices should be performed to ensure that:

a) malware protection software has not been disabled
b) the configuration of malware protection software is correct
c) updates are applied within defined timescales
d) emergency procedures are in place to deal with a malware-related information security incident.

CF10.3.8

The risk of downloading malware should be reduced by:

a) restricting the sources from which mobile code can be downloaded (eg by providing a blacklist of forbidden websites)
b) limiting the downloading of specific types of mobile code
c) configuring web browsers so that users are asked if they wish to install mobile code
d) allowing only trusted mobile code to be downloaded (ie signed with a trusted digital certificate)
e) running mobile code in a protected environment (eg a quarantine area such as a Java 'sandbox' or a proxy server in a 'Demilitarised Zone' (DMZ)).

Related content	ISF resources
CF10.2 Malware Awareness	No recent ISF material

FUNDAMENTAL

CONTROL FRAMEWORK

CF10.4 Security Event Logging

Principle Important security-related events should be recorded in logs, stored centrally, protected against unauthorised change and analysed on a regular basis.

Objective To help in the identification of threats that may lead to an information security incident, maintain the integrity of important security-related information and support forensic investigations.

CF10.4.1

Reliable security event logs should be established (eg to store messages about system crashes, unsuccessful login of authorised users, and unsuccessful changes to access privileges), which are supported by documented standards / procedures.

CF10.4.2

Standards / procedures should cover:

a) management of security event logging (eg setting policy, defining roles and responsibilities, signing off budget and reporting)
b) identification of business applications and technical infrastructure systems on which event logging should be enabled (eg critical business applications and systems that have experienced a major information security incident, or systems that are subject to legislative or regulatory mandates) to help identify security-related events
c) configuration of systems to generate security-related events (including event types such as failed login attempts, system crash, deletion of user account and event attributes such as date, time, UserID, file name, IP address)
d) storage of security-related events within event logs (eg using local systems, central servers, or by using storage provided by an external service provider)
e) analysis of security-related event logs (including normalisation, aggregation and correlation)
f) protection of security-related event logs (eg via encryption, access control and back-up)
g) retention of security-related event logs (eg to meet legal, regulatory and business requirements for possible forensic investigations).

CF10.4.3

Security event log management should include setting policy, defining roles and responsibilities, ensuring the availability of relevant resources, and guidance on the frequency and content of reports.

CF10.4.4

Security event logging should be performed on systems that:

a) are critical to the organisation (eg financial databases, servers storing medical records or key network devices)
b) have experienced a major information security incident
c) are subject to legislative or regulatory mandates.

CF10.4.5

Business applications and technical infrastructure systems should be configured to:

a) enable event logging
b) generate appropriate event types (eg system crashes, object deletion and failed login attempts)
c) incorporate relevant event attributes in event entries (eg IP address, username, time and date, protocol used, port accessed, method of connection, name of device and object name)
d) use a consistent, trusted date and time source (eg using global positioning system (GPS), atomic clocks or time-server on the Internet) to ensure event logs use accurate time-stamps.

CF10.4 Security Event Logging (continued)

CF10.4.6

Security-related event logging should be:

a) enabled at all times
b) protected from accidental or deliberate modification or overwriting.

CF10.4.7

Mechanisms should be established so that when event logs reach a maximum size, the system is not halted through lack of disk space and logging continues with no disruption.

CF10.4.8

Security-related event logs should be analysed regularly (eg using automated security information and event management (SIEM) tools or equivalent), and include:

a) processing of key security-related events (eg using techniques such as normalisation, aggregation and correlation)
b) interpreting key security-related events (eg identification of unusual activity)
c) responding to key security-related events (eg passing the relevant event log details to an information security incident management team).

> Security information and event management (SIEM) tools are also commonly referred to as security event management (SEM) tools, security information managers (SIM), core security event managers (CSEM) and enterprise security managers (ESM).

CF10.4.9

Security-related event logs should be:

a) reviewed regularly (eg to help identify suspicious or unauthorised activity)
b) retained according to retention standards / procedures
c) copied regularly on to portable storage media that can preserve the event log information (in electronic format) for long periods of time
d) stored securely for possible forensic analysis at a later date.

Related content	ISF resources
CF10.5 System / Network Monitoring	Security Event Logging

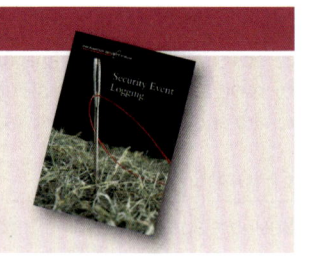

FUNDAMENTAL

CF10.5 System / Network Monitoring

Principle Business applications, computer systems and networks should be monitored continuously, and reviewed from a business user's perspective.

Objective To assess the performance of business applications, computer systems and networks, reduce the likelihood of system overload and detect potential or actual malicious intrusions.

CF10.5.1

The performance of business applications, information systems and networks should be monitored:

a) against agreed targets
b) by reviewing current utilisation of systems at normal and peak periods
c) using automated monitoring software
d) by reviewing event logs of system and network activity regularly (eg to help identify suspicious or unauthorised activity)
e) by investigating bottlenecks / overloads.

CF10.5.2

Key information relating to system / network monitoring should be retained long enough to meet legal / regulatory requirements (eg by archiving the information to portable storage media and storing it in a secure location).

CF10.5.3

Capacity planning activities should be undertaken to allow extra capacity to be commissioned before projected bottlenecks / overloads materialise.

CF10.5.4

System / network availability (ie response and up-time) should be measured from the perspective of business users (eg by monitoring information system and network performance).

CF10.5.5

System / network monitoring activities should be conducted regularly, and involve:

a) scanning information systems for known vulnerabilities (eg using automated tools)
b) checking whether powerful utilities / commands have been disabled on attached hosts (eg by using a 'network sniffer')
c) checking for the existence and configuration of unauthorised wireless networks (eg using automated tools)
d) discovering the existence of unauthorised systems (eg by using network discovery and mapping tools)
e) detecting unauthorised changes to electronic documents and configuration files (eg by using file integrity monitoring software).

CF10.5.6

The use of network analysis / monitoring tools should be restricted to a limited number of authorised individuals (eg network administrators or staff in a network operations centre (NOC) or security operation centre (SOC)).

CF10.5.7

Usage reports from service providers (eg invoices or service reports) should be examined to discover any unusual activity within information systems and networks (eg by reviewing patterns of activity).

CF10.5 System / Network Monitoring (continued)

CF10.5.8

System / network monitoring activities should be conducted to help identify:

a) unauthorised scanning of business applications, information systems and networks
b) successful and unsuccessful attempts to access protected resources (eg web portals and file shares)
c) unauthorised changes to user accounts and access rights (to detect privilege escalation)
d) extraction or modification of sensitive information (eg by checking the time-stamp of files and using file integrity checking software)
e) attempts to conceal unauthorised access and activity (ie to cover tracks)
f) the creation of back doors that provide unauthorised privileged access to business applications, information systems and networks at a later time.

CF10.5.9

The results of monitoring activities should be reviewed by the owners of business applications, information systems and networks, and presented to the business owners to whom services are provided.

Related content	ISF resources
CF10.4 Security Event Logging	*Security Event Logging*

FUNDAMENTAL

CF10.6 Intrusion Detection

Principle Intrusion detection mechanisms should be applied to critical systems and networks.

Objective To identify suspected or actual malicious attacks and enable the organisation to respond before serious damage is done.

CF10.6.1

Intrusion detection mechanisms should be employed for critical business applications, systems and networks to identify predetermined and new types of attack.

CF10.6.2

Intrusion detection methods should be supported by documented standards / procedures, which cover:

a) methods of identifying unauthorised activity
b) analysis of suspected intrusions
c) relevant responses to different types of attack (eg an information security incident management process).

CF10.6.3

Intrusion detection mechanisms should identify:

a) unplanned termination of processes or applications
b) activity typically associated with malware
c) known attack characteristics (eg denial of service and buffer overflows)
d) unusual system behaviour (eg identifying anomalies in standard protocols)
e) unauthorised access (actual or attempted) to systems or information.

CF10.6.4

Intrusion detection mechanisms should be configured to:

a) incorporate new or updated attack characteristics
b) provide alerts when suspicious activity is detected, supported by documented processes for responding to suspected intrusions
c) protect the intrusion detection software against attack (eg by hiding the presence of intrusion detection software).

CF10.6.5

Intrusion detection methods should be supported by specialist software, such as host intrusion detection systems (HIDS) and network intrusion detection systems (NIDS).

CF10.6.6

Network intrusion detection sensors (ie specialist hardware used to identify unauthorised activity in network traffic) should be protected against attack (eg by preventing the transmission of any outbound network traffic, or by using a network tap to hide the presence of the sensor).

CF10.6.7

Intrusion detection software should be:

a) updated automatically and within defined timescales (eg delivery of distribution attack signature files to intrusion detection sensors via a central management console)
b) configured to provide an alert when suspicious activity is detected (eg via a management console, email messages or SMS text messages to mobile telephones).

CF10.6 Intrusion Detection (continued)

CF10.6.8

Regular reviews should be performed to ensure that:

a) the configuration of intrusion detection software meets requirements
b) intrusion detection software has not been disabled or tampered with
c) updates have been applied within defined timescales.

CF10.6.9

Suspected intrusions should be analysed and potential business impact assessed. Initial analysis should include:

a) confirming whether an attack is actually occurring (eg by eliminating false positives)
b) determining the type of attack (eg worms, buffer overflows or denial of service)
c) identifying the original point of attack
d) quantifying the possible impact of an attack.

CF10.6.10

The status of an attack should be assessed in terms of:

a) time elapsed since the start of the attack and since detection of the attack
b) scale (eg the number and type of particular systems and networks affected).

CF10.6.11

There should be a documented method (eg an escalation process) for reporting serious attacks (eg to an information security incident management team or crisis management team).

Related content

CF10.4 Security Event Logging
CF10.5 System / Network Monitoring
CF11.1 Information Security Incident Management

ISF resources

Intrusion Detection: Establishing the Business Case

Intrusion Detection: Implementation Guide

Information Security Incident Management: Establishing an Information Security Incident Management Capability

FUNDAMENTAL CONTROL FRAMEWORK

AREA CF11 – Incident Management

List of Topics

CF11.1 Information Security Incident Management
CF11.2 Cybercrime Attacks
CF11.3 Emergency Fixes
CF11.4 Forensic Investigations

CF11.1 Information Security Incident Management

Principle Information security incidents should be identified, responded to, recovered from, and followed up using an information security incident management process.

Objective To identify and resolve information security incidents quickly and effectively, minimise their business impact and reduce the risk of similar incidents occurring.

CF11.1.1

A capability for governing the management of information security incidents (ie an event or chain of events that compromise the confidentiality, integrity or availability of information) should be established.

CF11.1.2

The information security incident management capability should be supported by documented standards / procedures, which:

a) cover the involvement of relevant stakeholders (eg legal department, public relations, human resources, law enforcement agencies, media and industry regulators)
b) detail the types of information needed to assist information security incident management (eg security event log data, network configuration diagrams and information classification details)
c) specify the tools needed to assist information security incident management (eg checklists, e-discovery software, log analysers, incident tracking software and forensic analysis software).

CF11.1.3

There should be a process for managing individual information security incidents, which includes:

a) identifying information security incidents (eg receiving information security incident reports, assessment of business impact, categorisation and classification of the information security incident, and recording of information about the information security incident)
b) responding to information security incidents (eg escalation to the information security incident management team, investigation, containment and eradication of the cause of the information security incident)
c) recovering from information security incidents (eg rebuilding systems and restoring data, and closure of the information security incident)
d) following up information security incidents (eg post-incident activities such as root cause analysis, forensic investigation, reporting to the business and notifying relevant authorities of a security breach).

CF11.1.4

Information security incidents should be:

a) reported to a predetermined contact (eg a helpdesk, telephone hot line or specialist IT team / department)
b) recorded in a log, or equivalent (eg using an automated information security incident management system)
c) categorised and classified (eg according to their severity and type).

CF11.1 Information Security Incident Management (continued)

CF11.1.5

The response to information security incidents should include:

a) analysing available information (eg application and system event logs)
b) handling necessary evidence (eg labelling it and storing it in a document / computer media fireproof safe location to prevent unauthorised tampering)
c) investigating the cause of information security incidents (eg with assistance from the information security incident management team)
d) containing and eradicating the information security incident (eg by making changes to access control systems, increasing network capacity, terminating or diverting network connections, or shutting down information systems).

CF11.1.6

The recovery from information security incidents should involve:

a) rebuilding systems or networks (and supporting IT facilities) to a previously known secure state (ie the same state they were in before the information security incident occurred)
b) restoring from information that has not been compromised by the information security incident
c) closure of the information security incident.

CF11.1.7

Following recovery from information security incidents:

a) reviews should be performed (involving an information security specialist) to identify the cause of the information security incident (eg by performing a root cause analysis)
b) assessments should be carried out (involving relevant business representatives and an IT specialist) to determine the business impact of the information security incident and corresponding recovery actions
c) forensic investigations should be performed, if required (eg for legal purposes or serious information security incidents, such as fraud)
d) existing security controls should be examined to determine their adequacy
e) corrective actions should be undertaken to minimise the risk of similar incidents occurring
f) details of the information security incident should be documented in a post-incident report.

CF11.1.8

Details about information security incidents experienced (eg incident type and category, information involved and events leading up to incidents) should be recorded and maintained on a continuous basis, using a consistent approach (eg using an agreed taxonomy).

CF11.1.9

Information about security incidents should be collated and reviewed regularly, to help:

a) determine patterns and trends of information security incidents
b) understand the costs and impacts associated with incidents
c) identify common factors that have influenced incidents (typically by performing a root cause analysis)
d) determine the effectiveness of controls (eg which controls are better at preventing, detecting and delaying incidents or minimising the business impact of incidents)
e) provide a comparison of internal and external incident information.

FUNDAMENTAL

CONTROL FRAMEWORK

CF11.1 Information Security Incident Management (continued)

CF11.1.10

There should be a defined individual / team responsible for managing information security incidents, who has:

a) defined roles and responsibilities
b) sufficient skills / experience in managing information security incidents
c) authority to make critical business decisions and escalate incidents (eg to the crisis management team)
d) methods of involving internal and external stakeholders (eg legal department, public relations, human resources, law enforcement agencies, media and industry regulators).

CF11.1.11

Information relevant to managing information security incidents (eg network diagrams, event logs, business processes and security audit reports) should be made available to help staff follow the information security incident management process, and as a result make important decisions.

CF11.1.12

Individuals responsible for managing information security incidents should be supported by tools (eg software for security information management, evidence handling, back-up and recovery, and forensic investigation) to help complete each stage of the information security incident management process.

Related content	ISF resources
CF10.2 Malware Awareness	*Information Security Incident Management: Introductory Guide*
CF10.3 Malware Protection Software	
CF10.6 Intrusion Detection	*Information Security Incident Management: Establishing an Information Security Incident Management Capability*

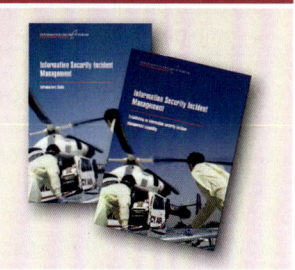

CONTROL FRAMEWORK

SPECIALISED

CF11.2 Cybercrime Attacks

Principle Arrangements should be made to protect the organisation's information and systems against cybercrime attacks.

Objective To reduce the frequency and impact of attempted and successful cybercrime attacks.

CF11.2.1

There should be documented standards / procedures for dealing with cybercrime attacks against the organisation.

> Many of the security activities associated with dealing with cybercrime attacks are based on fundamental information security incident management, and are covered in topics such as information security incident management and forensic investigations. However, cybercrime often involves sophisticated, targeted attacks against an organisation, and as such, additional security measures may be required to respond to specific cybercrime-related attacks.

CF11.2.2

Standards / procedures should take into account the threats associated with each stage of a cybercrime attack, which include:

a) reconnaissance – where parts of the organisation or key individuals (eg executive management) are the target of research by criminals (often using social engineering and research techniques)
b) development of attacks – where criminals construct one or more attacks against the organisation (often using a combination of social engineering and developed and purchased attack tools, and malware)
c) extraction of information – where criminals (often referred to as 'miners') execute attacks to extract information such as personal details, credit card details or product details
d) exploitation of information – where criminals take advantage of extracted information to perform acts such as acquiring money (eg by committing credit card fraud, currency fraud and identity theft) or disrupting business processes
e) money laundering – where criminals (often referred to as 'mules' or 'smurfs') conceal the origin of the money (eg by moving it through legitimate bank accounts or fake transactions between illegitimate organisations).

CF11.2.3

Threats relating to reconnaissance should be mitigated by:

a) identifying and protecting information that is likely to be targeted (eg personal contact details of staff on websites or details of systems and applications used within the organisation that are publicly accessible, such as advertising on websites, references in vendor material or details of IP addresses)
b) briefing internal staff who may be targeted by criminals (eg members of the governing body, executive management or staff that are likely to have privileged access such as key holders and cleaning staff) on the information that they are entitled to and not entitled to disclose, and how to identify and deal with cybercrime
c) implementing specialised security arrangements (eg 'honeypots' and 'tarpits' with fake database records) to detect and monitor cybercriminals, and collect forensic information about their activity.

CF11.2.4

Threats relating to development of attacks should be mitigated by:

a) establishing and maintaining a formal relationship with groups that are typically involved when preparing for and responding to cybercrime-related attacks (eg 'cyber-intelligence service providers', law enforcement agencies, government and industry regulators, representatives from organisations in the same industry sector, security experts in computer / software companies and service providers, and important contacts in the media)
b) obtaining cybercrime-related intelligence from a range of different sources (including law enforcement agencies, external cyber-intelligence service providers and specialist security vendors) to help identify imminent or actual cybercrime-related attacks and support an effective response
c) performing security tests (eg using specialised attack kits) that simulate real targeted attacks to test the strength of security controls and the organisation's incident management process.

SPECIALISED

CF11.2 Cybercrime Attacks (continued)

CF11.2.5

Cybercrime-related intelligence relating to the development of attacks should be reviewed on a regular basis (eg by a cybercrime specialist and business representative) to determine:

a) the extent to which the organisation is at risk of a cybercrime-related attack (eg review of discovered code on the Internet or discussions in underground groups)
b) how targeted information could be used by criminals (eg creating false passports, false accounts, credit cards or online scams)
c) the techniques used by criminals to perform cybercrime-related attacks (to help detect them).

CF11.2.6

Threats relating to extraction of information should be mitigated by:

a) augmenting the organisation's information security incident management process (eg by adding specific cybercrime-related procedures and guidelines)
b) sharing security incident information within the industry
c) performing cybercrime-specific forensic analysis and root cause analysis activities.

CF11.2.7

Threats relating to exploitation of information should be mitigated by:

a) monitoring online forums for details of stolen information (eg the sale of stolen credit card numbers)
b) marking sensitive information (eg using digital watermarking or information hiding techniques) to help investigators follow the information flow and identify connections between different individuals or groups involved in an attack
c) communicating warnings to external parties (eg customers and organisations in the same industry sector)
d) forwarding relevant information to law enforcement agencies.

CF11.2.8

Threats relating to money laundering should be mitigated by:

a) enhancing due diligence measures for external parties (eg by identifying and verifying the identity of external parties when establishing business relations, and assessing if external organisations have been subject to a money laundering or a terrorist financing investigation)
b) verifying client records (eg records of domestic and international transactions) to identify false or counterfeit documentation
c) developing anti-money laundering programmes (involving the development of internal policies, procedures and controls, producing an ongoing employee training programme and following appropriate legislation)
d) liaising with external party specialists in money laundering prevention.

Related content	ISF resources
CF11.1 Information Security Incident Management	ISF Briefing: Profit-Driven Attacks Cyber Security Strategies: Achieving cyber resilience Information Security Incident Management: Establishing an Information Security Incident Management Capability

CONTROL FRAMEWORK

FUNDAMENTAL

CF11.3 Emergency Fixes

Principle — Emergency fixes to business information, business applications and technical infrastructure should be tested, reviewed and applied quickly and effectively, in accordance with documented standards / procedures.

Objective — To respond to emergencies in a timely and secure manner, while reducing disruption to the organisation.

CF11.3.1

There should be documented standards / procedures for applying emergency fixes to business information, business applications and technical infrastructure (including systems software and computer equipment).

CF11.3.2

Standards / procedures should cover:

a) applying emergency fixes to business application software, systems software, parameter settings and business and system information within the live environment
b) emergency access for key individuals (eg business owners or users, system administrators, systems development staff and suppliers of equipment, software or services).

CF11.3.3

A method of applying emergency fixes to software and business applications should be established, which includes applying them to:

a) operating system and virtualisation software
b) enterprise software (eg enterprise resource planning (ERP) and customer relationship management (CRM) applications)
c) commercial-off-the-shelf (COTS) software
d) security software (eg data leakage protection (DLP), digital rights management (DRM) and intrusion detection software (IDS)).

CF11.3.4

A method of applying emergency fixes to technical infrastructure should be established, which includes applying them to:

a) computer equipment (including servers, desktop computers, ultrabooks, laptops and netbooks)
b) consumer devices (including tablets and smartphones)
c) virtual systems (eg virtual servers and virtual desktops)
d) network storage systems (including storage area network (SAN) and network-attached storage (NAS))
e) network equipment (eg routers, switches, wireless access points and firewalls)
f) telephony (including VoIP) and conferencing equipment
g) office equipment (eg network printers, photocopiers, facsimile machines, scanners and multifunction devices (MFDs))
h) specialist equipment (eg information systems that support or enable the organisation's critical infrastructure such as SCADA systems, process control PCs and embedded systems).

CF11.3.5

Emergency fixes should be approved by an appropriate business representative, logged, and carried out in accordance with standards / procedures.

CF11.3.6

Once an emergency is over:

a) authorisation for emergency access should be revoked immediately
b) emergency fixes should be documented
c) emergency fixes should be subject to standard change management disciplines and reviewed by the installation owner
d) emergency fixes should be checked to ensure that they are not left permanently in place.

FUNDAMENTAL

CONTROL FRAMEWORK

CF11.3 Emergency Fixes (continued)

Related content

CF7.6 Change Management

CF10.1 Patch Management

ISF resources

Patch Management SIG Digest

CF11.4 Forensic Investigations

Principle   A process should be established for dealing with information security incidents or other events (eg e-discovery requests) that require forensic investigation.

Objective   To identify perpetrators of malicious acts and preserve sufficient evidence to prosecute them if required.

CF11.4.1

A process should be established for dealing with information security incidents that may require forensic investigation.

CF11.4.2

There should be documented standards / procedures for dealing with information security incidents that may require forensic investigation, which cover:

a) planning the collection of electronic evidence
b) immediate preservation of evidence on discovery of an information security incident (eg to support the need for a chain of custody to show who handled evidence from the time of discovery to the time of legal proceedings)
c) compliance with a published standard or code of practice for the collection of admissible evidence
d) maintenance of a log of evidence recovered and the investigation processes undertaken
e) the need to seek legal advice where evidence is recovered
f) actions that may be monitored during the investigation.

CF11.4.3

Evidence should be collected:

a) with the intention of possible legal action
b) with respect for individuals' privacy and human rights
c) from IT sources relevant to the information security incident (eg active, temporary and deleted files on storage media, email or Internet usage, memory caches and event logs)
d) from non-IT sources relevant to the information security incident (eg CCTV recordings, building access logs and eye witness accounts).

CF11.4.4

Evidence collected should include passwords and encryption keys needed to access password protected or encrypted areas of storage containing electronic evidence.

CF11.4.5

Electronic evidence should be collected in accordance with legal constraints by:

a) creating a list of possible privacy implications (eg human rights and data protection)
b) identifying constraints in employment legislation
c) complying with legal conditions in which investigations are allowed (eg Regulation of Investigatory Powers Act 2000 (UK)).

CF11.4.6

The forensic investigation should be supported by recording important information about the investigation (eg in a forensics tool, work log or equivalent), including:

a) attributes (eg type, owner and location of equipment) of electronic evidence
b) a chronological sequence of events
c) investigative actions.

SPECIALISED

CONTROL FRAMEWORK

CF11.4   Forensic Investigations (continued)

CF11.4.7

The sources of forensic information should be protected by:

a) restricting physical and logical access to target computer equipment to a limited number of authorised individuals
b) preventing individuals tampering with possible evidence
c) establishing a 'litigation hold' (eg by stopping document 'housekeeping routines' such as deleting emails) to prevent deletion of documents and record archives which might contain electronic evidence.

CF11.4.8

The integrity of evidence should be protected by:

a) demonstrating that appropriate evidence has been collected, preserved and that it has not been modified
b) analysing evidence in a controlled environment (eg using a copy or a 'forensic image' of the computer media to avoid corruption of the original)
c) having evidence reviewed by an impartial, independent expert to ensure that it meets legal requirements
d) ensuring that processes used to create and preserve evidence can be repeated by an independent external party
e) limiting information about an investigation to nominated individuals and ensuring it is kept confidential.

CF11.4.9

Results from a forensic investigation should be reported to relevant internal parties (eg executive management, heads of business units / departments, in-house legal counsel) and appropriate external parties (eg external legal counsel, regulators or counterparties).

Related content	ISF resources
CF11.1 Information Security Incident Management	*ISF Briefing: Electronic Evidence*

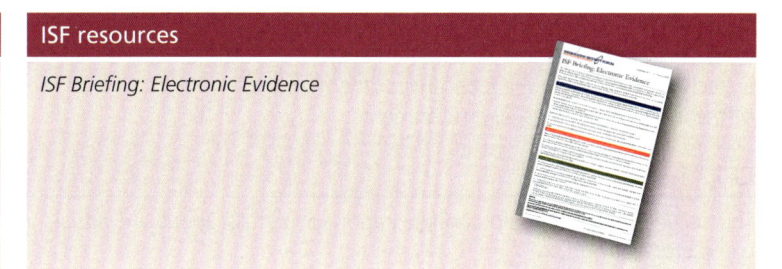

CONTROL FRAMEWORK

SPECIALISED

AREA CF12 – Local Environments

List of Topics
CF12.1 Local Environment Profile
CF12.2 Local Security Co-ordination
CF12.3 Office Equipment

CF12.1 Local Environment Profile

Principle A security profile for each local environment should be documented and maintained, which contains important business and security details about business users, information, technology and locations.

Objective To provide a high-level picture of the type and importance of business conducted in the local environment, which helps support security decisions about activities relating to the local environment.

CF12.1.1

A security profile for each local environment should be documented and maintained, providing an overall picture of the environment, which helps support risk-based decisions and information security-related activities at both a corporate and local level.

CF12.1.2

The security profile should help to identify potential business impacts, threats and vulnerabilities by including important details about:

a) individuals operating in the local environment
b) business processes and information associated with the local environment
c) technology used in the local environment
d) the location of the local environment.

CF12.1.3

The security profile should contain important details about individuals in the local environment (eg staff and contractors), including:

a) main business contact(s)
b) individuals with information security responsibilities (including local security co-ordinators and information protection champions)
c) types of individual operating in the local environment (eg regular users, operational staff, individuals with special privileges and external parties such as contractors)
d) use of consumer devices such as tablets and smartphones (and other gadgets including media players, e-book readers and cameras)
e) level of security awareness (ie the extent to which individuals understand the importance of information security, the level of security required by the organisation and their individual security responsibilities)
f) degree of responsibility for, and level of access to, information (eg from basic access to high security clearance)
g) those who have not been subject to standard / central vetting procedures, so that background checks can be performed.

SPECIALISED

CF12.1 Local Environment Profile (continued)

CF12.1.4

The security profile should contain important details about business processes and information, including:

a) their level of importance to the organisation (eg very low to very high or mission critical, business operational or business administrative)
b) the types of information handled in the local environment (eg intellectual property, financial information and personally identifiable information (PII))
c) ownership and accountability for critical and sensitive information (ie the person who is ultimately responsible within the local environment for the protection of each type of critical and sensitive information)
d) external suppliers used to support the local environment (eg outsource providers or cloud service providers).

CF12.1.5

The security profile should contain important details about the technology used in the local environment, including:

a) business applications (eg enterprise software, commercial-off-the-shelf (COTS) software and desktop applications)
b) computer equipment such as, servers, laptop computers, ultrabooks, portable storage devices, multifunction printers and specialist equipment
c) consumer devices (eg tablets and smartphones)
d) communications and telephony equipment (eg Voice over IP, wireless networks, Internet connections and teleconferencing).

CF12.1.6

The security profile should contain important details about the location of the local environment, for example when the local environment:

a) is accessible by the public (eg retail shops and airports)
b) involves co-sharing with one or more other organisations (eg in a business park)
c) is operated in a hazardous region (eg earthquake or hurricane zone).

CF12.1.7

Details about the security profile should be:

a) recorded (eg in a spreadsheet, tailor-made database or Document Management System (DMS))
b) kept up-to-date (eg by a local security co-ordinator, information protection champion or equivalent)
c) made available to authorised individuals (eg information risk analysts, auditors, and business continuity practitioners) to help them understand the local environment
d) protected against unauthorised change
e) updated regularly or as circumstances change (eg change of role or department, acquisition of new skills or access privileges or upon termination of employment)
f) reported to the corporate information security function.

Related content

CF12.2 Local Security Co-ordination

CF19 Physical and Environmental Security

ISF resources

Protecting Information in the End User Environment

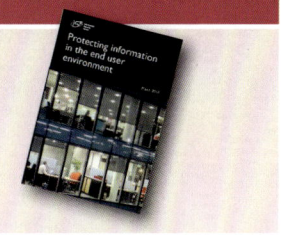

CONTROL FRAMEWORK

SPECIALISED

CF12.2 Local Security Co-ordination

Principle Arrangements should be made to co-ordinate information security activity in individual business units / departments.

Objective To ensure that security activities are carried out in a timely and accurate manner, throughout the organisation, and that security issues are resolved effectively.

CF12.2.1

Responsibility for information security should be assigned to the individual in charge of each local business unit or department.

CF12.2.2

Local information security co-ordinators should be appointed to co-ordinate information security in local environments throughout the organisation.

CF12.2.3

Local information security co-ordinators should have:

a) a clear understanding of their roles and responsibilities (eg by including details in their job description)
b) sufficient technical skills, time, necessary tools (eg checklists and specialist software products) and authority to carry out their assigned roles
c) access to in-house or external expertise in information security
d) documented standards / procedures to support day-to-day information security activities
e) up-to-date information related to information security issues (eg users' security requirements, emerging threats and newly discovered vulnerabilities) and techniques (eg information risk assessment methodologies, forensic investigation software and an enterprise-wide security architecture)
f) a channel of communication with the information security function (eg via regular reporting of duties and results of activities).

CF12.2.4

Local information security co-ordinators should be supported within each local environment by one or more 'information protection champions'.

Information protection champions are individuals who work in local environments (eg a business manager or a well-respected member of staff) and act as ambassadors or promoters for information security. Information protection champions should have:

- a fundamental understanding of the organisation and related business processes
- detailed knowledge of the local environment, including the types information handled, roles of individuals, technology used and the different physical locations associated with the environment
- good communication skills to help ensure they can engage with business owners and users
- technical skills (eg relating to the use of business applications and computing devices in the local environment)
- a strong understanding of information risk and information security concepts (eg threats and vulnerabilities, and the security controls required to reduce information risk)
- support from corporate function representatives with tools such as templates, checklists and specialist software
- authority (from business owners and corporate functions) to support security-related activities.

SPECIALISED

CF12.2 Local Security Co-ordination (continued)

CF12.2.5

Information protection champions should support local information security co-ordinators by facilitating information security-related activities, such as:

a) identifying critical and sensitive information
b) assessing information risks in the local environment
c) selecting and implementing security controls to mitigate information risks
d) delivering information security awareness messages to promote information security in the local environment
e) managing actual and suspected information security incidents.

> In some cases, the information protection champion and local security co-ordinator can be the same person.

CF12.2.6

An organisation-wide group of information protection champions (ie champions from different locations in the organisation) should be established (supported by mailing lists, regular teleconference calls and meetings) to help them:

a) understand common security challenges
b) share successful approaches to working with business owners and users
c) identify effective solutions to addressing security threats
d) determine the best approach to apply security measures in the local environment.

CF12.2.7

Local information security co-ordinators should meet regularly with business owners (ie people in charge of particular business applications or processes) to review the status of information security in business applications and systems, and to agree information security activities to be performed.

Related content	ISF resources
CF2 Human Resource Security CF12.1 Local Environment Profile	*Protecting Information in the End User Environment* *Beyond the clear desk policy: Releasing untapped potential in your staff*

SPECIALISED

CF12.3 Office Equipment

Principle Office equipment (eg network printers and multifunction devices) should be approved, protected by software controls and located in physically secure locations.

Objective To ensure information stored in or processed by office equipment is not disclosed to unauthorised individuals.

CF12.3.1

Office equipment should be supported by documented standards / procedures, which cover:

a) deployment and physical protection of office equipment
b) restricting access to sensitive equipment
c) monitoring the use of office equipment
d) encrypting information transmitted to and processed by office equipment
e) decommissioning office equipment in a secure manner.

> Office equipment includes printers, photocopiers, facsimile machines, scanners and multifunction devices (MFDs). Office equipment often contains the same components as a server (eg operating system, hard disk drives and network interface cards) and run services such as web, mail and ftp. As a result, sensitive information processed by or stored on office equipment is subject to similar threats to servers, yet this equipment is often poorly protected.

CF12.3.2

Office equipment should be:

a) assigned an owner (eg a facilities department or equivalent) who is responsible for maintaining and protecting information stored on or processed by them
b) deployed according to a standard, technical configuration (eg disabling unnecessary services such as web, mail and ftp and changing default administration passwords).

CF12.3.3

Information associated with office equipment should be protected against physical access and tampering by:

a) locating equipment in a physically secure environment (eg restricted area or locked office)
b) restricting access to USB ports
c) preventing the unauthorised removal of hard disk drives (eg by using padlocks).

CF12.3.4

Office equipment should be connected to a dedicated network (eg a virtual LAN (VLAN)) for print servers and multifunction devices to prevent access from unauthorised computing devices (including servers, desktop computers, mobile devices and consumer devices).

CF12.3.5

Access to office equipment by business users should be:

a) authenticated (eg password, token, biometric or RFID badge) to reduce the likelihood of confidential documents being left uncollected on the device
b) restricted to specific functionality (eg printing, scanning, faxing or photocopying).

CF12.3.6

Office equipment should be monitored (eg using intrusion detection and network discovery and mapping tools) on a regular basis to help identify tampering (eg removal of hard disks or memory), misuse (eg unauthorised printing) and theft.

CF12.3 Office Equipment (continued)

CF12.3.7

Sensitive information being processed by office equipment (eg to print, scan or fax) should be encrypted, to prevent viewing by unauthorised individuals, when:

a) transmitted over the network (eg using IPSec)
b) stored on print servers (eg servers used to store print jobs and scanned images)
c) cached on the processing device (eg while a print job is waiting to be printed by a multifunction device) to prevent unauthorised viewing of documents on the hard disk at a later date (eg when the hard disk is replaced).

CF12.3.8

Each piece of office equipment should be subject to a strict maintenance contract / service level agreement that covers:

a) security requirements for protecting information
b) physical access (ie attending equipment on the organisation's premises)
c) remote access for maintenance purposes
d) securely destroying information when equipment is decommissioned, sold or sent back to the supplier (eg for maintenance).

CF12.3.9

Access to office equipment by maintenance staff (including remote access by external service providers) should be:

a) restricted to a limited number of authorised individuals who are competent to perform maintenance and configuration tasks
b) subject to authentication (eg password, token, biometric or RFID badge) to prevent unauthorised access and provide accountability.

CF12.3.10

Office equipment should be configured to securely destroy (sometimes referred to as secure purge) files stored in printing queues and in network folders (eg where scanned documents are stored) after a defined period, regardless of whether they have been printed or retrieved.

CF12.3.11

Sensitive information stored on office equipment should be securely destroyed (eg by using deletion software or physically destroying the hard disk drives) before the equipment is decommissioned, sold or transferred to an external party (eg a leasing company or equivalent).

Related content	ISF resources
CF16.2 Hardware / Software Acquisition	*Protecting Information in the End User Environment*

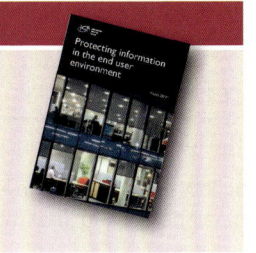

CONTROL FRAMEWORK **SPECIALISED**

AREA CF13 – Desktop Applications

List of Topics
CF13.1 Inventory of Desktop Applications
CF13.2 Protection of Spreadsheets
CF13.3 Protection of Databases
CF13.4 Desktop Application Development

CF13.1 Inventory of Desktop Applications

Principle Critical desktop applications (eg those developed using spreadsheet and database programs) should be recorded in an inventory, or equivalent.

Objective To maintain an accurate and up-to-date record of critical desktop applications, enabling them to be protected accordingly.

CF13.1.1

Details of critical desktop applications (eg those developed using spreadsheet and database programs that are used to support critical business processes such as processing high-value transactions, handling sensitive information and managing a production line) should be recorded in an inventory, or equivalent.

> Desktop applications are typically developed using spreadsheet programs, such as Microsoft Excel, OpenOffice Calc or IBM Lotus 1-2-3; database programs, such as Microsoft Access, OpenOffice Base or IBM Lotus Approach; or similar.

CF13.1.2

Details recorded in the inventory should include:

a) a description of each critical desktop application
b) the identity of the individual with primary responsibility for designing and maintaining each critical desktop application
c) the individuals who use each critical desktop application
d) the intended purpose of each critical desktop application (eg processing of: operational information, such as tracking and monitoring operational workflow; analytical / management information to support decision-making; or financial information such as balances populated in a general ledger)
e) the type of information processed by each critical desktop application (eg customer details, product data or financial transaction information)
f) the department / individual responsible for the development of each critical desktop application (eg individuals in the local environment or an IT function that specialises in spreadsheet and database programs)
g) any changes made to each critical desktop application.

CF13.1.3

The inventory should include details about the level of complexity of each critical desktop application, such as:

a) low (eg desktop applications that are used to maintain basic lists)
b) moderate (eg desktop applications that perform simple calculations or provide information for analytical review)
c) high (eg desktop applications that support complex calculations, valuations and modelling tools).

SPECIALISED

CF13.1 Inventory of Desktop Applications (continued)

CF13.1.4

The inventory should be:

a) kept up-to-date
b) checked for accuracy on a regular basis (eg to ensure that content is complete, comprehensive, correct and timely)
c) signed off by an appropriate business representative.

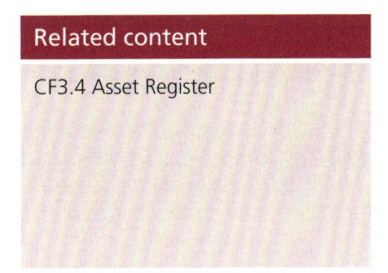

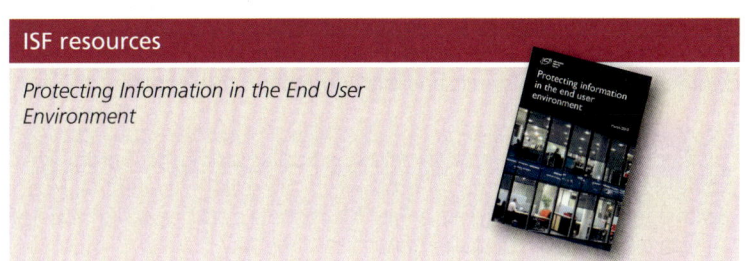

Related content	ISF resources
CF3.4 Asset Register	*Protecting Information in the End User Environment*

SPECIALISED

CF13.2 Protection of Spreadsheets

Principle Critical desktop applications created using spreadsheet programs should be protected by validating input, implementing access control and restricting access to powerful functionality.

Objective To assure the accuracy of information processed by critical spreadsheets, and protect that information from disclosure to unauthorised individuals.

CF13.2.1

Critical spreadsheets should be supported by documented standards / procedures, which cover:

a) training of individuals who use spreadsheets
b) validation of information input into spreadsheets
c) protection of spreadsheets and the information they contain.

> Critical spreadsheets are often developed using spreadsheet programs (eg Microsoft Excel, OpenOffice Calc or IBM Lotus 1-2-3). Often, macros (which are small, user defined, routines or pieces of code) are developed within the spreadsheet to automate functions like routine tasks, importing data, performing calculations and creating new menus and shortcuts.

CF13.2.2

Individuals who use and develop critical spreadsheets should be trained in how to:

a) use them effectively
b) protect the information they store and process
c) develop security-related functionality (eg when writing macros, conducting error checking and performing calculations in cells).

CF13.2.3

Information input into critical spreadsheets should be subject to integrity checks using validation routines, which:

a) require particular spreadsheet cells to contain a non-null value (ie the cell contains a value of some type, and is not empty)
b) restrict the type of information entered (eg requiring entered information to be in the format of date, currency, number or text)
c) use range checks to ensure information entered into the spreadsheet is within a predefined range (eg checking that a number that should be positive is not negative)
d) generate hash totals, to allow the integrity of information to be checked at various stages of being processed
e) perform consistency checks (eg on a formula that is repeated throughout a spreadsheet).

CF13.2.4

The risk of inaccurate entry of information should be reduced by the use of:

a) default values (eg pre-agreed values that will automatically be entered when a new record is added)
b) drop-down lists consisting of predefined values (eg to help users of spreadsheets select the correct information)
c) error messages (eg error codes and descriptive text provided to inform users when a mistake may have occurred)
d) special coding routines to check input values (eg macros and automated error checking routines).

SPECIALISED

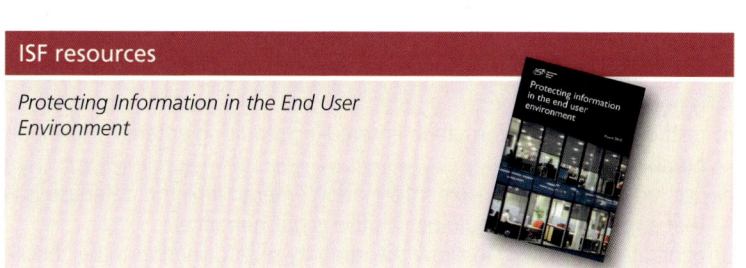

CF13.2 Protection of Spreadsheets (continued)

CF13.2.5

Critical spreadsheets should be protected by:

a) storing them on a central server (eg to reduce the risk of accidental and deliberate modification, and to help ensure spreadsheets are backed up centrally)
b) limiting access to authorised individuals (eg by using password protection and creating access control lists that limit access to spreadsheets or folders that contain spreadsheets)
c) assigning privileges to restrict the functions authorised individuals can perform in spreadsheets (eg by defining different passwords for separate functions, such as opening, reading and modifying spreadsheets)
d) using only approved versions of spreadsheets (eg using the current spreadsheet version, or an approved spreadsheet program such as Microsoft Excel, OpenOffice Calc or IBM Lotus 1-2-3).

CF13.2.6

The integrity of information contained in spreadsheets should be assured by:

a) using separate areas for calculation cells and data entry cells
b) restricting access to calculation areas (eg by using passwords)
c) conducting reconciliations of information entered into the spreadsheet (eg by manually checking against source information or physical records, or by implementing an automated process that checks information as it is downloaded or transferred from another application)
d) restricting access to, or removing standard menus (eg by hiding the standard menus or replacing standard menus with a customised menu to prevent access to developer functions)
e) restricting changes to coding routines that are used to produce additional functionality developed in the spreadsheet (eg writing macros, conducting error checking or performing calculations in cells).

Related content	ISF resources
CF4 Business Applications	*Protecting Information in the End User Environment*

CF13.3 Protection of Databases

Principle Critical desktop applications created using database programs should be protected by validating input, implementing access control, and restricting access to powerful functionality.

Objective To assure the accuracy of information processed by critical databases, and protect that information from disclosure to unauthorised individuals.

CF13.3.1

Critical databases should be supported by documented standards / procedures, which cover:

a) training of individuals who use databases
b) validation of information input into databases
c) protection of databases and the information they contain.

> Critical databases are often developed using commercial-off-the-shelf (COTS) database programs (eg Microsoft Access, OpenOffice Base or IBM Lotus Approach).

CF13.3.2

Individuals who use and develop critical databases should be trained in how to:

a) use them effectively
b) protect the information they store and process
c) develop required functionality securely.

CF13.3.3

Information input into critical databases should be subject to integrity checks using validation routines, which:

a) require particular database fields to contain a non-null value (ie the field contains a value of some type, and is not empty)
b) restrict the type of information entered (eg requiring entered information to be in the format of date, currency, number or text)
c) use range checks to ensure information entered into the database is within a predefined range (eg checking that a number that should be positive is not negative)
d) generate hash totals, to allow the integrity of information to be checked at various stages of being processed
e) perform consistency checks (eg on a calculation that is repeated throughout a database).

CF13.3.4

The risk of inaccurate entry of information should be reduced by the use of:

a) default values (eg pre-agreed values that will automatically be entered when a new record is added)
b) drop-down lists consisting of predefined values (eg to help users of databases select the correct information)
c) error messages (eg error codes and descriptive text provided to inform users when a mistake may have occurred).

CF13.3.5

The integrity of information in the database should be protected by employing data concurrency methods, to ensure that information is not corrupted when modified by more than one user.

SPECIALISED

CF13.3 Protection of Databases (continued)

CF13.3.6

Critical databases should be protected by:

a) storing them on a central server (eg to reduce the risk of accidental and deliberate modification, and to help ensure databases are backed up centrally)
b) limiting access to authorised individuals (eg using password protection and creating access control lists to limit access to databases or folders that contain databases)
c) assigning privileges to restrict the functions authorised individuals can perform in databases (eg defining user profiles and user privileges for individuals who need to open, read and modify the contents of databases)
d) using only approved versions of databases (eg using the current database version, or an approved database program, such as Microsoft Access, OpenOffice Base or IBM Lotus Approach).

CF13.3.7

The integrity of databases (including script code, triggers and schema) should be protected by:

a) compiling databases (eg to create a run-time executable)
b) using a separate password to access the design.

CF13.3.8

Access to database functionality should be restricted by using password protection to prevent unauthorised creation of declarations, statements, and procedures that perform operations or calculate values within a database.

CF13.3.9

Information contained in databases should be protected by restricting access to, or removing standard menus (eg by hiding the standard menus or replacing standard menus with a customised menu to prevent access to developer functions).

Related content	ISF resources
CF4 Business Applications	Protecting Information in the End User Environment

CF13.4 Desktop Application Development

Principle Development of desktop applications should be carried out in accordance with a documented development methodology.

Objective To ensure desktop applications function correctly and meet security requirements.

CF13.4.1

There should be documented standards / procedures for developing critical desktop applications, which cover: specifying requirements; designing, building and testing the desktop application; distributing the desktop application; and training users of the desktop application.

CF13.4.2

Development of critical desktop applications should include a definition of security requirements, which:

a) includes an assessment of the need for confidentiality, integrity and availability of information
b) takes into account an information classification scheme (ie the method of classifying information according to its level of confidentiality such as top secret, company-in-confidence and public).

CF13.4.3

Security requirements for critical desktop applications should be documented and signed off by an appropriate business representative (eg the individual in charge of the local environment).

CF13.4.4

Critical desktop applications should be subject to information risk assessment, in accordance with enterprise-wide standards / procedures for information risk assessment (eg using a structured Information Risk Analysis Methodology, such as the ISF's *IRAM* approach).

CF13.4.5

The results of the information risk assessment should be signed off by an appropriate business representative.

CF13.4.6

The design of critical desktop applications should include the identification and selection of security controls.

CF13.4.7

The build of critical desktop applications should be subject to:

a) approved methods of developing desktop applications (eg when creating macros and similar user-defined routines in spreadsheets, databases, and other desktop applications)
b) documented version control (eg by using incremental version numbers following a change to the desktop application)
c) review by an independent desktop application specialist (eg an individual that does not work in the local environment, and is highly skilled in the functionality of desktop applications).

CF13.4.8

Critical desktop applications should be tested to ensure that they:

a) function as required
b) meet security requirements.

CF13.4.9

Testing of critical desktop applications should be supplemented by the use of automated tools (eg macros, defined routines and scanning tools) to examine the integrity of formulae and code.

SPECIALISED

CF13.4 Desktop Application Development (continued)

CF13.4.10

Before critical desktop applications are made available to users, checks should be performed to ensure that they can be supported on a continuing basis (eg by an individual or a group of individuals skilled in developing desktop applications).

CF13.4.11

Changes to critical desktop applications should be:

a) performed in accordance with a change management process
b) reviewed to ensure that they do not adversely affect intended functionality or compromise security controls.

Related content	ISF resources
CF17 System Development Management	*Protecting Information in the End User Environment*
CF18 Systems Development Lifecycle	*Securing Business Applications*

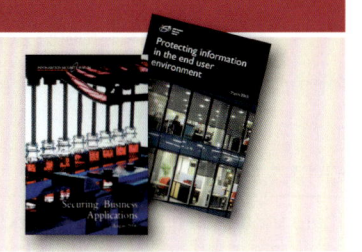

CONTROL FRAMEWORK　　　　　　　　　　　　　　　　　　　　　　　　　　　　　　　　　　　　**SPECIALISED**

AREA CF14 – Mobile Computing

List of Topics
CF14.1 Remote Environments
CF14.2 Mobile Device Configuration
CF14.3 Mobile Device Connectivity
CF14.4 Portable Storage Devices
CF14.5 Consumer Devices

CF14.1　Remote Environments

Principle　Staff working in remote environments (eg in locations other than the organisation's premises) should be subject to authorisation, supported by security awareness material and supplied with approved, robust and secure computing devices.

Objective　To ensure that critical and sensitive information handled by staff working in remote environments is protected against the full range of security threats.

CF14.1.1

There should be documented standards / procedures covering staff who work in remote environments, including public areas (eg hotels, trains, airports and Internet cafes) or work from home, which cover:

a) authorisation by an appropriate business representative for staff to work remotely
b) security requirements associated with remote working
c) the types of device that can be used by staff working in remote environments, such as computing devices (eg desktop computers, laptop computers, ultrabooks, tablets and smartphones) and other devices (eg printers or specialist equipment)
d) implementation and maintenance of computing devices located in remote environments
e) software configuration (eg employing standard 'builds' and relevant web browser settings)
f) provision of software to protect computing devices (eg system management tools, access control mechanisms, malware protection software and encryption capabilities)
g) protection against loss or theft.

CF14.1.2

Staff who work in remote environments should be:

a) authorised to work only in specified locations and informed of locations not approved for remote working (eg bars, public transportation and open spaces)
b) equipped with the necessary skills to perform required security tasks (eg restricting access, performing back-ups and encrypting key files)
c) made aware of the additional risks associated with remote working (including the increased likelihood of theft of equipment or accidental unauthorised disclosure of sensitive information)
d) provided with adequate technical support (eg via a helpdesk)
e) in compliance with legal and regulatory requirements (eg health and safety laws, and data privacy regulations)
f) provided with alternative working arrangements in case of emergency.

CF14.1.3

Staff who work in remote environments should only use computing devices that are:

a) purchased from approved suppliers (eg those with a proven record of providing robust and resilient equipment)
b) tested prior to use
c) supported by maintenance arrangements.

SPECIALISED

CONTROL FRAMEWORK

CF14.1 Remote Environments (continued)

CF14.1.4

Computing devices used by staff working in remote environments should be supplied with:

a) standard, technical configurations (eg pre-configured to run a standard operating system, standard applications and common communications software)
b) a comprehensive set of system management tools (eg maintenance utilities, remote support, patch management, enterprise management tools and back-up software)
c) access control mechanisms to restrict access to the device (eg using device capabilities or external party products)
d) up-to-date malware protection software, to protect against computer viruses, worms, trojan horses, spyware, rootkits, botnet software, keystroke loggers and adware
e) encryption software to protect information stored on the computer (eg using hard disk encryption) or transmitted by the device (eg using a virtual private network (VPN) when connecting to the organisation's network)
f) a security screen filter (often referred to as a privacy filter) to protect against the threat of shoulder surfing.

CF14.1.5

Access to computing devices used in remote environments should be restricted by encrypting passwords and preventing logical access to the capabilities of unattended computing devices (eg by using password-protected screen savers and configuring computers with a terminal lock-out).

CF14.1.6

Computing devices should be protected against loss and theft by:

a) providing users with physical cable locks, anti-theft alarms or equivalent security devices
b) attaching tamper-proof labels, with identification details (eg a unique asset number, bar code or QR code)
c) removing any markings / labels that indicate the owner of the device (eg individual's name or organisation's name)
d) the use of indelible marking
e) issuing instructions on how to return the equipment in the event of loss or theft (eg indicating a 'finders fee' or reward for safe return).

CF14.1.7

Staff travelling to 'high-risk' countries or regions should protect sensitive information from targeted attack by:

a) using temporary or loan mobile devices (including laptops, netbooks, tablets and smartphones)
b) limiting the amount of business information stored on mobile devices (eg by using a new build or securely deleting all previous information stored on the device before travelling)
c) storing sensitive information on an approved encrypted portable storage device, which is kept with the individual (to help ensure the information is protected when the mobile device is unattended)
d) avoiding the use of unknown equipment (eg equipment provided by unknown individuals or available in Internet cafes or kiosks) for communicating or processing sensitive information
e) limiting the number and duration of verbal and electronic business discussions that involve sensitive information.

Related content

CF16.2 Hardware / Software Acquisition

ISF resources

Best Practice in Securing Endpoint Computing Devices

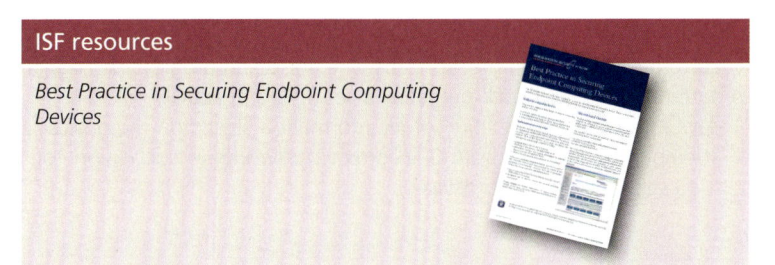

CONTROL FRAMEWORK

FUNDAMENTAL

CF14.2 Mobile Device Configuration

Principle Mobile devices (including laptops, netbooks and consumer devices, such as tablets, and smartphones) should be configured to function as required, protect against unauthorised disclosure of information and help prevent loss or theft.

Objective To ensure mobile devices do not compromise the security of information stored on them or processed by them, and prevent unauthorised access to information in the event they are lost or stolen.

CF14.2.1

Mobile devices (including laptops, netbooks and consumer devices, such as ultrabooks, tablets, and smartphones) should be supported by documented standards / procedures, which cover:

a) software configuration (eg securing the firmware and employing standard builds)
b) provision of software to protect them (eg system management tools, access control mechanisms, malware protection software and encryption capabilities)
c) using a Mobile Device Management (MDM) system.

CF14.2.2

Mobile devices should be provided with standard firmware configurations that include:

a) pre-configured BIOS settings (eg disabling the boot menu, USB facility and DVD boot option)
b) restricting access to the BIOS functions (eg password protection) to authorised administrators.

CF14.2.3

Mobile devices should be subject to 'system hardening' by:

a) removing or restricting unnecessary applications (eg unapproved games, non-business software and utilities)
b) disabling unnecessary services and user accounts (eg guest)
c) changing default administration passwords
d) disabling the 'auto-run' feature (eg from CDs, DVDs and portable storage devices).

CF14.2.4

Mobile devices should be provided with standard technical build configurations that include:

a) running a standard operating system, trusted applications and reliable communications software
b) preventing unauthorised applications from running (eg by using 'whitelists' that allow only specified, permitted applications to run or 'blacklists' that forbid specified applications from running)
c) preventing access to the workstation by unauthorised remote control software.

CF14.2.5

Mobile devices should be protected by the use of:

a) a comprehensive set of system management tools (eg maintenance utilities, remote support, patch management, enterprise management tools and back-up software)
b) access control mechanisms (eg passwords, tokens or biometrics) to restrict access by users and administrators to the device
c) up-to-date malware protection software (including programme code and signature files)
d) automatic time-out (lock-out) after a set period of activity
e) device lock-out and deletion of all information stored on the device following multiple failed authentication attempts (eg ranging from 3 incorrect passwords in succession for laptops to 10 incorrect passwords in succession for consumer devices).

FUNDAMENTAL

CF14.2 Mobile Device Configuration (continued)

CF14.2.6

Mobile devices should protect the confidentiality of stored information by:

a) using full hard-disk encryption to safeguard (by default) all data stored on internal hard disk drives
b) deploying file-based encryption software to safeguard individual files and folders (including files on portable storage media and flash memory cards, such as secure digital (SD)) by the user when required.

CF14.2.7

Mobile devices should protect the confidentiality of stored information by restricting the copying of files:

a) only to authorised portable storage devices
b) based on attributes about information (eg based on file type, information classification or content, such as credit card numbers or social security numbers).

CF14.2.8

Mobile devices should be protected in the event of loss or theft using centralised Mobile Device Management (MDM) software that provides remote:

a) lock-out (to prevent unauthorised access to the device)
b) device tracking (eg software that will attempt to locate the equipment using GPS, or automatically contact a designated location if the equipment can connect to the Internet or a mobile operator network)
c) retrieval of information (that may not have been backed up)
d) monitoring of device activity (in the event evidence is required for forensic analysis)
e) deletion (often referred to as 'remote wipe') by securely destroying all information stored on the device and any attached storage (eg flash memory cards such as secure digital (SD) and compact flash).

> Mobile Device Management (MDM) software provides the capability to centrally manage large numbers of mobile devices. A MDM system typically comprises a server component, a management console and client software ('agents') that are installed / active on each mobile device. MDM typically provide a range of system management features to enable the configuring of system settings, updating software, synchronising and backing up information. Security features typically include:
>
> - protecting information stored on the device (eg by performing a remote lock-out or remote delete)
> - providing a protected 'sandbox' environment (a logically separate area on the device), in which business applications can be used and information processed
> - logging of activity on the device (eg copying information).

CF14.2.9

Mobile devices used to access business applications should protect sensitive information against unauthorised access (eg from unauthorised or rogue applications) by:

a) preventing application information from being stored on the device (eg by deploying business applications using terminal servers (eg thin client) or web browsers)
b) protecting application information when it is stored on the device (eg by deploying business applications using a 'sandbox' or virtual desktop).

CF14.2.10

Mobile devices should be configured to log important events (eg when sensitive information is copied to another device).

CONTROL FRAMEWORK

FUNDAMENTAL

CF14.2 Mobile Device Configuration (continued)

Related content
No direct references

ISF resources
Best Practice in Securing Endpoint Computing Devices

Security in Mobile Networking: SIG Digest

Securing Consumer Devices

FUNDAMENTAL   CONTROL FRAMEWORK

CF14.3   Mobile Device Connectivity

Principle   Mobile devices (including laptops, netbooks and consumer devices, such as tablets, and smartphones) should be provided with secure means of connecting to other devices and to networks.

Objective   To ensure mobile devices are protected against unauthorised access and prevent the unauthorised disclosure of information.

CF14.3.1

Mobile devices (including laptops, netbooks and consumer devices, such as ultrabooks, tablets, and smartphones) should be subject to documented standards / procedures for connectivity, which cover:

a) using portable storage devices
b) protecting wireless access
c) protecting against untrusted networks
d) establishing a virtual private network (VPN)
e) configuring web browsers
f) using web proxy servers.

CF14.3.2

Mobile devices should be configured to:

a) restrict the copying of sensitive files only to authorised portable storage devices (eg based on file type, information classification or content, such as credit card numbers or social security numbers)
b) detect and record details about the use of / connection to unauthorised portable storage devices (eg cameras, smartphones, e-book readers and audio / video media players)
c) monitor information copied to portable storage devices (eg using information leakage protection or data leakage protection (DLP) software) to help detect or block unauthorised transfer of business information
d) prevent the connection of personal equipment such as portable storage devices (including external hard disk drives and USB memory sticks).

CF14.3.3

Mobile devices should be protected from connecting to unauthorised networks and computing devices by restricting wireless connectivity such as Wi-Fi, 3G / 4G, Bluetooth and infrared.

CF14.3.4

Mobile devices that access the corporate network from remote environments should be configured to:

a) establish a virtual private network (VPN) between the device and the corporate network
b) prevent access to unprotected networks while the device is connected to the corporate network (ie to avoid bypassing the VPN)
c) prevent network bridging / routing (eg by using a second network interface card).

CF14.3.5

Mobile devices that may connect to untrusted networks (including the Internet) should be protected by:

a) installing and maintaining personal firewalls to restrict inbound and outbound network traffic (eg to authorised applications such as a web browser and protocols such as HTTP and HTTPS)
b) enabling additional logging (eg logging events associated with particular business applications or folders containing sensitive information)
c) deploying host-based intrusion detection software (HIDS) and host-based intrusion prevention software (HIPS) to detect unexpected application behaviour.

CF14.3 Mobile Device Connectivity (continued)

CF14.3.6

Mobile devices that require access to the Internet (typically using web browser software) should:

a) use a single, approved type of web browser software (to reduce the introduction of vulnerabilities associated with different browsers)
b) route web browser traffic via a web proxy server.

CF14.3.7

Web browser software should be configured to:

a) prevent users from disabling or modifying security options in the software settings
b) limit the caching of information
c) restrict pop-up windows
d) enable the web browsers privacy mode (or equivalent) to stop the browser storing authentication information, such as passwords or tracking information.

CF14.3.8

Web proxy servers (sometimes referred to as Internet gateways or web gateways) should be deployed and configured to:

a) require users to authenticate before gaining access to the Internet
b) restrict access to only authorised websites
c) inspect web traffic (eg to identify malware and web browser attacks)
d) record details about web content being accessed (eg in the event the information is required during an investigation).

Related content	ISF resources
No direct references	Best Practice in Securing Endpoint Computing Devices
	Security in Mobile Networking: SIG Digest
	Securing Consumer Devices

SPECIALISED

CF14.4 Portable Storage Devices

Principle The use of portable storage devices (eg USB memory sticks, external hard disk drives, MP3 players and e-book readers) should be subject to approval, access to them restricted, and information stored on them protected.

Objective To ensure that sensitive information stored on portable storage devices is protected from unauthorised disclosure.

CF14.4.1

There should be documented standards / procedures covering the use of portable storage devices.

> Portable storage devices include external hard disk drives, flash memory cards such as secure digital (SD) and compact flash, USB memory sticks, e-book readers, solid state storage and MP3 players with storage capacity for holding data. Methods of connecting portable storage devices to computer equipment (eg computing devices, laptop computers and netbooks) include USB and Bluetooth.

CF14.4.2

Standards / procedures should include:

a) the types of portable storage device permitted for storing business information (eg portable storage devices that are issued by the organisation)
b) restrictions on use of portable storage devices (eg prohibiting personal use and sharing of portable storage devices with other staff and external individuals, or only permitting storage of non-sensitive information)
c) the type of information that can be transferred to and from portable storage devices (eg restricted to non-classified information or encrypted files)
d) encryption of sensitive information stored on portable storage devices
e) the rights of the organisation regarding ownership of information stored on portable storage devices (eg all information stored on a portable storage device remains the property of the organisation)
f) the right of the organisation to recover information held on portable storage devices.

CF14.4.3

Portable storage devices should be protected by the use of:

a) access control mechanisms (eg by the use of UserID and password, tokens or biometrics)
b) access restrictions (eg whether the user is authorised to read, write or format the device)
c) encryption techniques (eg using encryption software installed on the device, or using file-encryption software on the computing device to which the portable storage device connects)
d) tamper-proof labels, with identification details (eg a unique asset number, bar code or QR code).

CF14.4.4

Users of portable storage devices should be instructed to:

a) store them in a secure location (eg locked cabinet or computer media fireproof safe) when not in use
b) review the contents of the device on a regular basis to identify out-of-date or unwanted files
c) securely destroy files when they are no longer needed
d) return devices to the organisation when no longer needed so that information stored on them can be securely destroyed (eg before the device is reissued) or the device can be physically destroyed (eg via incineration or crushing).

SPECIALISED

CF14.4 Portable Storage Devices (continued)

CF14.4.5

Users of portable storage devices should be prohibited from:

a) sharing the device with unauthorised individuals
b) disclosing passwords (for accessing the device and encrypting files) to unauthorised individuals.

Related content	ISF resources
No direct references	Securing Portable Storage Devices Protecting Information in the End User Environment

SPECIALISED

CF14.5 Consumer Devices

Principle Where an organisation allows the use of consumer devices (eg tablets and smartphones that are owned by employees) for business purposes (often referred to as consumerisation), this should be supported by documented agreements with staff, and technical security controls to protect business information.

Objective To ensure critical and sensitive business information handled on consumer devices receives the same level of protection as that provided by corporate-owned equipment.

CF14.5.1

Where an organisation allows the use of consumer devices for business purposes, this should be supported documented standards / procedures, which cover:
a) establishing an acceptable usage policy (eg covering obligations of users and the rights of the organisation)
b) delivering an awareness programme aimed specifically at users of consumer devices
c) providing secure deployment of business applications (eg using a web browser or a 'sandbox').

> Consumer devices should be subject to the same level of protection as devices provided by the organisation. As a result, the security controls specified in *CF14.2 Mobile Device Configuration* and *CF14.3 Mobile Device Connectivity* should also be applied to consumer devices.

CF14.5.2

Consumer devices should be:

a) permitted only if they meet an agreed specification of the types of device allowed (eg the manufacturer and model of the device, the operating system and security features required, such as complex passwords and device encryption)
b) authorised for use and signed off by a business owner.

CF14.5.3

There should be an acceptable usage policy (AUP) for the use of consumer devices, which:

a) includes the conditions for use of consumer devices (eg user obligations, waiver of liability and employer rights to inspect, remote audit and remote wipe)
b) users must agree to and sign before being granted access to the organisation's business applications and information systems.

CF14.5.4

The acceptable usage policy should specify the:

a) restrictions on the use of consumer devices (eg prohibiting the sharing of devices with other individuals, banning synchronisation with unauthorised devices or only permitting storage of non-sensitive information)
b) ownership of information stored on consumer devices (eg all information stored on a consumer device remains the property of the organisation).

CF14.5 Consumer Devices (continued)

CF14.5.5

The acceptable usage policy for consumer devices should inform users of their obligations to:

a) protect information throughout the lifecycle of the device (ie acquisition, use, maintenance, repair and decommission) and the lifecycle of information (eg when creating, processing, copying, printing, storing and destroying information)
b) provide physical security of the device by keeping it at hand at all times, or locking it away
c) refrain from tampering with security settings or approved software on the device (sometimes referred to as 'jailbreaking')
d) immediately report actual and suspected security incidents relating to the device (eg loss or theft of the device, unauthorised disclosure of information) to a helpdesk, specialist IT team / department or equivalent.

CF14.5.6

Users of consumer devices should be subject to a security awareness campaign so that they clearly understand and can comply with the acceptable usage policy.

CF14.5.7

The organisation should reserve the right to:

a) confiscate, audit or inspect consumer devices
b) access, recover or delete information stored on consumer devices
c) remotely manage the device (eg from a central management console)
d) enforce technical security controls such as access control, malware protection software and encryption
e) remotely delete all information in the event of a security incident, if the individual leaves the organisation or the device is lost or stolen.

CF14.5.8

Consumer devices used to access business applications should protect sensitive information against unauthorised access (eg from unauthorised or rogue applications) by:

a) restricting critical or sensitive application information from being stored on the device (eg by deploying business applications using terminal servers (eg thin client) or web browsers)
b) protecting application information when it is stored on the device (eg by deploying business applications using a 'sandbox' or virtual desktop).

Security technologies used to protect business applications and related information, such as 'sandboxes' and virtual desktops, may not be applicable to, or available on, all types of consumer device.

CF14.5.9

Consumer devices should be configured to log important events (eg when sensitive information is copied to another device).

Related content	ISF resources
CF14.2 Mobile Device Configuration	*Securing Consumer Devices*
	Cyber citizenship in an enterprise environment (Briefing paper)

FUNDAMENTAL

CONTROL FRAMEWORK

AREA CF15 – Electronic Communications

List of Topics
CF15.1 Email
CF15.2 Instant Messaging

CF15.1   Email

Principle   Email systems should be protected by a combination of policy, awareness, procedural and technical security controls.

Objective   To ensure that email services are available when required, the confidentiality and integrity of messages is protected in transit, and the risk of misuse is minimised.

CF15.1.1
The use of email should be signed off by an appropriate business representative.

CF15.1.2
There should be documented standards / procedures for the provision and use of email, which include:

a) methods of configuring mail servers (eg to limit the size of messages or user mailboxes)
b) scanning email messages (eg for malware, chain letters or offensive content)
c) enhancing the security of email messages (eg by the use of disclaimers, hashing, encryption or non-repudiation techniques)
d) guidelines for business and personal use (eg prohibition of personal use)
e) the types of email service permitted (eg corporate services such as IBM Lotus Notes or Microsoft Exchange)
f) user guidelines for acceptable use (eg prohibition of the use of offensive statements)
g) details of any monitoring activities to be performed (eg scanning the content of messages including attachments) to detect malicious activity or accidental leakage of business information.

CF15.1.3
Mail servers should be configured to prevent the messaging system being overloaded by limiting the size of messages / user mailboxes and automatically identifying and cancelling email loops.

CF15.1.4
Mail servers should be configured to prevent the accidental disclosure of email and attachments to unauthorised individuals by:

a) preventing users from configuring the 'auto-forward' feature
b) restricting the use of large distribution lists (eg every individual in the organisation)
c) presenting users with a warning before they are able to use the 'reply all' feature to a large number of recipients.

CF15.1.5
Email systems should be reviewed to ensure that requirements for up-time and future availability can be met.

CF15.1 Email (continued)

CF15.1.6

Email messages should be scanned for:

a) attachments that could contain malicious code (eg malicious code hidden in self-extracting zip files or MPEG video clips)
b) prohibited words (eg words that are racist, offensive, libellous or obscene)
c) phrases associated with malware (eg those commonly used in hoax viruses or chain letters).

CF15.1.7

Email systems should protect messages by:

a) blocking messages that are considered undesirable (eg by using an email blacklist consisting of known undesirable websites or email list servers)
b) using digital signatures to identify if email messages have been modified in transit, and encrypting confidential or sensitive email messages
c) ensuring non-repudiation of origin of important email messages (eg by using digital signatures)
d) providing non-repudiation of receipt of important messages (eg by returning a digitally signed receipt message).

CF15.1.8

The business integrity of email messages should be protected by:

a) appending legally required information and return address details (for misdelivered email) to business email (eg as a disclaimer)
b) warning users that the contents of email messages may be legally and contractually binding and that the use of email may be monitored.

CF15.1.9

The organisation should prohibit:

a) automatic email diversion to external email addresses
b) unauthorised private encryption of email or attachments
c) the opening of attachments from unknown or untrusted sources.

CF15.1.10

Personal use of business email should be clearly labelled as personal and subject to the terms of a user agreement.

CF15.1.11

Users should be educated in how to protect the confidentiality and integrity of email messages (eg by the use of encryption, digital certificates and digital signatures).

Related content	ISF resources
CF2.3 Security Awareness Messages	*Secure E-mail: Technology Report*
CF8.6 Public Key Infrastructure	*Using E-mail: Managing the Risks*

SPECIALISED

CF15.2 Instant Messaging

Principle Instant messaging services should be protected by setting management policy, deploying instant messaging application controls and correctly configuring the security elements of an instant messaging infrastructure.

Objective To ensure that instant messaging services are available when required, the confidentiality and integrity of messages is protected in transit, and the risk of misuse is minimised.

CF15.2.1

The use of instant messaging should be signed off by an appropriate business representative.

CF15.2.2

There should be documented standards / procedures for instant messaging services (ie the application and supporting technical infrastructure) which include:

a) guidelines for business and personal use (eg prohibition of personal use)
b) the types of instant messaging services permitted (eg public services or internal services)
c) user guidelines for acceptable use (eg prohibition of offensive statements)
d) details of any monitoring activities to be performed (eg scanning the content of messages including attachments) to detect malicious activity or accidental leakage of business information.

CF15.2.3

The security of instant messaging applications should be improved by:

a) disabling unauthorised features (eg saving transcripts, file sharing, video and audio)
b) using encryption to protect the contents of sensitive messages
c) enabling malware checking at the desktop (eg to compensate for port agile instant messaging software that might bypass malware checking at gateways)
d) logging important events (eg to maintain records for regulatory purposes)
e) directing instant messaging traffic through a content filter.

CF15.2.4

Protection of the instant messaging infrastructure should be improved by:

a) employing a standard client configuration for the instant messaging application
b) 'hardening' instant messaging servers (eg by locking down the operating system and application)
c) configuring firewalls to block unauthorised instant messaging traffic (eg by blocking known instant messaging ports).

CF15.2.5

Users should be educated in how to protect the confidentiality and integrity of instant messages (eg by the use of encryption, digital certificates and digital signatures).

Related content	ISF resources
CF2.3 Security Awareness Messages	*Securing Instant Messaging: Research Report*

AREA CF16 – External Supplier Management

List of Topics
CF16.1 External Supplier Management Process
CF16.2 Hardware / Software Acquisition
CF16.3 Outsourcing
CF16.4 Cloud Computing Policy
CF16.5 Cloud Service Contracts

CF16.1 External Supplier Management Process

Principle Information security requirements should be considered at all stages throughout the relationship with external suppliers.

Objective To protect critical and sensitive information when being handled by external suppliers or when being transmitted between the organisation and the supplier.

CF16.1.1

There should be a process for managing the security of relationships with external suppliers. This process should involve the information security function, and include:

a) identifying and categorising all types of external supplier used by the organisation, enterprise-wide
b) agreeing security arrangements (eg based on business security requirements and compliance needs) for each supplier
c) validating security arrangements for each supplier
d) handling termination of a relationship with a supplier.

> Organisations typically work with many external suppliers and agree different security arrangements depending on the products and services provided by the supplier. The types of external service provider an organisation may use include outsource providers, offshore service providers and cloud service providers. Managing the security of relationships with external suppliers can be supported with a tool such as the ISF's *Third Party Security Assessment Tool (TPSAT)*.

CF16.1.2

All external suppliers working with the organisation should be:

a) identified (typically by business owners) and recorded in a register (or equivalent)
b) categorised from an information security perspective (eg as critical, important or standard)
c) assigned a business owner and information security contact.

CF16.1.3

Critical suppliers should be subject to a relationship assessment (sometimes referred to as a due diligence review), which covers:

a) dealings with the supplier (eg details of provider history, previous and current business arrangements and dispute information)
b) contract requirements (eg non-disclosure agreements, sub-contracting, roles and responsibilities, and termination clauses)
c) implications of the service(s) provided (eg information handled, underlying technical infrastructure, business dependency and sub-contractors used)
d) their demonstrable level of maturity in relation to information security and their degree of commitment to information security.

CF16.1 External Supplier Management Process (continued)

CF16.1.4

A baseline set of security arrangements should be defined and used as the foundation for agreeing security arrangements with each external supplier.

> Baseline information security arrangements represent mandatory security controls and other measures an organisation would typically expect an external supplier to implement to protect the organisation's critical and sensitive information. Defining a set of baseline information security arrangements allows the organisation to focus on agreeing additional security controls, which are often risk-based and specific to the organisation, supplier, business purpose, or the industry sector / jurisdiction in which the organisation operates. Baseline security arrangements typically cover: governance, risk and compliance; system management; access management; security monitoring and response; network connections; electronic communications; and systems development.

CF16.1.5

Additional, specialised controls should be:

a) identified for each external supplier to meet particular business and security requirements (eg as a result of a business relationship assessment, an information risk assessment, legal or regulatory requirements, or contractual arrangements)
b) agreed and signed by both parties (ie the organisation and the external supplier)
c) defined in a contract
d) deployed in practice.

CF16.1.6

A contract should be established with each external supplier, which includes agreed security arrangements (baseline and additional), such as the 'right to audit' and contract termination / exit activities.

CF16.1.7

The information security status of each external supplier should be assessed / validated on a regular basis, using a consistent and approved methodology (eg based on an industry standard). The categorisation of the external supplier should be used to determine:

a) who will perform the assessment (eg an independent specialist or external auditor)
b) the level of detail the assessment will involve
c) the frequency with which the assessment is performed.

CF16.1.8

A consistent method for securely handling the termination of relationships with external suppliers should be established, which includes:

a) designating individuals responsible for managing the termination
b) revocation of physical and logical access rights to the organisation's information
c) return, transfer or secure destruction of assets (eg back-up media storage, documentation, hardware and authentication devices)
d) coverage of license agreements and intellectual property rights
e) rehearsal and refinement of termination activities.

CONTROL FRAMEWORK

FUNDAMENTAL

CF16.1 External Supplier Management Process (continued)

CF16.1.9

Alternative (contingency) arrangements should be established to ensure that the organisation's business processes can continue in the event that the external supplier is not available (eg due to contract termination, a disaster, a dispute with the external supplier or the supplier ceases trading). These arrangements should be based on the results of a risk assessment, and include:

a) the provision of alternative, secure facilities for business processes to continue
b) escrow of information and closed / proprietary technologies (eg application source code and cryptographic keys) using a trusted external party, such as a legal representative, lawyer or equivalent
c) recovery arrangements to ensure continued availability of information stored at an outsource provider or in the cloud
d) alignment with the organisation's business continuity programme.

Related content	ISF resources
CF9.3 External Network Connections	*Information Security in Third Party Relationship Management*
	Third Party Security Assessment Tool (TPSAT)
	Information security for external suppliers: A common baseline
	Baseline Maturity Assessment Tool

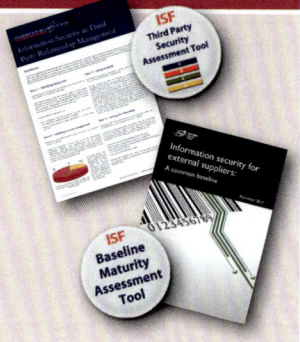

FUNDAMENTAL CONTROL FRAMEWORK

CF16.2   Hardware / Software Acquisition

Principle   Robust, reliable hardware and software should be acquired (eg purchased or leased) following consideration of security requirements and identification of any security deficiencies.

Objective   To ensure that hardware and software acquired from external suppliers provides the required functionality and does not compromise the security of the organisation's critical and sensitive information.

CF16.2.1

There should be documented standards / procedures for acquiring hardware / software, which specifies:

a) guidelines for selecting hardware / software (eg lists of approved suppliers, security considerations and contractual terms)
b) methods of identifying and addressing security weaknesses in hardware / software
c) the need to meet software licensing requirements
d) the process for reviewing and approving hardware / software.

CF16.2.2

Standards / procedures should apply to all hardware acquired throughout the organisation, including:

a) computer equipment (eg servers, desktop computers, ultrabooks, laptops and netbooks)
b) consumer devices (eg tablets and smartphones)
c) virtual systems (eg virtual servers and virtual desktops)
d) network storage systems (eg Storage Area Network (SAN) and Network-Attached Storage (NAS))
e) network equipment (eg routers, switches, wireless access points and firewalls)
f) telephony (including VoIP) and conferencing equipment
g) portable storage media (eg external hard disk drives and USB memory sticks)
h) authentication hardware (eg physical tokens, smartcards and biometric equipment)
i) office equipment (eg network printers, photocopiers, facsimile machines, scanners and multifunction devices (MFDs))
j) specialist equipment (eg equipment that is used to support or enable the organisation's critical infrastructure).

CF16.2.3

Standards / procedures should apply to all software acquired throughout the organisation, including:

a) operating system and virtualisation software
b) enterprise software (eg enterprise resource planning (ERP) and customer relationship management (CRM) applications)
c) commercial-off-the-shelf (COTS) software
d) security software (eg data leakage protection (DLP), digital rights management (DRM) and intrusion detection software (IDS)).

CF16.2.4

Hardware / software should be:

a) acquired (eg purchased or leased) from approved suppliers (ie those with a proven record of providing robust and resilient equipment)
b) tested prior to use (eg by performing penetration tests and vulnerability tests) to help identify and resolve security weaknesses
c) supported by maintenance arrangements.

CF16.2 Hardware / Software Acquisition (continued)

CF16.2.5

When acquiring hardware / software:

a) security requirements should be considered
b) a high priority should be placed on reliability in the selection process
c) contractual terms should be agreed with suppliers.

CF16.2.6

The risk of potential security weaknesses in hardware / software should be reduced by:

a) obtaining external assessments from trusted sources (eg external auditor's opinions and specified security criteria, such as the Information Technology Security Evaluation Criteria (ITSEC), 'Common Criteria' (CC), Federal Information Processing Standards (FIPS) and ISCA Labs)
b) identifying security deficiencies (eg by detailed inspection, reference to published sources, or by participating in user / discussion groups)
c) considering alternative methods of providing the required level of security (eg an alternative method of authentication or additional application and system monitoring).

CF16.2.7

Software licensing requirements should be met by obtaining adequate licenses for planned use and by providing proof of ownership of software (eg via 'blanket' licence agreements – one licence covering a large number of software deployments).

CF16.2.8

The acquisition of hardware / software should be reviewed by staff who have the necessary skills to evaluate them, and be approved by an appropriate business representative.

Related content	ISF resources
CF3.4 Asset Register	No recent ISF material

SPECIALISED

CF16.3 Outsourcing

Principle A process should be established to govern the selection and management of outsource providers (including cloud service providers), supported by documented agreements that specify the security requirements to be met.

Objective To ensure that security requirements are satisfied and maintained when a particular environment or service is delivered by an outsource provider.

CF16.3.1

A documented process should be established to govern the selection of outsource providers and the transfer of activity to them.

> Organisations typically use a range of external suppliers to support critical business processes. The security controls outlined in this topic apply to a broad range of external suppliers that an organisation may use including outsource providers, offshore service providers and cloud service providers.

CF16.3.2

When determining the requirements for outsourcing, the organisation should:

a) evaluate information risks associated with outsourcing arrangements and the particular business functions that may be outsourced
b) determine cross-border / multi-jurisdictional legislative and regulatory requirements
c) identify particularly critical or sensitive business environments
d) take into account the classification of information to be placed in the care of the outsource provider
e) assess the information security practices and standards of potential outsource providers
f) consider interdependencies between the function to be outsourced and other business functions
g) develop exit strategies from the relationship in the eventuality of an early termination of the agreement (eg due to a dispute with the outsource supplier or if the outsource supplier ceases trading).

CF16.3.3

Before the management of a particular business environment is transferred, information security controls should be agreed with the outsource provider and approvals for the transfer obtained from relevant business owners.

CF16.3.4

Contracts should be established with all outsource providers (including cloud service providers), which are:

a) reviewed independently (eg by a legal representative, lawyer or equivalent)
b) approved by executive management
c) agreed and signed by both parties
d) kept up-to-date.

CF16.3.5

Contracts with outsource providers should require them to:

a) comply with good practice for information security (eg apply common security architecture principles)
b) maintain the confidentiality of information gained through the outsourcing agreement
c) protect the integrity of information used in the course of work (ie to ensure it is complete, accurate and valid)
d) ensure the availability of information and systems (eg by providing resilient equipment and guaranteeing response times)
e) provide details about information security incidents in a timely manner.

CF16.3 Outsourcing (continued)

CF16.3.6

Contracts should require outsource providers to:

a) limit access to the assets of the organisation to authorised staff
b) protect personally identifiable information (PII)
c) meet legal and regulatory requirements (eg those relating to privacy, data protection, encryption export, data breach notification and the Payment Card Industry Data Security Standard (PCI DSS))
d) define the way in which they are permitted to further outsource to other external parties.

CF16.3.7

Contracts should specify that outsource providers are required to:

a) assure the quality and accuracy of work performed
b) follow a change management process
c) provide effective information security incident management
d) return or destroy information, software or equipment on an agreed date, or upon request
e) provide effective business continuity arrangements.

CF16.3.8

Contracts should specify:

a) details of licensing arrangements
b) the ownership of intellectual property rights and information
c) the right for the organisation to audit the outsource provider's activities (or provide agreed alternative assurance processes where an audit is not possible).

CF16.3.9

A process should be agreed, to deal with security issues via agreed point(s) of contact within the outsource provider, who is available at predetermined times (eg 24 hours a day, 365 days a year).

Related content	ISF resources
CF16.4 Cloud Computing Policy CF16.5 Cloud Service Contracts	*Information Risk Management in Outsourcing and Offshoring* *Outsourcing and Offshoring: Managing Information Risk* *Outsourcing and Third Party Risk Management – ISF deliverables*

SPECIALISED

CF16.4 Cloud Computing Policy

Principle A comprehensive, documented policy on the use of cloud services should be produced and communicated to all individuals who may purchase or use cloud services.

Objective To help ensure all relevant individuals throughout the organisation are aware of executive management's direction on and requirements regarding the purchase and use of cloud services.

CF16.4.1

There should be a documented corporate policy for the purchase and use of cloud services, which is:

a) based on the organisation's strategy for using cloud services
b) approved by executive management
c) distributed to all relevant individuals throughout the organisation
d) applied throughout the organisation.

> Cloud computing is a term used to describe distributed, on-demand computing services (Software as a Service (SaaS), Platform as a Service (PaaS) and Infrastructure as a Service (IaaS)), which are delivered across networks, typically using the Internet. Cloud services fall into three general types of service, which are:
>
> - generic (ie 'off-the-shelf')
> - configurable (ie supports some customisation)
> - specific (ie designed to meet particular requirements).
>
> Use of cloud services can be considered a form of outsourcing. Consequently, the security controls specified in *CF16.3 Outsourcing* should be applied for the use of cloud computing.

CF16.4.2

The information security function should assist business functions (eg procurement and legal) in the definition of standard / contractual requirements for the purchase and use of cloud services.

CF16.4.3

Specific awareness activities should be performed to help ensure staff:

a) are made aware of the organisation's corporate policy on the use of cloud services, particularly for generic, 'off-the-shelf' cloud services
b) are educated about the risks of using unapproved cloud services
c) demonstrate their compliance with the corporate policy for the purchase and use of cloud services.

> Cloud computing is able to deliver generic services (eg Salesforce.com, Google Apps, Hosted Microsoft Exchange or Amazon Web Services) that can be implemented quickly and easily. Consequently, business users often purchase new cloud services directly, avoiding the central IT procurement process, information security risk assessments and contractual reviews.

CF16.4.4

Prior to purchasing or using cloud services an information risk assessment should be performed, which takes into account:

a) the type, classification and importance of information that may be handled in the cloud
b) legal / regulatory risks to the organisation (eg copyright, data protection, financial regulation, privacy breach and corporate governance).

CF16.4 Cloud Computing Policy (continued)

CF16.4.5

The information risk assessment should help to identify the security arrangements required to protect information handled in the cloud, throughout its full lifecycle, including:

a) creation of information (eg classifying information as top secret, company-in-confidence or public)
b) processing (eg input validation and integrity checking)
c) storage (eg segregation and resilience)
d) transmission (eg encryption, non-repudiation and cross-border requirements)
e) destruction (eg 'secure erasure' and physical destruction).

CF16.4.6

Based on the results of the information risk assessment and the classification of information that may be handled in the cloud, a decision should be made on whether information needs to be:

a) prevented from entering the cloud (eg it has a very high-level of classification such as top secret or is subject to strict legal requirements such as personally identifiable information)
b) encrypted when stored and transmitted to / from the cloud
c) subject to restrictions when storing and processing in particular jurisdictions.

CF16.4.7

A process should be established that ensures that the use of cloud services (including generic cloud services) is:

a) identified and recorded in a register (or equivalent)
b) approved by both business owners and the corporate IT function (or equivalent)
c) supported by a contract
d) reviewed on a regular basis (eg by business representatives or information protection champions).

CF16.4.8

Sensitive information stored and processed in the cloud should be protected against co-mingling by separating the organisation's information from that of other organisations (eg so that it resides on a different virtual server, a separate hard disk partition or a physically isolated hard disk drive (often referred to as 'spindle separation')).

CF16.4.9

Organisations should provide technical means of protecting information placed in the cloud, which include:

a) developing a technical security infrastructure that is compatible with the architecture and infrastructure used by the cloud service provider
b) maintaining compatibility of client systems for each cloud service against organisational standards (eg by monitoring browser version and plug-in requirements)
c) using secure communication techniques between the organisation and cloud services used (eg by deploying VPN, TLS, HTTPS or similar).

CF16.4.10

The organisation should help to ensure the availability of access to information stored in the cloud by:

a) investing in robust, reliable Internet connectivity
b) establishing multiple methods of connection (eg wired network, wireless and 3G / 4G)
c) providing adequate network bandwidth
d) maintaining links with the organisation's legacy systems.

SPECIALISED

CF16.4 Cloud Computing Policy (continued)

Related content

CF16.3 Outsourcing
CF16.5 Cloud Service Contracts
CF20.3 Resilience

ISF resources

Security Implications of Cloud Computing

Securing Cloud Computing: Addressing the Seven Deadly Sins

ISF Briefing: Cloud Computing

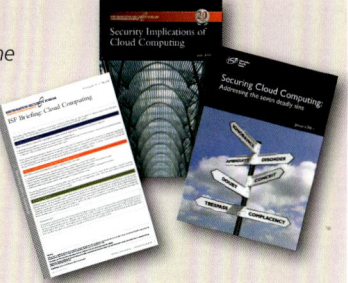

CF16.5 Cloud Service Contracts

Principle The organisation's use of cloud services should be supported by contracts that include cloud specific clauses beyond standard contracts with external suppliers.

Objective To help ensure cloud specific risks are reduced to a level acceptable by the organisation.

CF16.5.1

Each use of cloud computing services should be supported by a contract (including terms and conditions or equivalent), which covers all clauses that apply to standard external supplier contracts and include special provisions related to the use of cloud services.

> Use of cloud services can be considered a form of outsourcing. Consequently, the contractual arrangements specified in *CF16.3 Outsourcing* should be applied when establishing contracts for the use of cloud computing.

CF16.5.2

Contracts (including those for generic, 'off-the-shelf' cloud services) should be:

a) reviewed by a legal representative (eg a lawyer or equivalent) and an information security specialist
b) approved and signed by a senior business representative
c) subject to the organisation's standard acquisition processes
d) stored in a secure location (eg with the corporate legal function or equivalent) to enable them to be reviewed in the event of a dispute.

CF16.5.3

Contracts should require the cloud service provider to protect the organisation's information by:

a) providing a secure authentication service to meet the organisation's identity and access management (IAM) requirements (eg including any requirements for federated identity and access management)
b) restricting access to authorised users (eg using access control lists, 'whitelists' or 'blacklists')
c) preventing 'co-mingling' of information where required (ie by not storing the organisation's information in the same database as another organisation's information)
d) limiting access to cloud services when connections originate from outside the organisation's corporate firewall
e) managing access controls of the cloud service to meet the requirements of the organisation
f) implementing appropriate malware monitoring and protection solutions
g) providing a method of securely destroying the organisation's information stored in the cloud as soon as it is no longer required (eg according to the organisation's document retention policy, or equivalent).

CF16.5.4

Contracts should require the cloud service provider to share security-related information about unusual or malicious activity based on the organisation's requirements, including details about:

a) user / system activity (eg login, access to data or changing user permissions)
b) unauthorised changes to critical standing (or static) information, such as customer master files, manufacturing data, pricing tables and foreign exchange rates
c) event logs, alerts and reports produced by intrusion detection systems (IDS) and data leakage protection (DLP) systems
d) results of network traffic monitoring to provide early warning of potential attacks (including malicious network traffic).

SPECIALISED

CF16.5 Cloud Service Contracts (continued)

CF16.5.5

Cloud service contracts should require the provider to meet requirements for protecting the organisation's sensitive information by:

a) protecting the storage of personally identifiable information (eg by locating it in approved locations or within a particular jurisdiction)
b) providing solutions based on industry accepted standards for architecture and infrastructure.

CF16.5.6

Cloud service contracts should require the provider to meet the organisation's availability requirements by:

a) providing dedicated support (eg identified support staff and method of contacting them directly) in the event of a security incident in the cloud
b) ensuring that the organisation's security requirements are met in the event of cloud services being further sub-contracted to an external supplier or not allowing cloud services to be sub-contracted
c) supporting the organisation in the event of legal action that involves the organisation's information (eg e-discovery requests or forensic investigations)
d) providing an escrow facility (eg for information, proprietary technologies, application source code and cryptographic keys) using a trusted external party (eg a legal representative, lawyer or equivalent).

CF16.5.7

Contracts should require cloud service providers to provide advance notification prior to any changes being made to the way the service is delivered to the organisation, including:

a) changes to the technical infrastructure (eg major upgrades of operating systems or application software, or significant reconfiguration of systems such as virtual servers or Storage Area Networks (SANs))
b) relocation of the technical infrastructure to a different geographical region or legal jurisdiction
c) processing or storage of information in a new geographical or legal jurisdiction
d) reconfiguration of cloud services
e) use of other external parties (eg changing or using new sub-contractors to support the provision of services).

Related content
CF16.3 Outsourcing
CF16.4 Cloud Service Policy
CF20.3 Resilience

ISF resources
Security Implications of Cloud Computing

Securing Cloud Computing: Addressing the Seven Deadly Sins

Information Security in Third Party Relationship Management

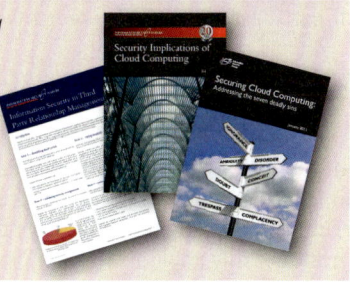

CONTROL FRAMEWORK

FUNDAMENTAL

AREA CF17 – System Development Management

List of Topics
CF17.1 System Development Methodology
CF17.2 System Development Environments
CF17.3 Quality Assurance

CF17.1 System Development Methodology

Principle Development activities should be carried out in accordance with a documented system development methodology.

Objective To ensure that business applications (including those under development) meet business and information security requirements.

CF17.1.1

There should be a documented system development methodology (often referred to as the systems development lifecycle (SDLC)), which is based upon sound systems development and project management practices (eg Structured Systems Analysis and Design Method (SSADM) and Jackson Structured Program (JSP)).

CF17.1.2

There should be documented standards / procedures for developing business applications (including those under development), which cover: specifying requirements; designing, building and testing applications; promoting applications into the live environment; and training users of business applications.

CF17.1.3

The system development methodology should ensure that applications are developed to comply with:

a) information security policies, standards, procedures and guidelines
b) legal and regulatory requirements, including privacy requirements
c) contractual requirements (eg those relating to external parties such as customers, clients and suppliers)
d) particular business requirements for security.

CF17.1.4

The system development methodology should require that:

a) good information security practices are not sacrificed in the interest of speed of delivery
b) initiatives are driven by business requirements (ie they are not technology-led)
c) dependence on immature technology is minimised
d) the security implications of implementing vendor solutions are assessed
e) testing is performed in an environment (eg a staging environment) which is separate from development and live environments
f) the duties of individuals responsible for development, testing and implementation are segregated.

FUNDAMENTAL

CF17.1 System Development Methodology (continued)

CF17.1.5

The system development methodology should be kept up-to-date to include new and emerging:

a) development techniques (eg rapid application development (RAD), agile software development, extreme programming and joint application design (JAD))
b) application platforms, such as Java, Microsoft .Net and HTML5
c) application architectures (eg Web 2.0, Service Oriented Architecture and Web Services)
d) security standards and techniques (eg Web Services Security, XML firewalls, data leakage protection, intrusion prevention and digital rights management).

CF17.1.6

The system development methodology should require the following activities to be performed at the start of each new project:

a) notification of the start of the project to the information security function (or equivalent)
b) assessment of the need for confidentiality, integrity and availability of information
c) clarification of the organisation's information classification scheme (ie the method of classifying information according to its level of confidentiality such as top secret, company-in-confidence and public) and how it will be applied
d) creation of a risk register related to the project
e) creation of a project management office (PMO) file (or equivalent), which contains all project control-related documentation.

CF17.1.7

Development staff should be trained in how to use and follow all aspects of the system development methodology.

CF17.1.8

The system development methodology should be:

a) applied by development staff in practice
b) used by external parties that are employed to develop parts or all of a system for the organisation (eg when using contractors, outsourced software developers, cloud providers or providers of Software as a Service).

CF17.1.9

Compliance with the system development methodology should be monitored at key stages in the system development lifecycle (eg during requirements, design, build, testing and deployment).

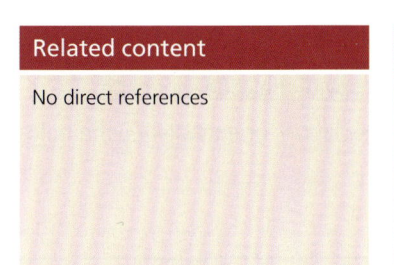

Related content	ISF resources
No direct references	Securing Business Applications ISF Briefing: Security implications of Web 2.0

CF17.2 System Development Environments

Principle System development activities should be performed in specialised development environments, which are isolated from the live and testing environments, and protected against unauthorised access.

Objective To provide a secure environment for system development activities, and avoid any disruption to business activity.

CF17.2.1

One or more environments (eg a dedicated network or a group of information systems) should be established, in which development and testing activities can be performed.

> Organisations often establish one or more separate test environments (also referred to as 'staging' areas) in which to perform different types of testing (eg functional testing, systems testing, unit testing and performance testing).

CF17.2.2

Development and test environments should be isolated from live environments and from each other (eg by hosting development and test systems on a separate, standalone network or segregating the network using a virtual local area network (VLAN) and a firewall).

CF17.2.3

Application source code (or equivalent) used in development environments should be protected by:

a) removing comments from programs (eg authentication details or sensitive information about the organisation) prior to deploying them in the live environment
b) preventing development staff from making unauthorised changes to live environments (eg by using access control software)
c) applying strict version control over systems development software (eg by using configuration management, recording access in a log and archiving old versions of software regularly)
d) employing malware detection / protection mechanisms
e) preventing malicious mobile code from being downloaded into development environments (eg by the use of filtering or blocking techniques).

CF17.2.4

Information and application source code used within development environments (including software under development, business information used in the development process and important system documentation) should be protected against unauthorised:

a) access (eg by using logical and physical access control mechanisms)
b) modification (eg by using integrity checking software and configuration management tools).

CF17.2.5

Where access to external party source code (or equivalent) is not granted, a copy of the code should be:

a) maintained in escrow by a trusted external party (eg a legal representative, lawyer or equivalent, who holds the source code until fulfilment of a contract)
b) checked regularly to ensure it is up-to-date and works correctly.

CF17.2.6

Changes to business applications (including those under development) should be:

a) performed in accordance with a formal, documented change management process
b) reviewed to ensure that they do not adversely affect intended functionality or compromise security controls.

Related content	ISF resources
No direct references	No recent ISF material

FUNDAMENTAL

CF17.3   Quality Assurance

Principle   Quality assurance of key security activities should be performed during the system development lifecycle.

Objective   To provide assurance that security requirements are defined adequately, agreed security controls are developed, and security requirements are met.

CF17.3.1

System development activities should be subject to quality assurance during all stages of the system development lifecycle (eg spot checks to ensure compliance with system development methodologies and supervisory review of new staff or critical activities).

CF17.3.2

Quality assurance of the system development methodology should include:

a) assessing development risks (ie those related to running a development project), which would typically include risks associated with business requirements, benefits, technology, technical performance, costing and timescale
b) checking that security requirements have been clearly defined
c) confirming that security controls (eg policies, methods, procedures, devices or programmed mechanisms intended to protect the confidentiality, integrity or availability of information) agreed during the information risk assessment process have been developed and are working correctly
d) confirming that individuals responsible for developing, testing and implementing systems under development are following the methodology.

CF17.3.3

Quality assurance of the system under development should be performed from the beginning, and throughout each stage, of the development process.

CF17.3.4

Quality assurance activities should ensure that any security deficiencies identified are:

a) documented
b) addressed in a timely manner
c) signed off by the head of system development (or equivalent).

CF17.3.5

The risk of developing insecure systems should be minimised by:

a) revising project plans / resources if security requirements are not being met effectively (eg by changing or adding staff, amending plans, delaying timescales or revising costs)
b) cancelling systems development and installation activities if security requirements cannot be met satisfactorily (eg the discovery of significant vulnerabilities in systems).

CF17.3.6

Quality reviews should be signed off at agreed checkpoints by the business owner of the system under development, an information security specialist, the head of system development (or equivalent) and the individual who will be responsible for maintaining systems in the live environment.

Related content	ISF resources
No direct references	No recent ISF material

AREA CF18 – Systems Development Lifecycle

List of Topics

CF18.1 Specifications of Requirements
CF18.2 System Design
CF18.3 System Build
CF18.4 Systems Testing

CF18.5 Security Testing
CF18.6 System Promotion Criteria
CF18.7 Installation Process
CF18.8 Post-implementation Review

CF18.1 Specifications of Requirements

Principle Business requirements (including those for information security) should be documented and agreed before detailed design commences.

Objective To ensure that information security requirements are treated as an integral part of business requirements, fully considered and approved.

CF18.1.1

Business requirements for systems under development should be documented in a specification of business requirements (or equivalent) and supported by an agreed process for handling changes to requirements.

CF18.1.2

Business requirements should cover the need for system:

a) performance (eg processing speeds and response times)
b) capacity (eg number of users or volume and size of transactions)
c) continuity (eg maximum length of time to recover key components following a system failure / outage)
d) scalability (eg to support future developments or changes)
e) connectivity (eg interfaces to existing systems, networks or external resources)
f) compatibility (eg with particular technical environments or components).

CF18.1.3

Business requirements should cover the need for confidentiality, integrity and availability of information throughout its lifecycle, including:

a) creation (eg input validation)
b) processing (eg integrity checking and performance)
c) storage (eg location and access control)
d) transmission (eg source and destination checking)
e) destruction (eg 'secure erasure' and physical destruction).

FUNDAMENTAL

CF18.1 Specifications of Requirements (continued)

CF18.1.4

Business requirements should cover:

a) compliance with contractual, legal and regulatory obligations
b) privacy requirements (eg the need to protect the confidentiality of customer records or personally identifiable information (PII) such as medical details)
c) adherence to an information classification scheme (ie the method of classifying information according to its level of confidentiality)
d) the provision of arrangements to support systems in the live environment (eg the need for a helpdesk or technical support)
e) fall-back / contingency plans
f) the reduction or elimination of single-points-of-failure.

CF18.1.5

Business requirements should take into account information security policies, standards, procedures and guidelines.

CF18.1.6

Business requirements should cover requirements for access:

a) by particular types of user (eg internal users, support staff, external parties or the general public)
b) from particular locations (eg home offices or external party premises or mobile environments)
c) to particular types of information (eg credit card details, personally identifiable information or trade secrets).

Related content	ISF resources
SR1 Information Risk Assessment	*Securing Business Applications*
CF8.1 Security Architecture	*Security Architecture: Workshop Report*
Appendix A: The ISF Business Impact Reference Table	

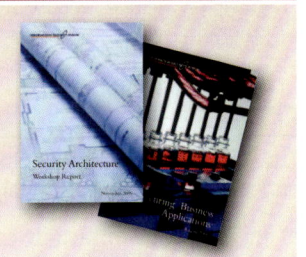

CONTROL FRAMEWORK

FUNDAMENTAL

CF18.2   System Design

Principle   Information security requirements for systems under development should be considered when designing systems.

Objective   To produce live systems based on sound design principles which have security functionality built-in, enable controls to be incorporated easily, and withstand malicious attacks, and help insure that no security weaknesses are introduced during the build process.

CF18.2.1

The system design phase should involve analysis of the information lifecycle in systems under development, including:

a) data inputs and connections to systems
b) transmission of data between system components
c) storage of information, access to databases and other types of storage
d) outbound connections to other systems and applications
e) inbound connections that provide application data from other systems
f) security of information outputs
g) secure erasure of information.

CF18.2.2

The system design phase should involve the integration of a security architecture that can support the technical security requirements, such as performance, capacity, continuity, scalability, connectivity and compatibility.

> Security architecture principles (sometimes referred to as guiding principles or design principles) represent fundamental security rules that should be met during the development of a security architecture for systems, and applied when the corresponding security controls are implemented. Examples of security architecture principles include 'secure by design', 'defence in depth', 'secure by default', 'default deny', 'fail secure', 'secure in deployment' and 'usability and manageability'.

CF18.2.3

The system design phase should involve consideration of potential threats (often referred to as 'threat modelling') and review of industry standards to help determine:

a) the full range of security controls required to protect live data (eg policies, methods, procedures, devices or programmed mechanisms intended to protect the confidentiality, integrity or availability of information)
b) specific security controls required by particular business processes supported by systems under development (eg encryption of sensitive information, integrity checking and digitally signing information)
c) where and how security controls are to be applied (eg by integrating with a security architecture and the technical infrastructure)
d) how individual security controls (manual and automated) work together to produce an integrated set of controls.

CF18.2.4

The system design phase should involve consideration of the security implications of how systems will interface with other systems (eg running as a standalone application, using two-tier or three-tier architecture, operating in a Web Services or Service Oriented Architecture (SOA) environment, or interacting with cloud services).

CF18.2.5

The system design phase should involve:

a) the use of security architecture principles, including 'secure by design', 'defence in depth', 'secure by default', 'default deny', 'fail secure', 'secure in deployment' and 'usability and manageability'
b) a review of designs to ensure security controls are specified, and comply with organisational security requirements
c) documentation of security controls that do not fully meet requirements.

FUNDAMENTAL

CF18.2 System Design (continued)

CF18.2.6

The evaluation of alternative designs for systems under development should take into account the:

a) need to integrate with a security architecture
b) technical security infrastructure (eg public key infrastructure (PKI), identity and access management (IAM), data leakage protection (DLP) and digital rights management (DRM))
c) capability of the organisation to develop and support the chosen technology
d) cost of meeting security requirements
e) skills needed to develop required security controls (eg policies, methods, procedures, devices or programmed mechanisms intended to protect the confidentiality, integrity or availability of information)
f) costs of deploying security controls.

CF18.2.7

Before coding or acquisition work begins, system designs should be:

a) documented
b) verified to ensure that they address security requirements
c) reviewed by an information security specialist (eg to check that security architecture principles have been applied)
d) signed off by the head of systems development (or equivalent) and the business owner of the system under development.

Related content	ISF resources
CF4.1 Application Protection	*Securing Business Applications*
CF8.1 Security Architecture	*Security Architecture: Workshop Report*
	ISF Briefing: Security of Service Oriented Architecture (SOA) and Web Services

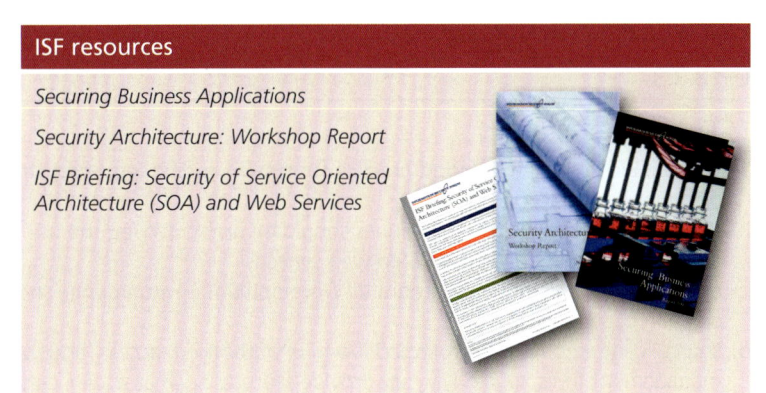

CONTROL FRAMEWORK

FUNDAMENTAL

CF18.3 System Build

Principle System build activities (including coding and package customisation) should be carried out in accordance with industry good practice; performed by individuals provided with adequate skills / tools; and inspected to identify unauthorised modifications or changes.

Objective To ensure that systems are built correctly, able to withstand malicious attacks, and help insure that no security weaknesses are introduced during the build process.

CF18.3.1

There should be documented standards / procedures for building systems (eg program coding, web page creation, customisation of packages and defining data structures), which specify:

a) approved methods of building systems (eg defining competence levels for staff writing or reviewing code; customising software packages; and documenting changes)
b) mechanisms for ensuring systems comply with good practice for system build (eg the use of structured programming techniques, methods of secure coding and documenting code)
c) methods of managing the use of code samples (eg defining acceptable sources for developers to obtain sample code and requiring a security review of any sample code before it can be used in the system)
d) 'secure' methods of making changes to the base code of software packages
e) review and sign-off processes (including those for software package customisation).

CF18.3.2

The build of systems under development should be inspected to identify unauthorised modifications or changes which may compromise security controls.

CF18.3.3

When building systems:

a) staff should comply with good practice for system coding (eg using structured programming techniques and documenting code)
b) the use of insecure design techniques should be prohibited (eg the use of hard coded passwords, unapproved code samples and unauthenticated web services)
c) development tools, such as Integrated Development Environments, should be configured to help enforce the creation of secure code
d) source code should be protected from unauthorised access and tampering (eg by using configuration management tools, which typically provide features such as access control and version control)
e) automated tools should be used to ensure adherence to coding standards.

CF18.3.4

Where modifications have to be made to the base code of external party software packages a documented customisation process should be applied, which takes into account the risk of:

a) suppliers refusing to support or maintain modified software
b) built-in security controls being compromised
c) incompatibility with updated versions of the base software package.

CF18.3.5

The customisation process should specify that modifications to the base code of external party software packages can only be made:

a) following approval by a systems development manager
b) with written permission from the supplier of the software package
c) to a clearly identified copy of the original code
d) following agreement with the supplier of the software package to change the support arrangements.

FUNDAMENTAL

CF18.3 System Build (continued)

CF18.3.6

System build activities (eg application coding and package customisations) should be reviewed by a systems development manager to ensure that systems function as intended, and to confirm that security weaknesses (eg those related to SQL / LDAP injection attacks, cross-site scripting (XSS), session token attacks and URL forgery) have not been introduced.

CF18.3.7

System build activities should be signed off by the person in charge of systems under development.

Related content	ISF resources
CF4 Business Applications CF8.1 Security Architecture	*Securing Business Applications*

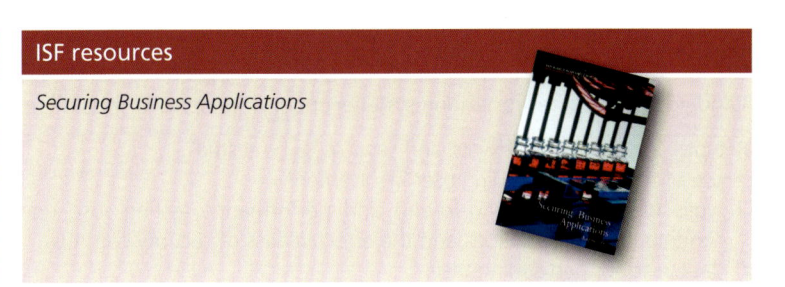

CONTROL FRAMEWORK

FUNDAMENTAL

CF18.4 Systems Testing

Principle Systems under development (including application software packages, system software, hardware, communications and services) should be tested in a dedicated testing area that simulates the live environment, before the system is promoted to the live environment.

Objective To ensure systems function as intended, meet predefined security requirements and do not compromise information security.

CF18.4.1

There should be a rigorous process for testing systems under development (system testing), which is supported by documented standards / procedures.

CF18.4.2

Standards / procedures for testing systems under development should cover the:

a) types of hardware, software and services to be tested
b) use of test plans, including user involvement
c) types of testing (eg end-to-end and performance testing, use under normal and exceptional business conditions, error situations and the effectiveness of security controls)
d) data used for performing tests
e) documentation, review and sign-off of the testing results.

CF18.4.3

Key components of all new systems should be tested before being installed in the live environment, including application software packages, system software, hardware, communications services and environmental facilities (eg air conditioning and back-up power supplies).

CF18.4.4

New systems should be tested in accordance with predefined, documented test plans, which should be cross-referenced to the system design / specification to ensure complete coverage. Key user representatives should be involved in planning tests, providing test data and reviewing test results.

CF18.4.5

System testing should:

a) be performed independently of system development staff
b) involve business users
c) simulate the live environment.

CF18.4.6

Tests should involve testing the complete system environment (eg end-to-end testing or compatibility testing) to identify any conflicts or dependencies with other systems, which includes:

a) using the underlying technical security infrastructure (eg identity and access management, public key infrastructure, patch management and security event logging)
b) interfacing with other applications (eg Service Oriented Architecture (SOA) components, Web Services, program calls, hyperlink references and browser software)
c) running on different operating systems (including those running on consumer devices such as tablets and smartphones) and browser software
d) interacting with databases and directory services, such as Lightweight Directory Access Protocol (LDAP)
e) processing on particular hardware platforms, including server / desktop computer / mobile device / consumer device configurations
f) communicating using different technologies (eg IP networks, the Internet, USB, Bluetooth, RFID, mobile applications and HTML5).

FUNDAMENTAL

CF18.4 Systems Testing (continued)

CF18.4.7

Tests should involve the system running in expected conditions, which include:

a) full integration testing, to ensure there will be no adverse effects on individual modules (eg Web Services) and existing, related systems
b) functional testing (ie testing the application functions against the business requirements)
c) performance testing when handling planned volumes of working (ie load testing with realistic numbers of users / volumes of transactions)
d) stress testing / volume testing (ie subjecting the system to large volumes of data to assess the performance under abnormal loads) to identify the maximum system capacity.

CF18.4.8

Tests should cover use under:

a) normal and special business conditions (eg financial year end or national holidays)
b) exceptional conditions (eg natural disasters, industrial action and denial of service attacks).

CF18.4.9

Tests should involve infrequent or unexpected conditions, which include:

a) installation / uninstallation testing (ie of system components and software using different hardware platforms, operating systems and software configurations)
b) application failure testing (eg to determine what happens if all or part of the system fails and how errors are handled)
c) recovery testing (ie how well new systems recover from events such as software malfunction and hardware failures)
d) testing of manual fall-back arrangements (ie revert to previous versions / procedures) or other contingency procedures.

CF18.4.10

Business information (eg customer data, medical records, product prices or manufacturing details) used for testing purposes should be protected by:

a) prohibiting the use of personally identifiable information (ie information that can be used to identify an individual person) in the testing process
b) using data masking to conceal real information (often referred to as data sanitisation)
c) requiring separate authorisation each time business information is copied from the live into the testing environment
d) restricting access to business information in the testing environment
e) logging the use of business information
f) securely destroying copies of business information once testing is complete.

CF18.4.11

Automated tools should be used to improve the testing process (eg to check the validity of system interfaces or simulate loading from multiple clients).

CF18.4.12

Test results should be documented, checked against expected results, approved by users and signed off by an appropriate business representative.

CONTROL FRAMEWORK

FUNDAMENTAL

CF18.4 Systems Testing (continued)

Related content
CF4 Business Applications

ISF resources
Securing Business Applications

ISF Briefing: Security of Service Oriented Architecture (SOA) and Web Services

FUNDAMENTAL

CF18.5 Security Testing

Principle Systems under development should be subject to security testing, using a range of attack types (including vulnerability assessments, penetration testing and access control testing).

Objective To identify security weaknesses in applications and determine how applications will behave under attack conditions.

CF18.5.1

There should be documented standards / procedures for testing the security of systems under development, which include:

a) performing independent checks of the application code
b) determining the effectiveness of security controls
c) performing specific attack tests to identify weaknesses in browser-based applications
d) using test data for security testing
e) resolving flaws and security weaknesses identified during testing.

CF18.5.2

Prior to security testing, independent checks of the application code should be performed (eg code analysis and unit testing) to ensure that:

a) vulnerabilities (eg 'back doors' or 'time bombs') have been identified and removed
b) programming features have not been used insecurely
c) sensitive information (eg comments by developers and customer details) has been removed from the application code.

CF18.5.3

Systems under development should be tested to determine the effectiveness of security controls, including:

a) vulnerability assessments (to identify weaknesses in software and security controls)
b) penetration testing (ie simulating attacks to demonstrate how vulnerabilities can be exploited)
c) access control testing (eg brute force attacks and dictionary attacks on passwords).

CF18.5.4

Browser-based applications should be subject to:

a) specific attack tests to identify weaknesses that are unique to browser-based applications (eg SQL / LDAP injection, cross-site scripting (XSS), session token attacks and URL forgery)
b) rigorous external content review (eg Web 2.0 content provided by external websites such as targeted advertising, digital maps and videos).

CF18.5.5

Security tests should include the use of:

a) transaction data (eg sales order, financial payments or foreign exchange deals)
b) standing data (eg customer master file, pricing tables or stock numbers)
c) specifically prepared test data (eg large numbers, URLs, command-line inputs and random data) designed to identify system faults or system weaknesses (eg buffer overflow and memory corruption).

CF18.5 Security Testing (continued)

CF18.5.6

There should be a process for ensuring that flaws or security weaknesses identified during the testing process are resolved in a consistent manner, which includes:

a) recording details of security weaknesses identified (eg in a test log or on a test results sheet)
b) assessing the associated risks
c) implementing actions to address these risks
d) repeating tests of the application following corrective actions.

Related content	ISF resources
SI1.2 Security Audit Process – Planning	*Securing Business Applications* *ISF Briefing: Security implications of Web 2.0*

FUNDAMENTAL

CONTROL FRAMEWORK

CF18.6 System Promotion Criteria

Principle Rigorous criteria (including security requirements) should be met before new systems are promoted into the live environment.

Objective To ensure that only security tested and approved versions of hardware and software are promoted into the live environment.

CF18.6.1

Rigorous and documented acceptance criteria should be met before new systems are promoted into the live environment.

CF18.6.2

Before new systems are promoted into the live environment, reviews should be performed, by implementation staff and business owners, to ensure that:

a) security assessments have been carried out
b) limitations of security controls have been documented
c) approval has been obtained from an appropriate business representative
d) service level agreements (SLAs) have been established to support systems in the live environment.

> A service level agreement (SLA) should include all key elements, such as: who is in charge of the application (ie the application owner); who is in charge of delivering the required service (eg an internal or external service provider); capacity requirements; maximum permissible down-time; criteria for measuring the level of service; and a warranty period for systems (to ensure support for systems after completion of its development).

CF18.6.3

Checks should be carried out to ensure that:

a) the application code (or equivalent) has been digitally signed to protect its integrity
b) performance and capacity requirements can be met
c) all necessary patches and updates have been tested and successfully applied
d) all development problems have been resolved successfully
e) there will be no adverse effects on existing live systems
f) the security of new systems can be supported on a continuing basis (eg through a predefined point of contact such as a helpdesk)
g) arrangements for fall-back have been established, in the event of new systems failing to function as intended
h) test data (including business information) has been securely destroyed.

CF18.6.4

Before new systems are promoted into the live environment:

a) error recovery and restart procedures should be established
b) contingency plans should be developed or updated
c) operating procedures should be documented and tested
d) users should be educated and trained to use systems correctly and securely
e) IT staff (eg computer operators / system administrators) should be trained in how to run systems correctly and apply required security controls effectively.

CF18.6.5

Arrangements should be in place to ensure that only tested and approved versions of hardware and software are promoted into the live environment.

CONTROL FRAMEWORK

FUNDAMENTAL

CF18.6 System Promotion Criteria (continued)

Related content
No direct references

ISF resources
Securing Business Applications

FUNDAMENTAL

CF18.7   Installation Process

Principle   New systems should be installed in the live environment in accordance with a documented installation process.

Objective   To minimise disruption to the organisation when new systems are installed in the live environment.

CF18.7.1

The promotion of new systems to the live environment should be governed by a documented installation process (or deployment plan).

CF18.7.2

The installation process should cover required technical activities, which include:

a) applying security architecture principles, such as 'secure by design', 'defence in depth', 'secure by default', 'default deny', 'fail secure', 'secure in deployment' and 'usability and manageability'
b) integrating with the organisation's technical security infrastructure (eg public key infrastructure (PKI), identity and access management (IAM), data leakage protection (DLP) and digital rights management (DRM))
c) validating the load or conversion of data
d) restricting the installation of new or significantly changed software to executable code.

CF18.7.3

The installation process should cover required user-related activities, which include:

a) providing new or revised documentation
b) informing the individuals involved of their roles and responsibilities
c) making users aware of their responsibilities for using new systems securely
d) providing ongoing technical support (eg via electronic help screens, a telephone helpdesk or hot-line support)
e) implementing new or revised standards / procedures
f) handing over responsibility to individuals running the live environment.

CF18.7.4

The installation process should cover required housekeeping activities, which include:

a) discontinuing old software, procedures and documentation
b) arranging for fall-back in the event of system failure
c) recording installation activity
d) archiving previous versions of software, together with corresponding information (including configuration settings, operations procedures, and supporting software).

CF18.7.5

The installation of new systems should be scheduled in advance, to avoid disrupting the live environment.

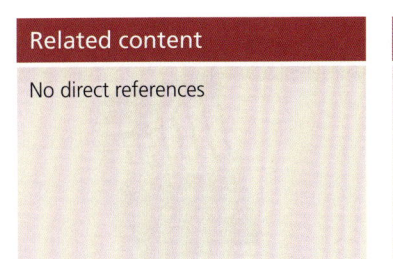

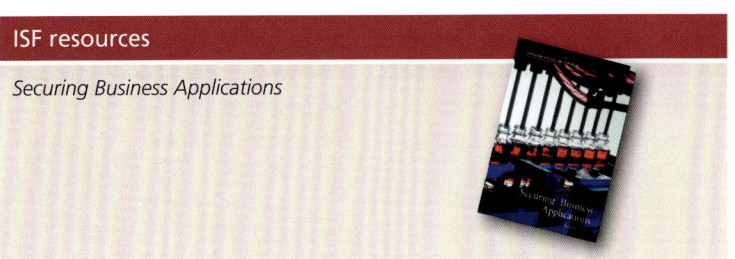

Related content	ISF resources
No direct references	*Securing Business Applications*

CONTROL FRAMEWORK   **FUNDAMENTAL**

CF18.8   Post-implementation Review

Principle   Post-implementation reviews (including coverage of information security), should be conducted for all new systems.

Objective   To provide assurance that information security was considered and addressed throughout each stage of the systems development lifecycle (SDLC) and built-in security controls are working as expected.

CF18.8.1

Post-implementation reviews should be conducted for all new systems.

CF18.8.2

Post-implementation reviews should cover:

a) fulfilment of business (including information security) requirements
b) the efficiency, effectiveness and cost of security controls
c) scope for improvement of security controls
d) information security incidents that occurred during system development.

CF18.8.3

Post-implementation reviews should provide assurance that:

a) information risks associated with new systems have been identified and treated (eg accepted, avoided, transferred or mitigated)
b) selected security controls have been reviewed and built into new systems
c) outstanding security issues have been or are being addressed.

CF18.8.4

Post-implementation reviews should:

a) identify successful approaches to information security (eg new software development techniques, security protocols or technologies)
b) provide recommendations for improving the systems development lifecycle (SDLC).

CF18.8.5

The findings of post-implementation reviews should be:

a) signed off by the person in charge of systems under development, an appropriate business representative and an information security specialist
b) communicated to individuals involved in the development of new systems, business owners of the new system and executive management
c) used to update information security policies, standards and procedures.

Related content	ISF resources
No direct references	*Securing Business Applications*

FUNDAMENTAL — CONTROL FRAMEWORK

AREA CF19 – Physical and Environmental Security

List of Topics
CF19.1 Physical Protection
CF19.2 Power Supplies
CF19.3 Hazard Protection

CF19.1 Physical Protection

Principle All critical facilities (including locations that house computer systems such as data centres, networks, telecommunication equipment, sensitive physical material and other important assets) should be physically protected against accident or attack and unauthorised physical access.

Objective To restrict physical access to authorised individuals, ensure that critical equipment is available when required and to prevent important services from being disrupted by loss of, or damage to, equipment or facilities.

CF19.1.1
There should be documented standards / procedures for the physical protection of critical facilities (including locations that house information systems such as data centres, networks, telecommunication equipment, sensitive physical material and other important assets) within the organisation.

CF19.1.2
Standards / procedures should cover:

a) protecting critical facilities against unauthorised access
b) locating critical facilities away from public access or approach
c) restricting access to critical facilities that support or enable the organisation's critical infrastructure
d) managing authorisation for physical access to critical facilities
e) restricting visitor access to critical facilities.

CF19.1.3
Buildings that house critical facilities should be protected against unauthorised access by:

a) providing locks, bolts (or equivalent) on vulnerable doors and windows, and employing security guards
b) installing closed-circuit television (CCTV), or equivalent
c) locating intruder detection systems on accessible external doors and windows, and testing regularly.

CF19.1.4
Critical facilities should be protected by locating them away from public access or approach and keeping details about them confidential (eg by using discrete signs and excluding details from directories or telephone books).

CF19.1.5
Physical access to critical facilities should be protected by:

a) defining and strengthening the physical security perimeter (eg by using solid construction walls, alarmed fire doors, armoured windows and physical barriers)
b) keeping buildings under constant surveillance (eg using closed-circuit television (CCTV) or Physical Security Information Management (PSIM) software)
c) locating computer equipment (eg server console screens, computing devices and printers) so that sensitive information cannot be overlooked
d) isolating holding areas for receipt of deliveries.

CF19.1 Physical Protection (continued)

CF19.1.6

Physical access to critical facilities (including those that support or enable the organisation's critical infrastructure (eg SCADA systems, process control PCs and embedded systems)) should be restricted to authorised individuals by:

a) installing locks activated by keypads, swipe cards or equivalent
b) locking doors / windows when the environment is vacated
c) fitting intruder alarms
d) ensuring all individuals wear visible means of identification
e) requiring staff to challenge strangers
f) employing security guards.

CF19.1.7

Authorisation to gain physical access to critical facilities should be:

a) issued in accordance with documented standards / procedures
b) reviewed regularly, to ensure that only appropriate individuals are allowed access
c) revoked promptly when no longer needed.

CF19.1.8

Visitors to critical facilities should be:

a) permitted access only for defined and authorised purposes
b) monitored by recording arrival and departure times
c) obliged to wear identity badges at all times when on the organisation's premises
d) supervised at all times
e) issued with instructions explaining the security requirements of the area, detailing emergency procedures and stating that audio and other recording (eg filming or photography) is prohibited.

CF19.1.9

Individuals should be required to obtain written approval before leaving the organisation's premises with critical IT equipment (eg servers, network devices, printers and specialist equipment).

CF19.1.10

Staff who may be subject to intimidation (eg engineers, bank tellers or pharmacists) should be protected by the:

a) provision of 'duress alarms' (or equivalent)
b) establishment of a process for responding to emergency situations.

Related content	ISF resources
CF3.4 Asset Register	*Securing Critical Infrastructure: Workshop Report*

FUNDAMENTAL

CF19.2 Power Supplies

Principle Critical facilities (including locations that house computer systems such as data centres, networks, telecommunication equipment, sensitive physical material and other important assets) should be protected against power outages.

Objective To prevent services provided by computer systems from being disrupted by loss of power.

CF19.2.1

Power cables to critical facilities (including locations that house information systems such as data centres, networks, telecommunication equipment, sensitive physical material and other important assets) should be protected by:

a) segregating them from communications cables to prevent interference
b) concealed installation
c) locked inspection / termination points
d) alternative feeds or routing
e) avoidance of routes through public areas.

CF19.2.2

The power supply to critical facilities should be protected by:

a) using uninterruptible power supply (UPS) devices
b) installing surge protection equipment (eg lightning protection filters and radio frequency interference (RFI) filters)
c) providing back-up electricity generators (supplied with adequate quantities of fuel) in the event of extended power failure
d) installing emergency lighting in case of main power failure
e) locating emergency power-off switches near emergency exits to facilitate rapid power-down in case of an emergency.

CF19.2.3

Uninterruptible power supply (UPS) devices should have the battery capacity to allow critical information systems, network equipment, voice facilities and supporting systems to shut down in an orderly manner.

CF19.2.4

Emergency equipment (eg UPS equipment, back-up electricity generators and emergency lighting) should be:

a) serviced in accordance with manufacturer recommendations
b) tested regularly.

Related content	ISF resources
No direct references	*Securing Critical Infrastructure: Workshop Report*

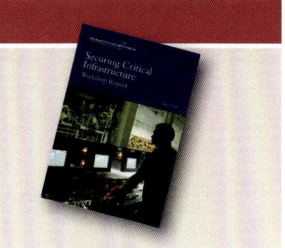

CONTROL FRAMEWORK

FUNDAMENTAL

CF19.3   Hazard Protection

Principle — Critical facilities (including locations that house computer systems such as data centres, networks, telecommunication equipment, sensitive physical material and other important assets) should be protected against fire, flood, environmental and other natural hazards.

Objective — To prevent services being disrupted by damage to critical facilities caused by fire, flood and other types of hazard.

CF19.3.1

Critical facilities should be located in a safe environment and in rooms that are:

a) constructed using fire resistant materials for walls, doors, windows and furniture
b) free from intrinsic fire hazards (such as combustible paper or flammable chemicals)
c) fitted with fire detection systems (eg using a combination of smoke detectors, optical detectors and temperature sensors)
d) protected with fire suppression systems (eg using water, carbon dioxide or FM 200 suppression systems)
e) protected against natural hazards (eg storm and flood damage) and man-made hazards (eg fire, explosions, civil unrest, building collapse or damage from neighbouring activities).

CF19.3.2

Fire alarms should be monitored continuously, tested regularly and serviced in accordance with manufacturer specifications.

CF19.3.3

The impact of hazards should be minimised by:

a) locating hand-held fire extinguishers so that minor incidents can be tackled without delay
b) training staff in the use of fire extinguishers and other emergency / safety equipment, and in emergency evacuation procedures
c) conducting fire drills so that staff know how to safely exit the organisation's premises
d) protecting computer equipment (including the organisation's critical infrastructure) against damage from environmental hazards (eg smoke, dust, vibration, chemicals, electrical interference / radiation, food, drink and nearby industrial processes)
e) monitoring and controlling the temperature and humidity of data centres and computer rooms (or equivalent) in accordance with equipment manufacturer recommendations.

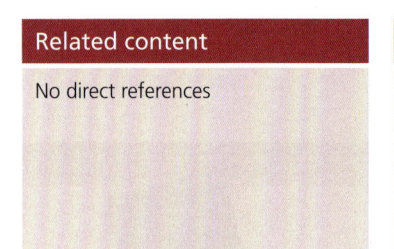

Related content	ISF resources
No direct references	*Securing Critical Infrastructure: Workshop Report*

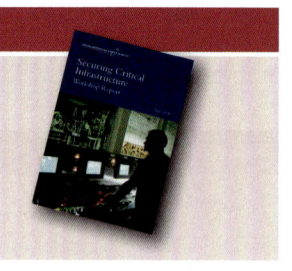

SPECIALISED

CONTROL FRAMEWORK

AREA CF20 – Business Continuity

List of Topics

CF20.1 Business Continuity Strategy
CF20.2 Business Continuity Programme
CF20.3 Resilience
CF20.4 Crisis Management

CF20.5 Business Continuity Planning
CF20.6 Business Continuity Arrangements
CF20.7 Business Continuity Testing

CF20.1 Business Continuity Strategy

Principle A business continuity strategy covering the whole organisation should be established, which promotes the need for business continuity management, embeds business continuity management into the organisation's culture, and is implemented in the form of a business continuity programme.

Objective To help align business continuity goals with the organisation's business goals, provide resilience against disruption and minimise impact to the organisation in the event of a disaster or emergency.

CF20.1.1

A business continuity strategy covering the whole organisation should be developed and maintained, which is aligned with both the organisation's business strategy and information security strategy.

> Business continuity and information security are complementary approaches to managing an organisation's operational risks, and their objectives and focus often overlap. The objective of business continuity is to provide executive management with assurance that critical business processes (whether automated or not) will continue operating at acceptable levels by focussing on the availability of information and infrastructure. Information security complements business continuity by providing executive management with assurance that information risks are being managed within acceptable levels by ensuring sensitive information is not disclosed to unauthorised parties and critical information is not corrupted.

CF20.1.2

A representative of the organisation's governing body (eg a board member or equivalent) should be appointed business continuity owner, who is ultimately accountable for business continuity across the organisation.

CF20.1.3

A business continuity management team (or equivalent) should be established which:

a) includes representatives of executive management
b) is responsible for developing, implementing and maintaining the organisation's business continuity strategy
c) oversees a programme of business continuity activities (ie a business continuity programme).

CONTROL FRAMEWORK

SPECIALISED

CF20.1 Business Continuity Strategy (continued)

CF20.1.4

The business continuity strategy should be based on a sound understanding of the organisation, including:

a) the organisation's risk appetite (ie the amount of risk the organisation is prepared to accept / tolerate)
b) the changes to threats the organisation faces (eg hactivism, corporate espionage and denial of service attacks)
c) stakeholder requirements (eg to maintain business operations and comply with legal, regulatory and contractual requirements relating to business continuity)
d) requirements for protecting the integrity of information (eg against corruption) and the confidentiality of information (eg against unauthorised disclosure)
e) the goals and objectives of the organisation from a business continuity perspective
f) major business environments (including the culture of local environments and the jurisdictions in which those environments operate), critical business processes and products / services offered
g) arrangements with external parties (eg outsource and cloud service providers and customers).

CF20.1.5

The business continuity strategy should help to ensure that:

a) business continuity management is embedded in the organisation's culture (eg by promoting business continuity via regular communications throughout the organisation and training / educating staff in business continuity activities)
b) critical business processes are supported by a resilient technical infrastructure (eg by duplicating business applications, information systems and networks and removing 'single points of failure')
c) the organisation is able to manage a major crisis (eg by having an incident management capability and establishing a crisis management team)
d) business continuity planning is performed throughout the organisation as a formal programme of work (eg a business continuity programme)
e) systems supporting critical business processes can be recovered within acceptable timeframes
f) sensitive information is not disclosed to unauthorised parties and critical information is not corrupted.

Related content

SG2.1 Information Security Strategy

CF11.1 Information Security Incident Management

Appendix A: The ISF Business Impact Reference Table

ISF resources

Aligning Business Continuity and Information Security

Hacktivism (Briefing paper)

SPECIALISED　　　　　　　　　　　　　　　　　　　　　　　　　　　CONTROL FRAMEWORK

CF20.2 Business Continuity Programme

Principle A business continuity programme should be established, which includes developing a resilient technical infrastructure, creating a crisis management capability, and co-ordinating and maintaining business continuity plans and arrangements across the organisation.

Objective To enable the organisation to withstand the prolonged unavailability of critical information, business applications and related technical infrastructure, and provide individuals with a documented set of actions to perform in the event of a disaster.

CF20.2.1

The business continuity management team should establish a business continuity programme to support the organisation's business continuity strategy.

CF20.2.2

The business continuity programme should determine the individual business environments to be supported by business continuity plans and arrangements by identifying and recording relevant details (eg in a central business continuity risk register) about:

a) major business areas throughout the organisation
b) critical business processes (ranked in order of priority) and associated business applications
c) underlying technical infrastructure (eg information systems and networks)
d) key internal and external stakeholders (including executive management, business representatives and relevant external parties).

> The approach taken to determine individual business environments throughout an organisation, which require business continuity plans and arrangements, can vary. As a result, individual business environments can represent one or more:
>
> - business units (eg a manufacturing, investment banking or retail division of a conglomerate, or significant operating regions)
> - major operational sites (eg head office building, trading floor, call centre, manufacturing plant or data centre)
> - critical business processes (eg enterprise resource planning (ERP), sales order processing or airline reservation).

CF20.2.3

Business owners should be appointed for each individual business environment, who are responsible for the corresponding business continuity plan and arrangements, and are supported by a local team of individuals.

CF20.2.4

The business continuity programme should require:

a) roles and responsibilities of individuals involved in business continuity to be identified
b) business continuity risk assessments to be performed for each individual business environment (which include the assessment of potential business impacts, threats and vulnerabilities) to identify the availability requirements
c) risk treatment options for business continuity to be identified and selected (ie accepting risks, avoiding risks, transferring risks or mitigating risks).

CONTROL FRAMEWORK

SPECIALISED

CF20.2   Business Continuity Programme (continued)

CF20.2.5

The business continuity programme should apply across the organisation and require each individual business environment to:

a) follow the organisation's central crisis management process (sometimes referred to as an emergency response process) at a local level
b) maintain links with the organisation's central crisis management team
c) build resilient business applications and a resilient technical infrastructure (eg duplicate information systems and networks) to support critical business processes and protect them against targeted attacks, such as denial of service attacks
d) develop and maintain comprehensive business continuity plans for critical parts of the organisation (based on a business continuity risk assessment)
e) provide alternative arrangements to support critical business processes in the event of a major incident or disaster (eg by maintaining a hot, warm or cold site where business operations can continue running)
f) review and test business continuity plans and arrangements on a regular basis (eg as part of a business continuity exercise)
g) keep business continuity plans and arrangements up-to-date.

Organisations typically choose one or more of the following three main options when establishing an alternative facility to support business operations in the event of a major disruption or disaster. These options are a:

- hot site – a fully functioning facility that will be ready to support business operations within a few hours of invoking a business continuity plan, by ensuring the hardware, software and information remains up-to-date and compatible with the live environment
- warm site – consisting of a partially configured facility that typically requires hardware and software to be provided and configured, and backed up information restored before business operations can be recovered following the invocation of a business continuity plan
- cold site – a basic facility, which comprises electrical wiring, air conditioning, plumbing and flooring, which would involve significant effort, resource and time to restore business operations following the invocation of a business continuity plan.

CF20.2.6

The business continuity management team should maintain a central inventory for each individual business environment, which includes:

a) the results of business continuity risk assessments (including details of the key threats, availability requirements and risk treatment options chosen)
b) business continuity plans
c) details about business continuity arrangements
d) the results of testing business continuity plans and arrangements
e) other important documents, such as business continuity awareness and training material, incident management plans, contracts and test schedules.

Related content	ISF resources
Appendix A: The ISF Business Impact Reference Table	*Aligning Business Continuity and Information Security*

SPECIALISED

CF20.3 Resilience

Principle Critical business applications and underlying technical infrastructure should be run on robust, reliable hardware and software, and be supported by alternative or duplicate facilities.

Objective To ensure critical business processes that rely on business applications and technical infrastructure are available when required.

CF20.3.1

Critical business processes should be supported by business applications and technical infrastructure (eg information systems, networks or voice facilities) that use robust, reliable hardware and software, and are supported by alternative or duplicate facilities.

CF20.3.2

The likelihood of critical business applications and technical infrastructure malfunctioning should be reduced by:

a) employing up-to-date makes / models of hardware and software (ie rather than using obsolete and unsupported products) that are easily maintained and can meet the requirements of critical business processes
b) giving high priority to reliability, compatibility (eg with other hardware / software used by the organisation) and capacity (eg network bandwidth) during the acquisition process
c) ensuring compliance with common or industry security standards for hardware and software
d) using telecommunication network links, and services that are proven to be robust and resilient.

CF20.3.3

The availability of critical business processes should be improved by:

a) running critical business applications simultaneously at multiple locations (eg using hot stand-by or virtualisation)
b) providing alternative locations from which business applications, information systems, networks and voice facilities can be run and administered
c) automatically identifying and recovering transactions following a business application / system failure.

CF20.3.4

The resilience of critical business processes should be improved by using fault tolerant:

a) information systems (eg by using multiple processors, hard disk drives, network interface cards, memory and expansion cards)
b) data storage systems (eg by using disk mirroring, RAID technology, hot swappable hard disk drives, and creating multiple access paths to storage using multiple dual host bus adaptors and switches)
c) telephone exchange components (eg processors and function cards).

CF20.3.5

Critical business processes should be protected against disruption from incompatible business applications by:

a) running critical business applications on a dedicated computer, mainframe partition or virtual server (ie a partition on a server running virtualisation software)
b) supporting critical business applications through a dedicated network or sub-network
c) preventing the transfer of information from any connected systems that do not have acceptable security controls (eg by using firewalls).

CF20.3.6

The resilience of critical business processes should be improved by reducing single points of failure in the network by:

a) re-routing network traffic automatically when critical network equipment or links fail
b) installing duplicate or alternative network components (eg routers, hubs, bridges, concentrators, switches, firewalls and network traffic filters) to critical communications equipment
c) arranging for fall-back to alternative points of connection and links with external service providers.

CONTROL FRAMEWORK   SPECIALISED

CF20.3 Resilience (continued)

CF20.3.7

The availability of communication services used to access external information systems, networks and voice facilities (including those provided in the cloud) should be protected by:

a) providing duplicate or alternative points of connection to external communications carriers
b) routing critical links to more than one external exchange or switching centre
c) arranging for use of an alternative communications carrier (eg using alternative communication technologies such as satellite, microwave and WiMAX)
d) deploying emergency bypass for in-house telephone exchanges, so that they can fall back to direct calls.

CF20.3.8

The resilience of technical infrastructure should be improved by applying standard servicing and maintenance disciplines, which include:

a) maintaining consistent versions of software (eg using standard change management disciplines)
b) servicing equipment in accordance with manufacturers' recommended service intervals
c) prohibiting servicing of equipment by unqualified individuals
d) maintaining an adequate supply of system consumables (eg data storage media, printer ink cartridges and stationery)
e) ensuring equipment that supports critical business processes or is particularly susceptible to failure can be replaced quickly (eg by holding a stock of spares on-site).

CF20.3.9

The resilience of technical infrastructure should be improved by providing a method of dealing with faults, which includes:

a) recording all actual or suspected faults
b) disabling equipment, software and services with suspected faults until remedied
c) ensuring that critical information systems, networks and voice facility components are repaired or replaced within critical timescales.

CF20.3.10

Critical business applications and underlying technical infrastructure should be protected against targeted attacks that may disrupt business processes by:

a) reviewing intelligence information (eg to help understand key threats and related motivations, types and methods)
b) determining how the threats affect the business environment in which business processes are running
c) increasing monitoring activity for critical business applications to help prevent, detect or delay disruptive activity when it occurs (eg denial of service attacks or repeated attempts to gain unauthorised access).

Related content	ISF resources
CF19.2 Power Supplies	Securing Critical Infrastructure: Workshop Report
	Cyber Security Strategies: Achieving cyber resilience

SPECIALISED

CONTROL FRAMEWORK

CF20.4   Crisis Management

Principle   A crisis management process should be established, supported by a crisis management team, which details actions to be taken in the event of a major incident or serious attack.

Objective   To respond to major incidents and serious attacks quickly and effectively, reducing any potential business impact including brand and reputational damage.

CF20.4.1

There should be a crisis management process for dealing with major incidents and serious attacks in each individual business environment (supported by a business continuity plan or business continuity arrangements).

> Crisis management is the process by which major information security and cyber incidents (or potential major incidents) – that impact or threaten the continuity of the organisation and require executive intervention for decision-making and coordination – are managed. Major incidents can be a result of a man-made or natural disaster or when an information security incident or cyber attack escalates into a crisis or emergency.
>
> The role of crisis management includes coordination and communication with: the governing body and executive management; staff; organisations in the supply chain (eg customers, suppliers and business partners); government, intelligence and law enforcement agencies; industry groups and regulators; the media and other stakeholders.

CF20.4.2

The crisis management process should be supported by a predetermined high-level team (eg a crisis management team), which includes:

a) a member of the organisation's governing body
b) representatives from executive management
c) individuals skilled in responding to major incidents and serious attacks.

CF20.4.3

The crisis management process should:

a) include clearly defined steps to be taken in a crisis or emergency situations
b) provide contact details for all key individuals (including those in the crisis management team and those associated with external parties such as law enforcement agencies, industry regulators and organisations in the supply chain)
c) be rehearsed and tested on a regular basis, using real life simulations.

CF20.4.4

Individuals involved in crisis management should be made aware of:

a) the definition of a crisis or emergency situation
b) their allocated roles and responsibilities.

CF20.4.5

The crisis management process should include a method of:

a) gaining approval for recommended actions within a critical timescale
b) enabling critical decisions to be made promptly
c) permitting investigators to react quickly.

CF20.4 Crisis Management (continued)

CF20.4.6

The crisis management process should include a method of engaging with business environments, specialist functions (eg major operational risk, internal audit, legal or human resources) and external parties (eg in the supply chain), including:

a) law enforcement agencies
b) industry regulators
c) security experts in computer / software companies
d) cyber-partners to share intelligence and collaborate.

CF20.4.7

Special arrangements should be established for dealing with the media (eg television, radio, newspapers and Internet media organisations), which includes:

a) developing public relations policies and procedures for helping to manage with major incidents clearly and rapidly
b) identifying one or more predetermined internal points of contact (eg a spokesperson) who is trained and experienced in managing communications with the media
c) establishing an external point of contact (eg a specialist public relations or communications organisation) through which communications with the media will be managed
d) providing guidelines on developing draft statements (and any relevant documentation) for sharing with the media in a timely manner throughout a crisis
e) establishing a suitable environment in which to liaise with the media.

CF20.4.8

The crisis management process should ensure that, after a crisis (or emergency) has been resolved:

a) any business applications and underlying technical infrastructure (eg information systems and networks) affected are restored to their previous state
b) the likelihood of a similar crisis occurring is minimised
c) security controls are reviewed
d) internal staff involved in the cause of the incident (eg through inappropriate, careless or criminal activity) are treated according to the organisation's crisis management process (eg by providing training, advice or warnings)
e) information regarding the crisis is shared with relevant external parties (eg service providers, cyber-intelligence service providers, industry regulators, and organisations in the supply chain)
f) action is taken to stop illegal activity (eg establishing injunctions against attacking Internet domains and having websites that are masquerading as the organisation shutdown).

Related content	ISF resources
CF11.1 Information Security Incident Management	*Cyber Security Strategies: Achieving cyber resilience*

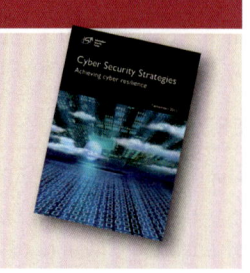

FUNDAMENTAL

CONTROL FRAMEWORK

CF20.5 Business Continuity Planning

Principle   Business continuity plans should be developed and documented to support all critical business processes throughout the organisation.

Objective   To provide relevant individuals with a documented set of actions to perform in the event of a disaster or emergency affecting business applications and technical infrastructure, enabling critical business processes to be resumed within critical timescales.

CF20.5.1

An individual business continuity plan should be created for each individual business environment across all parts of the organisation, and form part of a wider business continuity programme.

CF20.5.2

Each business continuity plan should be based on the results of a risk assessment (eg using the ISF's *Information Risk Analysis Methodology (IRAM)*), which includes:

a) assessing the potential business impacts associated with disruption to critical business processes, by performing a business impact assessment (BIA)
b) evaluating the likelihood of critical business processes being disrupted, by performing a threat and vulnerability assessment
c) obtaining executive management sign-off for selecting suitable business continuity plans and arrangements to treat the risks identified.

> The business impact assessment would typically identify the maximum period of time the organisation can withstand a disruption to one or more critical processes. This is typically referred to as the 'maximum tolerable period of disruption', and is used to help determine the objectives for recovering critical business processes following a disruption.

CF20.5.3

Each business continuity plan should be:

a) developed in conjunction with business representatives
b) based on a set of scenarios of possible disasters
c) the responsibility of a specific individual or working group
d) distributed to all individuals who would require them in case of emergency.

CF20.5.4

Individuals should be informed of their responsibilities regarding the business continuity plan and provided with relevant training / tools to fulfil them.

CF20.5.5

The business continuity plan should include arrangements for resuming critical business processes by using alternative facilities (eg via reciprocal arrangements with another organisation or a contract with a specialist provider of business continuity arrangements).

CF20.5.6

Business continuity plans should clearly state the:

a) services / activities and information to be recovered
b) timescales in which services / activities and information need to be recovered
c) order in which services / activities and information should be recovered.

CONTROL FRAMEWORK   **FUNDAMENTAL**

CF20.5 Business Continuity Planning (continued)

CF20.5.7

Business continuity plans should include:

a) conditions for their invocation
b) sufficient detail so that they can be followed by individuals who do not normally carry them out
c) arrangements for the secure storage of plans (eg off-site), and their retrieval in case of emergency.

CF20.5.8

Business continuity plans should cover details about key activities, which include:

a) a schedule of recovery tasks and activities to be carried out including emergency, fall-back and resumption procedures (in priority order)
b) the responsibilities for carrying out each task and activity (including deputies)
c) information security controls to be applied following invocation of the business continuity plan (eg to protect the confidentiality and integrity of information)
d) details of tasks to be undertaken following recovery and restoration (eg checking that systems and information are restored to the same state they were in before the business continuity plan was invoked).

CF20.5.9

Business continuity plans should include the reconfiguring or restoring of the relevant elements of technical security infrastructure, including:

a) identity and access management systems and access control mechanisms
b) network protection tools, such as firewalls, intrusion detection systems (IDS) and corporate network gateways
c) malware protection software (including programme code and signature files)
d) cryptographic solutions and public key infrastructure components (eg Certification Authorities (CAs) and Registration Authorities (RAs)).

CF20.5.10

Each business continuity plan should be:

a) reviewed regularly by business representatives, IT staff and information security specialists to identify any need for changes (often referred to as a checklist test)
b) approved and signed off by an appropriate business representative
c) subject to standard change management practices
d) tested on a regular basis.

CF20.5.11

Business continuity plans should be updated on a regular basis, and:

a) following significant changes to business processes (such as to network services / facilities or legal, regulatory or contractual obligations)
b) in response to problems encountered during tests / rehearsals
c) as a result of invoking business continuity plans.

Related content	ISF resources
Appendix A: The ISF Business Impact Reference Table	Aligning Business Continuity and Information Security

FUNDAMENTAL

CONTROL FRAMEWORK

CF20.6 Business Continuity Arrangements

Principle — Alternative business continuity arrangements (sometimes referred to as disaster recovery plans) should be established for individual business environments, and made available when required.

Objective — To enable critical business processes to be resumed to an agreed level, within an agreed time following a disruption, using alternative processing facilities.

CF20.6.1

Alternative information processing arrangements should be established for each individual business environment to enable critical business processes (and related services) to continue (at an acceptable level) in the event of a disaster or emergency affecting the underlying business applications, information systems or networks.

CF20.6.2

Each business continuity plan should be supported by the provision of business continuity arrangements, such as separate processing facilities, reciprocal arrangements with another organisation or a contract with a specialist provider of business continuity arrangements.

CF20.6.3

Business continuity arrangements should cover all business locations and users associated with the organisation's critical business processes.

CF20.6.4

Alternative arrangements should:

a) involve separate, alternative processing facilities (within the organisation, at an external party site or as part of a contract with a specialist business continuity arrangements provider)
b) be ready for immediate use.

CF20.6.5

Business continuity arrangements should enable critical business processes to continue in the event of prolonged unavailability of:

a) key individuals (eg due to illness, injury, vacation or travel)
b) critical information (eg business information, documentation or back-up files) in paper or electronic form
c) company premises and office accommodation (eg buildings or equipment rooms)
d) access to information systems or buildings (eg due to police, military or terrorist action, natural disaster, or withdrawal of transport services).

CF20.6.6

Business continuity arrangements should enable critical business processes to continue in the event of prolonged unavailability of technical infrastructure, including:

a) business applications, information systems or communications software
b) important computer, communications and environmental control equipment (eg servers, Internet connections, cabling and air conditioning units).

CF20.6.7

Business continuity arrangements should enable critical business processes to continue in the event of prolonged unavailability of services, including:

a) services provided to or required by external parties (eg the organisation's supply chain)
b) public utilities (eg electricity, gas or water supplies)
c) network services (eg due to loss of voice, data or other communications systems)
d) IT operations centre(s) (eg network operations centres (NOCs) or security operations centres (SOCs))
e) system documentation (including operating procedures and parameter settings).

CF20.6 Business Continuity Arrangements (continued)

CF20.6.8

Contracts with specialist providers of business continuity arrangements (or equivalent) should be established, which require the provider to:

a) provide facilities and premises immediately following invocation of the organisation's business continuity plan
b) protect the confidentiality, integrity and availability of information (using both physical and logical controls) for the duration of using alternative facilities
c) securely destroy all information (on hard disk drives and portable storage devices) once alternative arrangements are no longer required (eg main processing has resumed on the organisation's premises).

CF20.6.9

Contracts with specialist providers of business continuity arrangements (or equivalent) should be:

a) reviewed independently (eg by a legal representative, lawyer or equivalent)
b) approved by executive management
c) agreed and signed by both parties
d) kept up-to-date.

CF20.6.10

Each business continuity arrangement should be:

a) reviewed regularly by key staff (eg information security specialists and user representatives) to identify any need for change
b) approved and signed off by an appropriate business representative
c) tested on a regular basis.

CF20.6.11

Business continuity arrangements should be updated on a regular basis, as well as:

a) following significant changes to business processes (such as to network services / facilities or legal, regulatory or contractual obligations)
b) in response to problems encountered during tests / rehearsals
c) a result of invoking business continuity plans.

Related content	ISF resources
No direct references	*Aligning Business Continuity and Information Security*

FUNDAMENTAL

CONTROL FRAMEWORK

CF20.7 Business Continuity Testing

Principle — Business continuity plans and arrangements should be tested on a regular basis.

Objective — To provide assurance that business continuity plans and arrangements will work as required, so that critical business processes can resume within predefined timescales.

CF20.7.1

Business continuity plans and arrangements should be tested on a regular basis, and at least annually.

CF20.7.2

Business continuity tests (or exercises) should be approved by:

a) the business owner (eg the owner of the related critical business process)
b) relevant IT, network and facilities management
c) the central business continuity management team.

CF20.7.3

Tests of business continuity plans and arrangements should include realistic scenarios (involving both business users and IT staff) to demonstrate that critical business processes can be resumed within critical timescales (ie the timescale beyond which a loss of service would be unacceptable to the organisation).

CF20.7.4

Tests of business continuity plans and arrangements should be performed to ensure that following the invocation of business continuity plans:

a) critical information is protected (ie against corruption)
b) sensitive information is protected (ie against unauthorised disclosure).

CF20.7.5

Tests of business continuity plans and arrangements should include an assessment of the restored technical security infrastructure, including:

a) identity and access management systems and access control mechanisms
b) network protection tools, such as firewalls, intrusion detection systems (IDS) and corporate network gateways
c) malware protection software (including programme code and signature files)
d) cryptographic solutions and public key infrastructure components (eg Certification Authorities (CAs) and Registration Authorities (RAs)).

CF20.7.6

Tests of business continuity plans and arrangements should be based on the organisation's recovery requirements, and include:

a) simple tests – which often involve structured (step-by-step) walk-through tests (where stakeholders meet to rehearse the business continuity plan using different scenarios)
b) medium tests – which often involve simulation tests (where staff test the business continuity plan using a specific scenario) and parallel tests (where alternative facilities are used to avoid disrupting real business processes)
c) complex tests – which often involve full-interruption tests (where the original site is shut down and a complete test is performed at an alternative facility).

CF20.7 Business Continuity Testing (continued)

CF20.7.7

The results of business continuity testing should be:

a) documented by the team performing the test
b) checked against expected results
c) signed off by the business owner
d) compared with business continuity tests conducted in other areas of the organisation
e) reported to central business continuity management team and executive management.

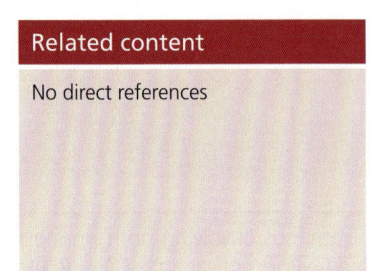

Related content	ISF resources
No direct references	*Aligning Business Continuity and Information Security*

SECURITY MONITORING AND IMPROVEMENT

Contents

SI1 Security Audit

SI1.1   Security Audit Management
SI1.2   Security Audit Process – Planning
SI1.3   Security Audit Process – Fieldwork
SI1.4   Security Audit Process – Reporting
SI1.5   Security Audit Process – Monitoring

SI2 Security Performance

SI2.1   Security Monitoring
SI2.2   Information Risk Reporting
SI2.3   Monitoring Information Security Compliance

SECURITY MONITORING AND IMPROVEMENT

FUNDAMENTAL

AREA SI1 – Security Audit

List of Topics

SI1.1 Security Audit Management
SI1.2 Security Audit Process – Planning
SI1.3 Security Audit Process – Fieldwork
SI1.4 Security Audit Process – Reporting
SI1.5 Security Audit Process – Monitoring

SI1.1 Security Audit Management

Principle The information security status of target environments (eg critical business environments, business processes, business applications (including those under development), information systems and networks) should be subject to thorough, independent and regular security audits.

Objective To ensure that security controls have been implemented effectively, that risk is being managed and to provide the owners of target environments and executive management with an independent assessment of their security status.

SI1.1.1

Independent security audits should be performed regularly for target environments that are critical to the success of the organisation, including:

a) business environments (eg business administration offices, trading floors, call centres, warehouses and retail environments)
b) business processes (eg processing high value transactions, manufacturing goods, handling medical records)
c) business applications (including those under development)
d) information systems and networks that support critical business processes
e) specialist systems that are important to the organisation (eg systems that support or enable the organisation's critical infrastructure, such as SCADA systems, process control PCs and embedded systems)
f) key enterprise-wide security activities (eg managing a security architecture, running awareness programmes or monitoring security arrangements)
g) office equipment (eg network printers, photocopiers, facsimile machines, scanners and multifunction devices (MFDs)).

SI1.1.2

Security audits should:

a) assess the business risks associated with target environments
b) consider the information security requirements of target environments (ie the need to protect the confidentiality, integrity and availability of business information).

FUNDAMENTAL   SECURITY MONITORING AND IMPROVEMENT

SI1.1 Security Audit Management (continued)

SI1.1.3

Security audits should be:

a) agreed with the owner of target environments
b) defined in scope, and documented
c) performed by experienced and qualified individuals who have sufficient technical skills (eg hold certifications for security audit and testing) and knowledge of information security
d) carried out independently of individuals running or supporting target environments (eg by an independent external specialist or by internal audit)
e) conducted frequently and thoroughly (in terms of scope and extent) to provide assurance that security controls function as required
f) focused on ensuring that controls are effective enough to reduce risks to acceptable levels
g) supplemented by the use of automated software tools
h) validated by competent individuals
i) complemented by reviews carried out by independent external parties.

SI1.1.4

Security audit activity should be managed by:

a) agreeing requirements for special processing routines or tests (eg performing vulnerability assessments and penetration tests) with the owner(s) of target environments
b) restricting access to business applications, information systems and networks by audit teams (eg by granting only 'read' access to business information and software files or granting increased levels of access only for isolated copies of business information and software files)
c) monitoring and logging the activities of audit teams
d) disposing of business information copied for the purpose of audits as soon as it is no longer required
e) protecting software tools used in carrying out audits (eg by keeping them separate from tools / utilities used in the live environment and holding them in secure storage facilities, such as restricted software libraries)
f) protecting documents and system files relating to audits.

SI1.1.5

There should be a repeatable and consistent process for performing security audits of target environments, which includes:

a) planning the security audit
b) conducting fieldwork (eg collecting relevant background material, performing security audit tests and recording the results of the tests)
c) reporting the results of the security audit
d) monitoring recommended actions related to the security audit.

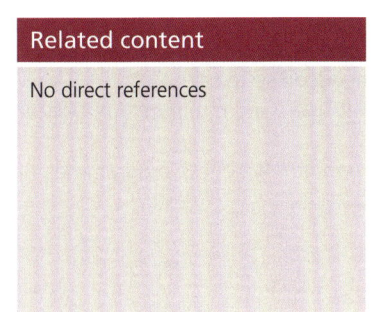

Related content	ISF resources
No direct references	*Security Audit of Business Applications* *Securing Business Applications*

SECURITY MONITORING AND IMPROVEMENT

FUNDAMENTAL

SI1.2 Security Audit Process – Planning

Principle
Security audits of target environments should be subject to thorough planning, which includes identifying risks, determining audit objectives, defining the approach and scope of security audits and preparing a security audit plan.

Objective
To ensure security audits are performed using an agreed methodology, can be completed within acceptable timescales and that no audit steps or activities are missed.

SI1.2.1

Security audits should be planned, and involve:

a) identifying the information risks associated with target environments (ie criticality of information, potential business impacts, level of threats and identified vulnerabilities (eg security control weaknesses))
b) documenting and agreeing the objectives of the security audit (eg using SMART criteria – specific, measurable, achievable, realistic and timed)
c) defining the approach and scope of the security audit (eg whether the audit involves a compliance-based approach, a threat-based approach or both)
d) preparing a security audit plan.

SI1.2.2

The planning of a security audit should involve identifying the information risks associated with the target environment by assessing:

a) the value or level of criticality of information associated with the target environment
b) potential business impacts (ie a business impact assessment)
c) threats related to the target environment (ie a threat assessment)
d) identified vulnerabilities (eg security control weaknesses).

SI1.2.3

The objectives of the security audit should be defined, which take into account the threats and security controls associated with related:

a) business environments (eg business administration offices, trading floors, call centres, warehouses and retail environments)
b) business processes (eg processing high value transactions, manufacturing goods, handling medical records)
c) business information (eg transactional information such as foreign exchange deals, sales orders and financial payments and credits, and standing (or static) data such as customer master files, manufacturing data, pricing tables and foreign exchange rates)
d) business applications (eg enterprise software such as ERP and CRM, commercial-off-the-shelf (COTS) software such as office productivity suites, and desktop applications such as those created using spreadsheet and desktop database programs)
e) information systems and networks (including operating system configuration, application settings and network device configuration) that support critical business processes
f) specialist systems that are important to the organisation (eg systems that support or enable the organisation's critical infrastructure, such as SCADA systems, process control PCs and embedded systems)
g) office equipment (eg network printers, photocopiers, facsimile machines, scanners and multifunction devices (MFDs))
h) enterprise-wide security activities (eg managing a security architecture, running awareness programmes or monitoring security arrangements).

FUNDAMENTAL

SECURITY MONITORING AND IMPROVEMENT

SI1.2 Security Audit Process – Planning (continued)

SI1.2.4

An approach to performing a security audit of the target environment should be agreed, taking into account the:

a) compliance-based approach, which typically examines the controls in place (eg by determining if controls are being applied by testing their effectiveness)
b) threat-based approach, which typically uses tests that mimic or closely match threats that attempt to exploit vulnerabilities (eg control weaknesses) or bypass security controls (eg by undertaking penetration testing, simulating social engineering attacks, inputting bad data or performing SQL injection attacks).

> Organisations often combine the compliance-based and threat-based approach when performing security audits (eg by selecting tests that probe compliance with a standard and tests that break or bypass the controls deployed) to help ensure all risks are fully addressed.

SI1.2.5

A plan for the security audit should be developed and documented, which clearly defines the:

a) scope and approach of the security audit (eg business environments, business processes, business applications (including those under development), information systems or networks to be audited)
b) objectives (ie what the audit aims to achieve).

SI1.2.6

The security audit plan should include details about:

a) resources required to conduct the audit (eg people, software and office space) – both from the perspective of the auditors and the business owner
b) reporting mechanisms (eg report, briefing and / or presentation) and reporting lines (eg who works for whom)
c) key tasks to be undertaken and responsibilities for those tasks (ie who will perform the tasks)
d) the timescale for the security audit (including milestones, 'stage gates' and key dates)
e) physical access required
f) logical access required
g) restrictions on the audit team (eg special processing routines that must not be run or business applications, information systems and networks that must not be accessed).

SI1.2.7

The security audit plan should be:

a) approved and signed off by the owner of the target environment and by the audit manager
b) tracked and regularly checked to ensure that the audit is progressing as expected.

Related content	ISF resources
CF18.5 Security Testing	*Security Audit of Business Applications*

SECURITY MONITORING AND IMPROVEMENT **FUNDAMENTAL**

SI1.3   Security Audit Process – Fieldwork

Principle Security audit fieldwork conducted for target environments should include collecting relevant background material, performing security audit tests and recording the results of the tests.

Objective To identify both non-compliances and information risks associated with target environments.

SI1.3.1

Conducting the fieldwork for a security audit should involve:

a) collecting background material, to help understand business processes and application(s), the operating environment and the technical characteristics associated with supporting system(s) and network(s)
b) determining audit tests
c) selecting and performing audit tests
d) documenting audit findings.

SI1.3.2

Background material to support security audits should be gathered, which includes:

a) audit-related material (eg audit scope documents and working papers, risk assessment reports, risk treatment measures, threat lists and previous security audits and findings)
b) business-related material (eg relating to business processes, legal and regulatory requirements, transactions, users, external parties, policies and procedures, management reports, asset inventories and business continuity planning)
c) information-related material (eg information classification scheme, incidents / events, transaction data and standing data)
d) technology-related material (eg application settings, access control, security and network diagrams, device inventories, data storage details and cryptography).

SI1.3.3

Security audit fieldwork should include:

a) reviewing audit material gathered (eg to help to determine the current state of business applications, information systems and networks, and how they are deployed and used)
b) conducting pre-fieldwork assessments (eg reviewing the results of vulnerability assessments and issuing control questionnaires)
c) selecting the audit tests to use (eg compliance-based tests or threat-based tests)
d) describing tests that will be carried out during the audit.

FUNDAMENTAL

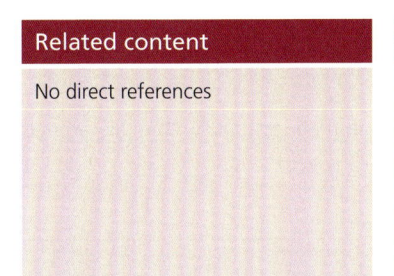

SECURITY MONITORING AND IMPROVEMENT

SI1.3 Security Audit Process – Fieldwork (continued)

SI1.3.4

The selection and performance of security tests should be based on examining:

a) how access to relevant information, associated with critical business environments, business processes, business applications (including those under development), information systems and networks is controlled (eg by access control)
b) whether critical business applications (including those under development), information systems and networks meet the requirements for confidentiality, integrity and availability of information
c) the controls associated with standing data (eg foreign exchange rates)
d) the validity of transactional data (eg input and output validation, reconciliation and recording of events processed by critical business applications)
e) how the critical business applications, information systems and network devices handle processing errors, data in unexpected formats, and whether the errors are logged for further investigation (ie error handling)
f) the controls, processes and mechanisms in place to guarantee availability of critical business applications, information systems and networks should a service interruption occur (ie resilience)
g) security controls that protect the software, hardware and network infrastructure.

SI1.3.5

Details of security audit fieldwork performed should be recorded, including the results of audit tests, issues identified and recommended actions made (eg by using test templates designed for specific target environments).

Related content	ISF resources
No direct references	*Security Audit of Business Applications*

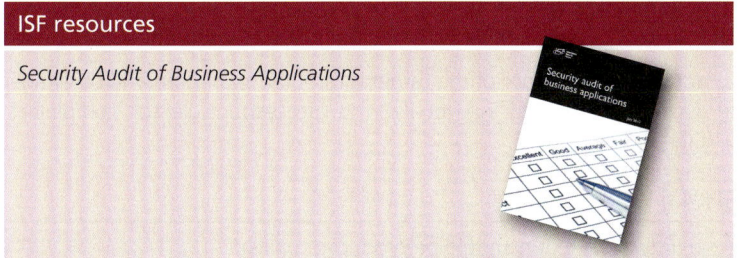

SECURITY MONITORING AND IMPROVEMENT

FUNDAMENTAL

SI1.4 Security Audit Process – Reporting

Principle
The results of security audits of target environments, including findings and recommendations, should be documented and reported to stakeholders.

Objective
To ensure stakeholders are informed about the risks associated with target environments and enable owners for actions to be identified and agreed.

SI1.4.1

The results of security audits should be reported to stakeholders, which involve:

a) agreeing findings and recommendations
b) producing the security audit report
c) presenting findings and recommendations to stakeholders.

SI1.4.2

The results of security audits should include important information and ratings about:

a) control effectiveness (eg very low to very high)
b) conformance classification (eg fully / partially / non-compliant)
c) risks (eg red / amber / green (RAG) or insignificant to critical)
d) implications (eg values entered in a business impact reference table such as very low to very high)
e) recommendations, actions and costs (eg priority, timescales and responsibilities).

SI1.4.3

Prior to producing the security audit report, the findings and recommendations should be:

a) agreed by the owner of the target environment and the audit manager
b) assigned to named individuals who are responsible for completing identified actions within an agreed timescale.

SI1.4.4

A security audit report should be produced, which:

a) describes significant audit findings (often using methods such as red / amber / green (RAG) colour scoring schemes)
b) provides a set of recommendations relating to each audit finding
c) details the owners of findings and recommendations
d) compares the results with the results of previous security audits to demonstrate trends (eg use of weak passwords by staff, increased theft of mobile devices or poor software development practices)
e) highlights good practice (eg use of information risk assessments, effective incident management or continued security awareness campaigns)
f) specifies the need for additional resources (eg to address particular audit findings).

SI1.4.5

The security audit report should be:

a) reviewed and agreed between the security audit manager, the owner of the target environment and an information security specialist
b) signed off as a final security audit report
c) presented to relevant individuals (eg information security specialists, business owners, executive management and developers)
d) made available to executive management (typically in the form of a written report).

FUNDAMENTAL

SECURITY MONITORING AND IMPROVEMENT

SI1.4 Security Audit Process – Reporting (continued)

Related content
SI2.2 Information Risk Reporting

ISF resources
Security Audit of Business Applications
Reporting Information Risk

SECURITY MONITORING AND IMPROVEMENT

FUNDAMENTAL

SI1.5 Security Audit Process – Monitoring

Principle Actions to address security audit findings should be incorporated into a programme of work and monitored continuously.

Objective To ensure the risks identified during security audits are treated effectively, compliance requirements are being met, and agreed security controls are being implemented within agreed timescales.

SI1.5.1

Monitoring of security audit actions should involve:

a) evaluating progress against audit findings
b) conducting follow-up reviews
c) identifying trends
d) tracking the results and actions from all security audits
e) reviewing the progress against audit findings.

SI1.5.2

The actions identified following a security audit should be incorporated into the organisation's information security programme (or equivalent).

SI1.5.3

The progress of actions to resolve each security audit finding should be monitored continuously by tracking the:

a) audit finding, its importance (eg the risk rating) and its context
b) responsibility for the audit finding
c) progress against plan, objectives and actions
d) steps taken to mitigate risks identified (eg implementation of technical or compensating controls)
e) current relevance of the risk rating (ie any changes)
f) level of residual risk to the organisation (ie the impact that would occur if confidentiality, integrity or availability of information was compromised even if all agreed controls are in place).

SI1.5.4

Security audits should be subject to follow-up reviews to check that:

a) major non-compliances have been addressed
b) critical risks have been treated effectively
c) identified risks are being managed on an ongoing basis.

SI1.5.5

The results across multiple security audits should be compared over time to:

a) identify trends (eg lack of information risk assessments being performed or weak access control across all business applications)
b) understand the risk profile of target environments and how they vary over time
c) assist in root cause analysis to identify possible security solutions that could be applied throughout the organisation.

Related content	ISF resources
SI2.1 Security Monitoring	No recent ISF material

AREA SI2 – Security Performance

List of Topics
SI2.1 Security Monitoring
SI2.2 Information Risk Reporting
SI2.3 Monitoring Information Security Compliance

SI2.1 Security Monitoring

Principle   The information security condition of the organisation should be monitored regularly and reported to executive management.

Objective   To provide executive management with an accurate, comprehensive and coherent assessment of the information security condition of the organisation.

SI2.1.1

There should be arrangements for monitoring the information security condition of the organisation, which are documented, agreed with executive management and performed regularly.

SI2.1.2

Analysis performed as part of security monitoring arrangements should be:

a) based on quantitative security metrics (eg the number, frequency and business impact of information security incidents; internal and external audit findings; operational security statistics, such as firewall log data, patch management details and number of spam emails; and costs associated with financial losses, legal or regulatory penalties and fraud)
b) presented in a standard format (eg security dashboards, cockpits or balanced scorecards).

SI2.1.3

Information collected as part of security monitoring arrangements should include details about all aspects of information risk (eg criticality of information, level of threats and identified vulnerabilities, potential business impacts and status of security controls in place).

SI2.1.4

Security monitoring should include obtaining information about the security condition of important environments (eg critical business environments, business applications, information systems and networks) throughout the organisation (eg via local security co-ordinators and information protection champions), which is:

a) aggregated to reflect the organisation as a whole
b) assessed to identify trends, strengths and weaknesses in information security
c) compared with information about the security condition of other organisations (eg using the ISF's Benchmark or information gathered via intelligence sharing activities and collaborating with 'cyber-partners' (eg ISPs, security analysts, government and industry regulators, law enforcement and intelligence agencies)).

SI2.1.5

Information about the security condition of the organisation should be provided to key decision-makers (including executive management, members of the organisation's high-level working group (or equivalent) and relevant external bodies).

SI2.1 Security Monitoring (continued)

SI2.1.6

Security monitoring arrangements should provide key decision-makers with an informed view of:

a) the effectiveness and efficiency of information security controls
b) areas where improvement is required
c) information and systems that are subject to an unacceptable level of risk
d) performance against quantitative, objective targets
e) actions required to help minimise information risk (eg reviewing the organisation's risk appetite, understanding the information security threat environment and encouraging business and system owners to remedy unacceptable risks)
f) details of progress made since previous monitoring reports.

SI2.1.7

Security monitoring arrangements should provide key decision-makers with financial information including:

a) the cost of security controls (eg acquisition and upgrade of security products and services, implementation costs, operational and maintenance costs, and the cost of staff)
b) the financial impact of information security incidents (eg loss of sales; cost of delayed deliveries; fraud; and cost of recovery, including staff time, hardware, software and services)
c) the return on security investment (ROSI) of deployed controls (eg tangible (financial) and intangible (non-financial) benefits).

SI2.1.8

Security monitoring arrangements should enable key decision-makers to:

a) manage information risk effectively
b) relate information risk to operational / business risk
c) demonstrate compliance with legal and regulatory requirements, and internal information security standards / procedures
d) make strategic decisions affecting information security governance.

SI2.1.9

Information generated by monitoring the information security condition of the organisation should be used to measure the effectiveness of the information security strategy, information security policy and security architecture.

Related content

SG1 Security Governance Approach

SG2 Security Governance Components

SI1.5 Security Audit Process – Monitoring

Appendix A: The ISF Business Impact Reference Table

ISF resources

Information Security Metrics

ISF Briefing: Key Performance Indicators for Information Security

ROSI – Return on Security Investment: Workshop Report

ISF Briefing: Information Security Maturity Models

Cyber Security Strategies: Achieving cyber resilience

SPECIALISED SECURITY MONITORING AND IMPROVEMENT

SI2.2 Information Risk Reporting

Principle Reports relating to information risk should be produced and presented to executive management on a regular basis.

Objective To provide executive management with an accurate, comprehensive and coherent view of information risk across the organisation.

SI2.2.1

There should be documented standards / procedures for reporting information risks (eg to executive management).

SI2.2.2

Standards / procedures should cover:

a) defining requirements of the audience that receive the reports
b) collecting and analysing information risk data
c) presenting reports (including details about risk treatment options) and obtaining approval for risk treatment actions that need to be performed
d) monitoring business changes that affect risk ratings
e) the relationship with (and alignment to) other risk reporting.

SI2.2.3

Information risk reports should be presented to or made available to key decision-makers (including executive management, members of a high-level working group and the governing body).

SI2.2.4

Information risk reporting mechanisms should be developed, which are relevant to each audience, and take into account requirements such as:

a) style of report expected
b) risk ratings used (eg aligned with risk ratings used for other types of business risk)
c) method of presentation (eg detailed report, balanced scorecard, cockpit / dashboard or diagrams using colour (red / amber / green) coding)
d) frequency of publication (eg monthly or quarterly).

SI2.2.5

Information risk reports should cover a broad range of information risk-based activities, which include:

a) identification of critical or sensitive information and supporting information systems
b) results of security assurance and security audit initiatives being reported to external parties (eg auditors and regulators), such as the International Standard on Assurance Engagements (ISAE) 3402 or the Statement on Standards for Attestation Engagements (SSAE), Reporting on Controls at a Service Organisation 16 (which replaces the Statement on Auditing Standards 70, Service Organisations (SAS 70))
c) risk treatment options (that have been agreed by executive management), such as accepting risks, avoiding risks, transferring risks or applying appropriate security controls to mitigate risks
d) actions required to help minimise information risk (eg reviewing the organisation's risk appetite, understanding the information security threat environment and encouraging business and system owners to remedy unacceptable risks)
e) performance against quantitative, objective targets
f) details about information security incidents, including assessment of business impact, root cause analysis (to identify control weaknesses) and forensic investigation (where applicable)
g) areas where security control improvement is required to manage information risk.

SECURITY MONITORING AND IMPROVEMENT

SPECIALISED

SI2.2 Information Risk Reporting (continued)

SI2.2.6

Information risk reports should be used to obtain business approval (eg from executive management) for risk treatment options.

SI2.2.7

Information risk reports should:

a) be aligned with other established corporate risk reporting methods (eg enterprise risk, operational risk or market risk)
b) use business language that is consistent with other risk reports
c) incorporate approved impact ratings that have been agreed by executive management (eg using business impact reference tables).

Related content	ISF resources
SR1.1 Managing Information Risk Assessment SR1.2 Information Risk Assessment Methodologies SR1.6 Information Risk Treatment SI2.3 Monitoring Information Security Compliance Appendix A: The ISF Business Impact Reference Table	*Reporting Information Risk* *ISF Briefing: Key Performance Indicators for Information Security* *Security Audit of Business Applications*

SPECIALISED SECURITY MONITORING AND IMPROVEMENT

SI2.3 Monitoring Information Security Compliance

Principle A security compliance management process should be established, which comprises information security controls derived from regulatory and legal drivers and contracts.

Objective To help ensure information security controls are consistently prioritised and addressed according to information security obligations associated with legislation, regulations, industry standards or organisational policy.

SI2.3.1

There should be documented standards / procedures for monitoring information security compliance across the organisation.

SI2.3.2

Standards / procedures should cover:

a) identifying the security compliance obligations (eg that are derived from laws, regulations, contractual obligations and industry standards)
b) translating obligations into compliance-related information security requirements and controls
c) implementing security controls to meet obligations
d) monitoring compliance-related information security controls
e) reporting results of monitoring activities and recommending actions to mitigate compliance risks.

SI2.3.3

Security compliance obligations should be identified by:

a) working with organisational functions (such as legal and compliance) to identify regulatory and legal compliance obligations for jurisdictions in which the organisation operates or has a presence
b) reviewing industry-specific standards and extracting relevant obligations (eg privacy, export, cryptography, import and joint ventures)
c) working with the organisational functions responsible for developing contracts with external parties to identify information security clauses and obligations in contracts
d) reviewing internal policies (eg HR policies, records management policies and document retention schedules) to determine if there are any information security-related obligations.

SI2.3.4

Security compliance obligations should:

a) include coverage of legal and regulatory requirements, contractual requirements, relevant information security-related standards (eg ISO/IEC 27001, COBIT or NIST SP 800-53) and organisational policies, standards and procedures for information security
b) be verified by legal and compliance functions (or equivalent) to help ensure the intent of the obligation(s) is accurately interpreted (eg from legal, regulatory and contractual perspectives)
c) be translated into compliance-related information security requirements.

SI2.3.5

Security compliance obligations, together with the associated information security requirements and security controls, should be recorded in a matrix (eg in a database, via a specialised piece of software or on paper), which is:

a) assigned an owner
b) fully populated
c) maintained (ie updated and reviewed) on a regular basis.

SI2.3 Monitoring Information Security Compliance (continued)

SI2.3.6

Methods of meeting security requirements should be defined, which include:

a) identification of compliance metrics
b) determination of what level of compliance should be monitored
c) identification of monitoring methods to be used
d) agreement on whether information security compliance metrics will be reflected in the organisation's overall compliance scorecard or equivalent.

SI2.3.7

A documented process for systematically monitoring security requirements and obligations should be established, which:

a) identifies information to be monitored from a broad range of sources
b) considers how, when and by whom the information to be monitored will be gathered
c) determines where information being monitored will be aggregated and stored
d) aggregates information gathered
e) enables interoperability issues that may impact the information collection process to be addressed.

SI2.3.8

Compliance gaps (eg in processes, systems and behaviour) should be identified and addressed, including:

a) reviewing information risks associated with compliance gaps
b) analysing the consequences of non-compliance
c) identifying and documenting corrective actions
d) presenting recommendations to executive management for approval.

Related content	ISF resources
SR2.1 Legal and Regulatory Compliance	*Monitoring Compliance: Workshop Report*

APPENDICES

Appendix A: The ISF Business Impact Reference Table

As part of the *Information Risk Analysis Methodology (IRAM)*, the ISF has developed the *Business Impact Reference Table (BIRT)*. This table is a powerful yet simple tool that is used, typically by information risk analysts, to help:

- assess the potential level of business impact that could occur as a result of the loss of confidentiality, integrity and availability of business information
- determine the security requirements for protecting information in a particular environment.

The Business Impact Reference Table contains a list of 15 business impact types, grouped in four impact categories. One of the main reasons for applying the security arrangements recommended in *the Standard* is to help prevent security incidents or to mitigate their impact.

This Appendix presents an example of a *Business Impact Reference Table*, showing completed values in key fields and the different levels of impact (from Very high to Very low) for each business impact type.

Full details about *IRAM* and related tools can be found in the *IRAM Group* on ISF LIVE

Business Impact Reference Table

	Property of information	Appropriate measure	Level of impact				
Ref.	Business impact type		A Very high	B High	C Medium	D Low	E Very low
Financial							
F1	Loss of sales, orders or contracts (eg sales opportunities missed)	Financial impact	20%+	11% to 20%	6% to 10%	1% to 5%	Less than 1%
F2	Loss of tangible assets (eg fraud, theft of money, lost interest)	Financial impact	$20m+	$1m to $20m	$100K to $1m	$10K to $100K	Less than $10K
F3	Penalties/legal liabilities (eg breach of legal, regulatory or contractual obligations)	Financial impact	$20m+	$1m to $20m	$100K to $1m	$10K to $100K	Less than $10K
F4	Unforeseen costs (eg recovery costs)	Financial impact	$20m+	$1m to $20m	$100K to $1m	$10K to $100K	Less than $10K
F5	Depressed share price (eg sudden loss of share value)	Loss of share value	25%+	11% to 25%	6% to 10%	1% to 5%	Less than 1%
Operational							
O1	Loss of management control (eg impaired decision-making)	Extent of loss of control	Severe loss of control	Serious loss of control	Significant loss of control	Moderate loss of control	Minor loss of control
O2	Loss of competitiveness (eg, delays in the introduction of new production capabilities)	Targets under-achieved	20%+	11% to 20%	6% to 10%	1% to 5%	Less than 1%
O3	New ventures held up (eg delayed new products or services)	Achieved	20%+	11% to 20%	6% to 10%	1% to 5%	Less than 1%
O4	Breach of operating standards (eg contravention of regulatory standards)	Extent of sanctions imposed	Closure of building or operation	Serious sanctions imposed	Significant sanctions imposed	Moderate sanctions imposed	Minor sanctions imposed
Customer-related							
C1	Delayed deliveries to customers or clients (eg failure to meet product delivery deadlines)	Extent of delay	Deliveries delayed by 6 months	Deliveries delayed by 3 months	Deliveries delayed by one month	Deliveries delayed by one week	Deliveries delayed by one day
C2	Loss of customers or clients (eg customer/client defection to competitors)	Percentage of customers lost	25%	11% to 25%	6% to 10%	1% to 5%	Less than 1%
C3	Loss of confidence by key institutions (eg adverse criticism by investors)	Extent of loss of confidence	Complete loss of confidence	Serious loss of confidence	Significant loss of confidence	Moderate loss of confidence	Minor loss of confidence
C4	Damage to reputation (eg confidential financial information published in media)	Extent of negative publicity	World-wide negative publicity	Continental-wide negative publicity	Nation-wide negative publicity	Local negative publicity	Minor negative publicity
Employee-related							
E1	Reduction in staff morale/productivity (eg reduced efficiency)	Extent of loss of morale	Complete loss of morale	Serious loss of morale	Significant loss of morale	Moderate loss of morale	Minor loss of morale
E2	Injury or death (eg harm to staff)	Number of incidents	10+	6-10	3-5	1-2	No injuries or deaths

Appendix B: The ISF Threat List

The ISF has developed a standard list of 39 information security threats, grouped in seven threat categories designed to cover the whole of information security. If any of these threats materialise they create a security incident that can have a significant impact on the business.

One of the main reasons for applying the security arrangements recommended in *the Standard* is to help prevent security incidents or to mitigate their impact.

This Appendix presents the individual threat types, provides more detailed information on each, so that Members can consider these threat types when applying *the Standard* in their organisation, and indicates the property of information most likely to be affected by the threat (confidentiality, integrity and availability of information).

> This standard set of 39 threats is used in a consistent manner across all ISF deliverables and is particularly used in the ISF's *Information Risk Analysis Methodology (IRAM)* and the *Benchmark* tool.

Coverage of the 39 Threats and ISF tools

The ISF's *Benchmark* is a powerful service that enables Members to assess the extent to which controls are implemented within Member environments and provides an indication of 'Benchmark' level security required to reduce the frequency and impact of security incidents. To gather this data, the Benchmark asks questions about the experience of security incidents related to the 39 threat types across all environments.

The ISF's *Information Risk Analysis Methodology (IRAM)* enables organisations to assess business information risk and select the right set of security controls to mitigate that risk. The methodology comprises three phases:

1. **Business Impact Assessment** – assesses the potential level of business impact and determines the security requirements for protecting information in critical business applications
2. **Threat and Vulnerability Assessment** – determines the likelihood of particular threats to exploit vulnerabilities and cause business impact
3. **Control Selection** – evaluates and selects security controls to mitigate threats.

The 39 threat types are used within both the Threat and Vulnerability and the Control Selection phases of the IRAM approach.

Appendix B: The ISF Threat List

Ref	Incident	Extended information	Property mostly affected*		
			C	I	A
A. Malware-related incidents					
Malware-related incidents are caused by malicious software, computer programs, code or equivalent (malware), which has been developed for the purpose of compromising information, harming computer systems and / or disrupting business processes.					
Malware-related incidents are related to threats that are malicious in nature and can be generic or targeted against an organisation or individual. They typically include viruses / worms, Trojan horses / rootkits and botnet clients.					
A1	Viruses / Worms	Self-replicating programs (often referred to as the payload) that propagate between computer systems and perform one or more unauthorised actions such as collecting or corrupting business information, or transmitting business information to unauthorised individuals.		X	X
A2	Trojan horses / Rootkits	Malicious software (including spyware, scareware, ransomware and adware) that masquerades as an authorised program or conceals its existence while carrying out one or more unauthorised actions, such as transmitting business information to unauthorised individuals.	X	X	
A3	Botnet Clients	Malicious software that makes the computer act as part of a 'robot network' (botnet) of similarly compromised devices (often referred to as 'zombies'). Botnet clients are remotely operated typically from a 'command and control' centre (or equivalent) and are typically used to conduct denial of service attacks, send large volumes of spam, or infect additional computer systems.	X	X	X
B. Hacking-related incidents					
Hacking-related incidents involve deliberate attempts (typically by one or more external individuals) to intentionally access or harm and organisation's networks and computer systems without authorisation or in excess of authorisation, typically by exploiting vulnerabilities and bypassing security controls (or equivalent).					
Hacking-related incidents are related to threats that are deliberate and often malicious in nature, and targeted against an organisation or individual. They include denial of service attacks; unauthorised access to, scanning of, interception of or alteration of information, software or websites; session hijacking; and theft of authentication credentials.					
B1	Denial of service attacks	Deliberately overloading systems and network devices (often by the use of repeated automated network information requests or other unauthorised network traffic) or re-directing network traffic. Denial of service attacks are often performed in order to degrade the operations of an organisation's networks and computer systems to the point that normal operations are impaired or prevented.			X
B2	Unauthorised use of access credentials	The unauthorised use of valid access credentials (ie user identity information and authenticator) by a malicious internal or external party to gain access to an organisation's applications, computer systems or networks (often as a result of 'identity theft').	X		
B3	Unauthorised network scanning and / or probing	Performing probes or scans (often referred to as reconnaissance) of network devices (eg routers, switches and firewalls), computer systems (eg web servers, mail servers and file servers) or applications to gather information that could be used to perform an attack.	X	X	
B4	Unauthorised tapping, interception, or alteration of network traffic	The unauthorised interception (often referred to as eavesdropping) or modification of information as it is transmitted over public or private networks, or between virtual machines, often using techniques such as cryptanalysis.	X	X	
B5	Session hijacking	The unauthorised control or manipulation of an existing legitimate network connection (eg between a web browser and a web server). Session hijacking is typically used to perform unauthorised activities with the credential(s) of the legitimate user.	X	X	
B6	Unauthorised website modification	The unauthorised alteration or replacement of information (content) on a website. Unauthorised website modification is typically referred to as website defacement.		X	
B7	Unauthorised software modification	The unauthorised changing, adding, or deleting of software, source code, plug-ins, application modules (or equivalent) typically to corrupt the software or cause unauthorised system behaviour / actions.		X	
B8	Unauthorised access to or modification of data	The unauthorised accessing, changing, adding, or deleting of information (including transactions, files, account records or database records) typically using techniques such as SQL injection, buffer overflows, or malware-based attacks.	X	X	
B9	Unauthorised decryption of sensitive information	The unauthorised decryption of encrypted information, typically by using techniques such as cracking passwords (ie determining the plaintext version of an encrypted password), using rainbow tables or brute force attack, or cracking encryption keys (determining the plaintext versions of encrypted keys such as WPA2 keys in wireless networks).	X		
B10	Theft of authentication credentials	Theft of access control information (eg user id, passwords, PIN numbers, private encryption keys or digital certificates).	X	X	

* Note: Other properties of information may be affected by an incident.

Appendix B: The ISF Threat List

Ref	Incident	Extended information	Property mostly affected*		
			C	I	A

C. Social-related incidents

Social-related incidents involve the use of social tactics (often referred to as social engineering) to exploit one or more individuals, and influence them into performing specific actions (typically disclosing authentication credentials or sensitive information). Social engineering typically involves using a variety of techniques against one or more individuals, including deception, manipulation and intimidation.

Social-related incidents are related to threats that are deliberate, often malicious in nature and involve activities such as blackmail, scams, threats and pretexting (where a false scenario is created to increase the likelihood of a targeted individual or group disclosing sensitive information). They include trademark spoofing, impersonation, phishing, spam, and unauthorised disclosure or modification of information.

Ref	Incident	Extended information	C	I	A
C1	Trademark spoofing	The unauthorised use of or masquerading as a legitimate organisation's name or brand, often by registering Internet domains and creating bogus websites to which unsuspecting users are directed.		X	
C2	Impersonation	An individual pretends to be another person in order to perform unauthorised actions or commit fraud.	X	X	
C3	Phishing	A method using social engineering where legitimate-looking communication messages (often via emails or websites) are used by attackers in an attempt to mislead recipients and deceive them into revealing sensitive information (eg personal details, authentication information or financial details). Variants of phishing include spear phishing (phishing attacks targeted at specific individuals or small groups of individuals), whaling (targeted phishing attacks of senior executives) and vishing (phishing attacks using VoIP).	X	X	
C4	Spam	Excessive volumes of unsolicited (commercial) messages (including e-mail, instant messaging and telephony).			X
C5	Unauthorised disclosure of information	Unauthorised (accidental or deliberate) disclosure of business information (eg project names, customer names, medical records and credit card numbers) or user access credentials (eg unique identifiers and authenticators), which should remain confidential.	X		

D. Misuse-related incidents

Misuse-related incidents involve unauthorised use of resources or privileges (typically by authorised internal individuals) to gain unauthorised access to and / or steal software, information or equivalent.

Misuse-related incidents are related to threats that are deliberate, can be malicious or non-malicious in nature, and are typically focussed on the software or information. They include unauthorised system activity, theft of software or business information and unauthorised physical access. Examples of misuse-related incidents include administrative abuse, policy violations and use of non-approved software.

Ref	Incident	Extended information	C	I	A
D1	Unauthorised modification of user access privileges	Unauthorised modification (typically escalation) of user access privileges (ie without approval or sign-off).		X	
D2	Unauthorised system activity	Unauthorised use of a computer system (often by an authorised individual) including: intentionally causing adverse system behaviour / performance (eg by changing or adding software, transactions, files or databases); committing fraud by diverting funds to unauthorised accounts; using a computer system in a malicious or excessive manner; or using authorised communication services (eg e-mail and instant messaging) to carry out unauthorised activities (eg downloading or sending of obscene, discriminatory or harassing content).	X	X	X
D3	Theft of software	Theft of software (eg programs, computer code, source code, and methodologies).	X		
D4	Theft of business information	Theft of business information (eg customer lists, product designs, trade secrets or intellectual property) or personally identifiable information (credit card numbers, employment IDs or medical records).	X		

E. Physical-related incidents

Physical-related incidents involve physical actions and / or physical access to computer / networking equipment, mobile devices or equivalent. These incidents are typically associated with loss or theft of equipment.

Physical-related incidents are related to threats that are typically deliberate acts of theft, tampering or sabotage, or negligence on the part of an individual (eg loss or misplacement of equipment).

Ref	Incident	Extended information	C	I	A
E1	Unauthorised physical access	Deliberately gaining unauthorised access to locations housing business information, applications, computer systems or networks (eg by tailgating, trespassing or pretending to be an authorised individual).	X		
E2	Theft or loss of computer equipment	Theft or loss of computer equipment (including servers, desktops, or laptops) typically from the organisation's premises.	X		X
E3	Theft or loss of mobile devices or portable storage devices	Theft or loss of portable computer equipment (eg equipment used by individuals in remote environments), such as ultrabooks, tablets, smartphones and portable storage devices.	X		X
E4	Theft or loss of physical authentication devices	Theft or loss of physical authentication devices, such as tokens and smartcards.	X		X

* Note: Other properties of information may be affected by an incident.

Appendix B: The ISF Threat List

Ref	Incident	Extended information	Property mostly affected*		
			C	I	A
F. Error-related incidents					
Error-related incidents are the result of mistakes by one or more individuals. The mistakes may have been due to performing an unintentional action (eg incorrect data entry, inadvertent programming error, misconfiguration of software, or malfunction of hardware) or failing to perform a necessary action (ie an omission).					
Error-related incidents are related to threats that involve weaknesses in the human element or hardware. They include staff or administrator errors, software malfunction, system overload, hardware failure and undesirable effects of change.					
F1	User errors	Mistakes made by staff or external individuals (eg consultants, contractors or employees of external parties) when using applications (eg mistakes when inputting data, incorrect operation of workstations, or sending material to the wrong address).	X	X	X
F2	Technical staff errors	Mistakes made by individuals responsible for designing, developing and maintaining applications, computer systems and networks (eg mistakes when writing software code, configuring computer systems, or maintaining network device settings).	X	X	X
F3	Software malfunction (internally produced software)	Incorrect execution or failure of software developed or integrated in-house. Software malfunctions are typically caused as a result of an application flaw, a software bug or equivalent.	X	X	X
F4	Software malfunction (externally acquired software)	Incorrect execution or failure of software acquired from an external party (eg enterprise applications and commercial-off-the-shelf (COTS) software, such as ERP, CRM, office productivity software, communications software and security software). Software malfunctions are typically caused as a result of an application flaw, a software bug or system equivalent.	X	X	X
F5	System overload	Excessive system activity or demand for services causing performance degradation or failure (often as a result of poor capacity planning).			X
F6	Hardware malfunction or failure	Malfunction of computer / network equipment (eg hard disk drives, memory, routers, hubs or switches).			X
F7	Undesirable effects of change	Adverse or damaging impact upon information and / or computer systems from significant changes within the organisation, including: organisational / environmental changes, updates to business processes or business information, newly implemented or recently changed software computer or network hardware.	X	X	X
G. Environmental-related incidents					
Environmental-related incidents are typically associated with natural events (eg storms, earthquakes, floods or atmospheric conditions) or man-made events (eg fire, explosion, electrical interference, pipe leaks, civil unrest or building collapse) and may affect computer systems, network and telecommunication equipment, or entire installations (eg data centres).					
Environmental-related incidents are related to threats that include accidental or malicious physical damage, tampering of computer systems or network / telecommunications equipment, power failure, damage to or loss of external communications, or malicious jamming or interference of wireless communications.					
G1	Natural hazard	Natural disasters include storms, earthquakes, fires and the effects of extreme weather (eg flooding or freezing).			X
G2	Accidental physical damage	Unintended material damage to computer systems, network equipment or the physical environment in which they are located affecting their normal function (eg fire, pipe leaks or building collapse).			X
G3	Malicious physical damage to or tampering with computing or network equipment	Deliberate material damage to computer systems, network equipment or the physical environment in which they are located affecting their normal function (eg fire, electrical interference or explosion).			X
G4	Power failure	Temporary withdrawal or failure of mains electricity or back-up power supply.			X
G5	Damage to or loss of external communications	Damage to or loss of communications links / services (eg Internet connections, wide area network (WAN), local area networks (LANs), satellite links, or wireless networks).			X
G6	Malicious jamming or interference of wireless communications	Malicious interference with wireless communications so as to impede or prevent communications from reaching intended recipients.			X

* Note: Other properties of information may be affected by an incident.

Appendix C: Description of external standards

This Appendix contains references to the information security-related standards that have been reviewed as part of developing *the Standard*.

ISO Standards relating to information security

Standard	Description
ISO/IEC 27001:2005 Information technology – Security techniques – Information security management systems – Requirements	A normative standard providing a mandatory set of steps as part of an Information Security Management System (ISMS), against which an organization can certify its security arrangements (eg 'Define target environment', 'Assess risks' and 'Select appropriate controls').
ISO/IEC 27002:2005 Information technology – Security techniques – Code of practice for information security management	An informative standard providing a framework of security controls which can be used to help select the controls required within an ISMS.
ISO/IEC 27005:2011 Information technology – Security techniques – Information security risk management	A normative standard detailing the mandatory steps required to perform an information security risk assessment, as part of an ISMS (eg 'Identify possible business impact', 'Evaluate threats and vulnerabilities', and 'Create a risk treatment plan').
ISO/IEC 27014* Information technology – Security techniques – Governance of information security	An informative standard that defines the governance of information security, explains the relationship with other types of governance (and with an ISMS) and details how information security governance can be applied in practice.
ISO/IEC 27036* Information technology – Security techniques – Information security for supplier relationships	An informative standard that outlines information security for external parties for both the acquirer and supplier. It supports organizations in implementing information security controls related to supplier relationships.

*in draft

Source: http://www.iso.org/iso/home.htm

Other information security-related standards

- BS 25999-1 Business Continuity Management Part 1 Code of Practice
- COBIT 5 for Information Security
- Payment Card Industry Data Security Standard (PCI DSS) v2.0
- NIST Special Publication 800-53 Recommended Security Controls for Federal Information Systems and Organizations Revision 3
- Cloud Security Alliance (CSA) Cloud Controls Matrix
- UK HMG Security Policy Framework (SPF)

Other information security-related material

- IT Infrastructure Library (ITIL) V3
- Financial Services Authority (UK) Data Security in Financial Services
- COSO – Enterprise Risk Management – Integrated Framework
- Open Compliance & Ethics Group (OCEG) GCR Capability Model "Red Book" 2.0

Appendix D: Templates

Organisations often have a need to focus on groups of topics when selecting, applying and reviewing security controls. For example, they may want to apply just the relevant part of *the Standard* to a particular environment, such as a critical business application, network or end user environment. To assist Members with this approach, *the Standard* can be viewed by grouping topics that are relevant to a particular type of environment. These groups can be represented as templates.

This Appendix contains six templates covering Security Management, Critical Business Applications, Computer Installations, Networks, Systems Development and End User Environment. Each template is shown as a table that includes the topics contained, grouped under area headings. Each table is presented using three headings outlined below:

- Template Reference – shows the template reference for the Topic or Area
- Title – presents the Topic or Area title
- Topic Reference – shows the Topic reference number that is used in *the Standard* and is contained in the main body of this report.

These templates can be used by Members as a basis of developing their own groups of topics for a particular purpose (eg by adding or removing those topics that better suit the environment to which *the Standard* is being applied).

SM – Security Management

The focus of this template is security management at the enterprise level, typically looking at the arrangements within a group of companies, part of a group or an individual organisation. It is designed to probe the commitment provided by executive management to promoting good information security practices across the enterprise, along with the allocation of appropriate resources.

Template Ref	Title	Topic Ref
SM1	Information Security Governance Approach	
SM1.1	Security Governance Framework	SG1.1
SM1.2	Security Direction	SG1.2
SM2	Security Governance Components	
SM2.1	Information Security Strategy	SG2.1
SM2.2	Stakeholder Value Delivery	SG2.2
SM2.3	Information Security Assurance Programme	SG2.3
SM3	Information Risk Management	
SM3.1	Managing Information Risk Assessment	SR1.1
SM3.2	Information Risk Assessment Methodologies	SR1.2
SM3.3	Confidentiality Requirements	SR1.3
SM3.4	Integrity Requirements	SR1.4
SM3.5	Availability Requirements	SR1.5
SM3.6	Information Risk Treatment	SR1.6
SM4	Compliance	
SM4.1	Legal and Regulatory Compliance	SR2.1
SM4.2	Information Privacy	SR2.2
SM5	Security Policy and Organisation	
SM5.1	Information Security Policy	CF1.1
SM5.2	Information Security Function	CF1.2
SM6	Human Resource Security	
SM6.1	Staff Agreements	CF2.1
SM6.2	Security Awareness Programme	CF2.2
SM6.3	Security Awareness Messages	CF2.3
SM6.4	Security Education / Training	CF2.4
SM6.5	Roles and Responsibilities	CF2.5
SM7	Asset Management	
SM7.1	Information Classification	CF3.1
SM7.2	Document Management	CF3.2
SM7.3	Sensitive Physical Information	CF3.3
SM7.4	Asset Register	CF3.4
SM8	Technical Security Infrastructure	
SM8.1	Security Architecture	CF8.1
SM8.2	Identity and Access Management	CF8.2
SM8.3	Critical Infrastructure	CF8.3
SM8.4	Cryptographic Solutions	CF8.4
SM8.5	Cryptographic Key Management	CF8.5
SM8.6	Public Key Infrastructure	CF8.6
SM8.7	Information Leakage Protection	CF8.7
SM8.8	Digital Rights Management	CF8.8
SM9	Threat and Vulnerability Management	
SM9.1	Patch Management	CF10.1
SM9.2	Malware Awareness	CF10.2
SM9.3	Malware Protection Software	CF10.3
SM9.4	Intrusion Detection	CF10.6

Template Ref	Title	Topic Ref
SM10	Incident Management	
SM10.1	Information Security Incident Management	CF11.1
SM10.2	Cybercrime Attacks	CF11.2
SM10.3	Forensic Investigations	CF11.4
SM11	Local Environments	
SM11.1	Local Environment Profile	CF12.1
SM11.2	Local Security Co-ordination	CF12.2
SM12	Mobile Computing	
SM12.1	Remote Environments	CF14.1
SM12.2	Mobile Device Configuration	CF14.2
SM12.3	Mobile Device Connectivity	CF14.3
SM12.4	Portable Storage Devices	CF14.4
SM12.5	Consumer Devices	CF14.5
SM13	Electronic Communications	
SM13.1	Email	CF15.1
SM13.2	Instant Messaging	CF15.2
SM14	External Supplier Management	
SM14.1	External Supplier Management Process	CF16.1
SM14.2	Hardware / Software Acquisition	CF16.2
SM14.3	Outsourcing	CF16.3
SM14.4	Cloud Computing Policy	CF16.4
SM14.5	Cloud Service Contracts	CF16.5
SM15	Physical and Environmental Security	
SM15.1	Physical Protection	CF19.1
SM15.2	Power Supplies	CF19.2
SM15.3	Hazard Protection	CF19.3
SM16	Business Continuity	
SM16.1	Business Continuity Strategy	CF20.1
SM16.2	Business Continuity Programme	CF20.2
SM16.3	Crisis Management	CF20.4
SM16.4	Business Continuity Planning	CF20.5
SM16.5	Business Continuity Arrangements	CF20.6
SM16.6	Business Continuity Testing	CF20.7
SM17	Security Audit	
SM17.1	Security Audit Management	SI1.1
SM17.2	Security Audit Process – Planning	SI1.2
SM17.3	Security Audit Process – Fieldwork	SI1.3
SM17.4	Security Audit Process – Reporting	SI1.4
SM17.5	Security Audit Process – Monitoring	SI1.5
SM18	Security Performance	
SM18.1	Security Monitoring	SI2.1
SM18.2	Information Risk Reporting	SI2.2
SM18.3	Monitoring Information Security Compliance	SI2.3

CB – Critical Business Applications

This template focuses on a business application of any type (including transaction processing, process control, funds transfer, customer service and desktop applications) or size (eg an application supporting thousands of users or just a few) that is critical to the success of the organisation.

The template probes the security requirements of the application and the arrangements made for identifying risks and keeping them within acceptable levels.

Template Ref	Title	Topic Ref
CB1	Business Requirements for Security	
CB1.1	Confidentiality Requirements	SR1.3
CB1.2	Integrity Requirements	SR1.4
CB1.3	Availability Requirements	SR1.5
CB1.4	Information Classification	CF3.1
CB1.5	Information Risk Assessment Methodologies	SR1.2
CB2	Human Resource Security	
CB2.1	Staff Agreements	CF2.1
CB2.2	Security Awareness Programme	CF2.2
CB2.3	Security Awareness Messages	CF2.3
CB2.4	Security Education / Training	CF2.4
CB2.5	Roles and Responsibilities	CF2.5
CB2.6	Local Security Co-ordination	CF12.2
CB3	Application Management	
CB3.1	Application Protection	CF4.1
CB3.2	Browser-based Application Protection	CF4.2
CB3.3	Information Validation	CF4.3
CB3.4	Change Management	CF7.6
CB3.5	Document Management	CF3.2
CB3.6	Sensitive Physical Information	CF3.3
CB4	Customer Access	
CB4.1	Customer Access Arrangements	CF5.1
CB4.2	Customer Contracts	CF5.2
CB4.3	Customer Connections	CF5.3
CB5	Access Management	
CB5.1	Access Control	CF6.1
CB5.2	Access Control Mechanisms	CF6.3
CB5.3	Access Control Mechanisms – Password	CF6.4
CB5.4	Access Control Mechanisms – Token	CF6.5
CB5.5	Access Control Mechanisms – Biometric	CF6.6
CB5.6	Sign-on Process	CF6.7

Template Ref	Title	Topic Ref
CB6	System Management	
CB6.1	Service Level Agreements	CF7.7
CB6.2	Resilience	CF20.3
CB6.3	External Network Connections	CF9.3
CB6.4	Back-up	CF7.5
CB7	Cryptography	
CB7.1	Cryptographic Solutions	CF8.4
CB7.2	Cryptographic Key Management	CF8.5
CB8	Incident Management	
CB8.1	Information Security Incident Management	CF11.1
CB8.2	Emergency Fixes	CF11.3
CB9	Business Continuity	
CB9.1	Business Continuity Planning	CF20.5
CB9.2	Business Continuity Arrangements	CF20.6
CB9.3	Business Continuity Testing	CF20.7
CB10	Security Audit	
CB10.1	Security Audit Management	SI1.1
CB10.2	Security Audit Process – Planning	SI1.2
CB10.3	Security Audit Process – Fieldwork	SI1.3
CB10.4	Security Audit Process – Reporting	SI1.4
CB10.5	Security Audit Process – Monitoring	SI1.5

CI – Computer Installations

This template focuses on a computer installation (of any size, running in a specialised environment and any kind of operating system) that supports one or more business applications. It probes how requirements for computer services are identified, and how the computers are set up and run in order to meet those requirements.

Template Ref	Title	Topic Ref
CI1	Human Resource Security	
CI1.1	Security Awareness Programme	CF2.2
CI1.2	Security Awareness Messages	CF2.3
CI1.3	Roles and Responsibilities	CF2.5
CI1.4	Local Security Co-ordination	CF12.2
CI2	Security Requirements	
CI2.1	Information Classification	CF3.1
CI2.2	Information Risk Assessment Methodologies	SR1.2
CI3	Asset Management	
CI3.1	Document Management	CF3.2
CI3.2	Sensitive Physical Information	CF3.3
CI3.3	Asset Register	CF3.4
CI4	Business Applications	
CI4.1	Application Protection	CF4.1
CI4.2	Browser-based Application Protection	CF4.2
CI5	Customer Access	
CI5.1	Customer Access Arrangements	CF5.1
CI5.2	Customer Contracts	CF5.2
CI5.3	Customer Connections	CF5.3
CI6	Access Management	
CI6.1	Access Control	CF6.1
CI6.2	User Authorisation	CF6.2
CI6.3	Access Control Mechanisms	CF6.3
CI6.4	Access Control Mechanisms – Password	CF6.4
CI6.5	Access Control Mechanisms – Token	CF6.5
CI6.6	Access Control Mechanisms – Biometric	CF6.6
CI6.7	Sign-on Process	CF6.7
CI7	System Management	
CI7.1	Computer and Network Installations	CF7.1
CI7.2	Server Configuration	CF7.2
CI7.3	Resilience	CF20.3
CI7.4	Mobile Device Configuration	CF14.2
CI7.5	Mobile Device Connectivity	CF14.3
CI7.6	Virtual Servers	CF7.3
CI7.7	Network Storage Systems	CF7.4
CI7.8	Back-up	CF7.5
CI7.9	Change Management	CF7.6
CI7.10	Service Level Agreements	CF7.7

Template Ref	Title	Topic Ref
CI8	Technical Security Infrastructure	
CI8.1	Identity and Access Management	CF8.2
CI8.2	Cryptographic Solutions	CF8.4
CI8.3	Cryptographic Key Management	CF8.5
CI8.4	Information Leakage Protection	CF8.7
CI8.5	Digital Rights Management	CF8.8
CI9	Threat and Vulnerability Management	
CI9.1	Patch Management	CF10.1
CI9.2	Malware Protection Software	CF10.3
CI9.3	Security Event Logging	CF10.4
CI9.4	System / Network Monitoring	CF10.5
CI9.5	Intrusion Detection	CF10.6
CI10	Incident Management	
CI10.1	Information Security Incident Management	CF11.1
CI10.2	Cybercrime Attacks	CF11.2
CI10.3	Emergency Fixes	CF11.3
CI10.4	Forensic Investigations	CF11.4
CI11	External Supplier Management	
CI11.1	Hardware / Software Acquisition	CF16.2
CI11.2	Cloud Computing Policy	CF16.4
CI11.3	Cloud Service Contracts	CF16.5
CI12	Physical and Environmental Security	
CI12.1	Physical Protection	CF19.1
CI12.2	Power Supplies	CF19.2
CI12.3	Hazard Protection	CF19.3
CI13	Business Continuity	
CI13.1	Business Continuity Planning	CF20.5
CI13.2	Business Continuity Arrangements	CF20.6
CI13.3	Business Continuity Testing	CF20.7
CI14	Security Audit	
CI14.1	Security Audit Management	SI1.1
CI14.2	Security Audit Process – Planning	SI1.2
CI14.3	Security Audit Process – Fieldwork	SI1.3
CI14.4	Security Audit Process – Reporting	SI1.4
CI14.5	Security Audit Process – Monitoring	SI1.5

NW – Networks

This template focuses on a network (eg a wide area network (WAN), a local area network (LAN), enterprise-wide, small scale, intranet, extranet and voice, data or integrated) that supports one or more business applications, probing how requirements for network services are identified, and how the network is set up and run in order to meet those requirements.

Template Ref	Title	Topic Ref
NW1	Human Resource Security	
NW1.1	Roles and Responsibilities	CF2.5
NW1.2	Security Awareness Programme	CF2.2
NW1.3	Security Awareness Messages	CF2.3
NW1.4	Local Security Co-ordination	CF12.2
NW2	Security Requirements	
NW2.1	Information Classification	CF3.1
NW2.2	Information Risk Assessment Methodologies	SR1.2
NW3	Access Management	
NW3.1	Access Control	CF6.1
NW3.2	Sign-on Process	CF6.7
NW4	Network Management	
NW4.1	Computer and Network Installations	CF7.1
NW4.2	Network Device Configuration	CF9.1
NW4.3	Physical Network Management	CF9.2
NW4.4	Service Level Agreements	CF7.7
NW4.5	External Network Connections	CF9.3
NW4.6	Firewalls	CF9.4
NW4.7	Remote Maintenance	CF9.5
NW5	Network Operations	
NW5.1	System / Network Monitoring	CF10.5
NW5.2	Intrusion Detection	CF10.6
NW5.3	Information Security Incident Management	CF11.1
NW5.4	Physical Protection	CF19.1
NW5.5	Back-up	CF7.5
NW5.6	Change Management	CF7.6

Template Ref	Title	Topic Ref
NW6	Electronic Communications	
NW6.1	Email	CF15.1
NW6.2	Instant Messaging	CF15.2
NW6.3	Wireless Access	CF9.6
NW6.4	Voice Over IP (VoIP) Networks	CF9.7
NW6.5	Telephony and Conferencing	CF9.8
NW7	Business Continuity	
NW7.1	Resilience	CF20.3
NW7.2	Business Continuity Planning	CF20.5
NW7.3	Business Continuity Arrangements	CF20.6
NW7.4	Business Continuity Testing	CF20.7
NW8	Security Audit	
NW8.1	Security Audit Management	SI1.1
NW8.2	Security Audit Process – Planning	SI1.2
NW8.3	Security Audit Process – Fieldwork	SI1.3
NW8.4	Security Audit Process – Reporting	SI1.4
NW8.5	Security Audit Process – Monitoring	SI1.5

SD – System Development

This template focuses on a systems development unit / department or a particular systems development project, including projects of all sizes, any type of development and those based on tailor-made software or application packages. It applies to how business requirements (including information security requirements) are identified, and how systems are designed and built to meet those requirements.

Template Ref	Title	Topic Ref
SD1	System Development Management	
SD1.1	Roles and Responsibilities	CF2.5
SD1.2	System Development Methodology	CF17.1
SD1.3	System Development Environments	CF17.2
SD1.4	Quality Assurance	CF17.3
SD2	Local Security Management	
SD2.1	Local Security Co-ordination	CF12.2
SD2.2	Security Awareness Programme	CF2.2
SD2.3	Security Awareness Messages	CF2.3
SD3	Business Requirements	
SD3.1	Specifications of Requirements	CF18.1
SD3.2	Confidentiality Requirements	SR1.3
SD3.3	Integrity Requirements	SR1.4
SD3.4	Availability Requirements	SR1.5
SD3.5	Information Risk Assessment Methodologies	SR1.2
SD4	System Design and Build	
SD4.1	System Design	CF18.2
SD4.2	System Build	CF18.3
SD4.3	Hardware / Software Acquisition	CF16.2
SD4.4	Application Protection	CF4.1
SD4.5	Browser-based Application Protection	CF4.2
SD4.6	Information Validation	CF4.3

Template Ref	Title	Topic Ref
SD5	Testing	
SD5.1	Security Testing	CF18.5
SD5.2	Systems Testing	CF18.4
SD6	Implementation	
SD6.1	System Promotion Criteria	CF18.6
SD6.2	Installation Process	CF18.7
SD6.3	Post-implementation Review	CF18.8
SD7	Security Audit	
SD7.1	Security Audit Management	SI1.1
SD7.2	Security Audit Process – Planning	SI1.2
SD7.3	Security Audit Process – Fieldwork	SI1.3
SD7.4	Security Audit Process – Reporting	SI1.4
SD7.5	Security Audit Process – Monitoring	SI1.5

UE – End User Environment

This template focuses on any environment (eg head office department, general business unit, factory floor or call centre) in which individuals use corporate business applications and / or critical desktop applications to support business processes. An environment could be of any size (eg several individuals to groups of more than one hundred) and include individuals with varying degrees of IT skills and / or awareness of information security.

Template Ref	Title	Topic Ref
UE1	User Awareness	
UE1.1	Security Awareness Programme	CF2.2
UE1.2	Security Awareness Messages	CF2.3
UE1.3	Security Education / Training	CF2.4
UE1.4	Malware Awareness	CF10.2
UE2	Local Environment Management	
UE2.1	Local Environment Profile	CF12.1
UE2.2	Roles and Responsibilities	CF2.5
UE2.3	Local Security Co-ordination	CF12.2
UE2.4	Office Equipment	CF12.3
UE2.5	Physical Protection	CF19.1
UE3	Asset Management	
UE3.1	Information Classification	CF3.1
UE3.2	Document Management	CF3.2
UE3.3	Sensitive Physical Information	CF3.3
UE3.4	Hardware / Software Acquisition	CF16.2
UE3.5	Asset Register	CF3.4
UE4	Corporate Business Applications	
UE4.1	Access Control	CF6.1
UE4.2	Access Control Mechanisms	CF6.3
UE4.3	Access Control Mechanisms – Password	CF6.4
UE4.4	Access Control Mechanisms – Token	CF6.5
UE4.5	Access Control Mechanisms – Biometric	CF6.6
UE4.6	Sign-on Process	CF6.7
UE5	Desktop Applications	
UE5.1	Inventory of Desktop Applications	CF13.1
UE5.2	Protection of Spreadsheets	CF13.2
UE5.3	Protection of Databases	CF13.3
UE5.4	Application Protection	CF4.1
UE5.5	Information Validation	CF4.3
UE5.6	Desktop Application Development	CF13.4
UE6	Computing Devices	
UE6.1	Remote Environments	CF14.1
UE6.2	Mobile Device Configuration	CF14.2
UE6.3	Mobile Device Connectivity	CF14.3
UE6.4	Consumer Devices	CF14.5
UE6.5	Portable Storage Devices	CF14.4

Template Ref	Title	Topic Ref
UE7	Electronic Communications	
UE7.1	Email	CF15.1
UE7.2	Instant Messaging	CF15.2
UE7.3	Wireless Access	CF9.6
UE7.4	Voice Over IP (VoIP) Networks	CF9.7
UE7.5	Telephony and Conferencing	CF9.8
UE8	Incident and Change Management	
UE8.1	Information Security Incident Management	CF11.1
UE8.2	Change Management	CF7.6
UE8.3	Back-up	CF7.5
UE8.4	Emergency Fixes	CF11.3
UE9	Business Continuity	
UE9.1	Business Continuity Planning	CF20.5
UE9.2	Business Continuity Arrangements	CF20.6
UE9.3	Business Continuity Testing	CF20.7

INDEX

The Standard of Good Practice for Information Security Index

This Index presents an extensive list of information security-related terms found in the Standard. It provides references to topics where each term is covered, using the relevant topic reference (eg *SG2.1* for the topic *SG2.1 Information Security Strategy*).

- Terms included in this Index refer to those found in one or more of the four categories (ie Security Governance, Security Requirements, Control Framework and Security Monitoring and Improvement).
- This Index does not include references to terms found in the Introduction or Appendices.

A

Acceptable usage policy / use

SR2.2, CF1.1, CF2.1, CF14.5, CF15.1, CF15.2

Access

Arrangements   CF5.1
Control   CF5.3, CF6.1, CF6.3, CF7.5, CF9.3, CF13.2, CF13.3, CF16.5, CF17.2, CF18.5
External   CF9.3
Privileges   CF2.1, CF2.5, CF4.1, CF5.3, CF6.1, CF6.2, CF6.4, CF8.1, CF8.2, CF8.8
Rights   CF2.5, CF5.1, CF6.1, CF8.2, CF9.5, CF10.5, CF16.1
Unauthorised   CF4.1, CF7.2, CF7.4, CF7.5, CF8.1, CF8.5, CF9.1, CF9.3, CF9.5, CF9.8, CF10.5, CF10.6, CF12.3, CF14.2, CF14.3, CF14.5, CF17.2, CF18.3, CF19.1

Access control mechanisms

CF6.3
Biometric   CF6.6
Password   CF6.4
Token   CF6.5

Access management

CF6.1, CF6.2, CF6.3, CF6.4, CF6.5, CF6.6, CF6.7

Accountability

CF2.5, CF6.1, CF7.4, CF9.1, CF9.3, CF12.1, CF12.3

Acquisition

CF14.5, CF16.2, CF16.5, CF18.2, CF20.3, SI2.1

Application

Controls   CF15.2
Desktop   CF13.1, CF13.2, CF13.3, CF13.4
Development   CF13.4, CF17.1
Owner(s)   CF5.1, CF6.1, CF18.6
Software   CF11.3, CF18.4

Asset management / register

CF3, CF3.4

Audit

SR2.1, SR2.2, SI1.1, SI1.2, SI1.3, SI1.4, SI1.5

Authentication

CF6.4, CF6.5, CF6.6, CF8.8, CF9.8, CF12.3, CF14.2
Details   CF5.1, CF6.1, CF6.7, CF17.2
Device   CF9.6
Hardware   CF2.1, CF3.4, CF5.3, CF8.6, CF16.2
Information   CF6.5, CF6.6, CF8.2, CF14.3
Mechanisms   CF6.3
Methods   CF6.3, CF7.7
Services   CF1.2, CF8.1, CF16.5
Strong   CF6.1, CF8.4, CF8.6, CF9.1, CF9.3
System   CF9.3
User   CF9.6

Authorisation

CF2.3, CF5.3, CF6.1, CF6.2, CF7.2, CF7.3, CF11.3, CF14.1, CF18.4, CF19.1

Awareness

CF2.2, CF2.3, CF10.2

B

Back-up

CF7.2, CF7.5, CF14.1, CF14.2

Business

Application   CF4.1, CF4.2, CF4.3
Impact   SR1.2, SR1.3, SR1.4, SR1.5, SR1.6, CF11.1, CF20.4
Manager   SG2.2, CF1.2, CF2.5, CF7.6 CF8.4
Owner   SG1.2, SR1.1, SR1.6, SR2.1, CF3.1, CF3.3, CF5.1, CF7.1, CF9.4, CF10.5, CF11.3, CF12.2, CF14.5, CF16.1, CF16.3, CF16.4, CF17.3, CF18.2, CF18.6, CF18.8, CF20.2, CF20.7, SI1.2, SI1.4
Representative   SR1.2, CF1.1, CF2.2, CF3.3, CF3.4, CF6.1, CF6.7, CF7.6, CF7.7, CF9.6, CF9.7, CF11.1, CF11.2, CF11.3, CF13.1, CF13.4, CF14.1, CF15.1, CF15.2, CF16.2, CF16.4, CF16.5, CF18.4, CF18.6, CF18.8, CF20.2, CF20.5, CF20.6
Requirements   SG2.3, SR1.3, SR1.4, SR1.5, SR1.6, CF3.1, CF5.1, CF6.1, CF7.5, CF7.7, CF17.1, CF17.3, CF18.1
Risks   CF5.1, SI1.1, SI2.1, SI2.2

Business continuity

CF20.1, CF20.2, CF20.3, CF20.4, CF20.5, CF20.6, CF20.7
Arrangements   CF16.3, CF20.2, CF20.6
Plans   CF20.1, CF20.2, CF20.5, CF20.6, CF20.7
Programme   CF16.1, CF20.2
Strategy   CF20.1
Testing   CF20.7

C

Capacity

CF4.1, CF7.1, CF7.7, CF9.8, CF10.5, CF18.1, CF18.2, CF18.4, CF18.6, CF20.3

Certification Authority (CA)

CF4.2, CF8.6, CF20.5, CF20.7

Certification Revocation Lists (CRL)

CF8.6

Change management

CF7.2, CF7.4, CF7.7
Discipline   CF4.1, CF11.3, CF20.3
Practices   CF20.5
Process   CF7.3, CF7.6, CF13.4, CF16.3, CF17.2, CF20.5
System   CF8.2

Chief Information Security Officer (CISO)

CF1.2

Clear desk policy

CF2.4

Cloud

CF16.4, CF16.5

Commercial-off-the-shelf (COTS) software

CF2.4, CF3.4, CF11.3, CF12.1, CF13.3, CF16.2, SI1.2

Communications equipment

CF8.3, CF9.2, CF20.3
See also Network equipment

Compliance

SR2.1, SR2.2
Requirements   SG2.1, SG2.3, SR1.2, SR1.6, CF3.4, SI1.5

Computer Emergency Response Team (CERT)

CF9.1, CF10.1

Computer media

CF7.5, CF11.1, CF11.4, CF14.4

Confidentiality

SR1.2, SR1.3, CF1.1, CF2.3, CF2.4, CF3.1, CF3.2, CF4.3, CF5.3, CF7.1, CF8.3, CF8.4, CF9.5, CF9.7, CF11.1, CF13.4, CF14.2, CF15.1, CF15.2, CF16.3, CF17.1, CF17.3, CF18.1, CF18.2, CF20.1, CF20.5, CF20.6, SI1.1, SI1.3, SI1.5
Agreements   CF2.1
Requirements   SR1.3, CF7.3

Consumer devices

CF14.5

Consumerisation

SG1.2, SG2.2, SR1.1, CF1.2, CF14.5

Contingency

Arrangements   CF16.1
Plans   CF8.6, CF18.1, CF18.6
Procedures   CF18.4

Contract(s)

SR1.3, SR1.4, SR1.5, CF1.1, CF1.2, CF2.1, CF3.1, CF3.4, CF5.1, CF5.2, CF7.7, CF9.5, CF12.3, CF16.1, CF16.3, CF16.4, CF16.5, CF17.2, CF18.1, CF20.2, CF20.6, SI2.3

Contractor(s)

SR1.1, CF1.1, CF2.1, CF9.6, CF12.1, CF17.1

Contractual

SG2.3
Conditions   CF5.3, CF6.1
Obligations   SR1.3, SR1.4, SR1.5, CF1.1, CF6.1, CF8.3, CF8.8, CF18.1, CF20.5, CF20.6, SI2.3
Terms   SR1.2, CF16.2

Corporate governance

SR2.1, CF16.4

Crisis management

CF20.4

Critical

Equipment   CF19.1
Information   CF1.1, CF2.3, CF2.4, CF2.5, CF3.2, CF4.3, CF5.3, CF7.7, CF8.3, CF8.4, CF20.1, CF20.2, CF20.6, CF20.7
Infrastructure   CF8.3
Timescales   CF5.2, CF7.5, CF7.7, CF20.3, CF20.5, CF20.7

Criticality

CF5.1, CF6.3, CF7.7, CF8.3, SI1.2, SI2.1

Cryptographic

Algorithms   CF8.4, CF8.8
Key management   CF8.5
Services   CF1.2, CF8.1
Solutions   CF8.4, CF20.5, CF20.7
Techniques   CF8.1

Cryptography

CF1.2, CF8.4, CF8.8, SI1.3, SI2.3

Customer

Access   CF5.1, CF5.2, CF5.3
Access arrangements   CF5.1
Connections   CF5.3
Contracts   CF5.2
Relationship Management (CRM)   CF3.4, CF11.3, CF16.2, SI1.2

INDEX

Customer(s) / client(s)
CF5.1, CF5.2, CF5.3

Cyber
SG1.2, SR1.1, CF1.2, CF11.2, CF20.4
Intelligence Service Providers   CF11.2
Partners   CF1.2, CF20.4, SI2.1
Threat   CF11.2

D

Data protection
EU directive   SR2.2
Legislation   SR2.2, CF2.1, CF5.2, CF8.4, CF11.4, CF16.3, CF16.4
Manager   SR2.2

Data storage
CF7.4, CF20.3, SI1.3

Demilitarised Zone (DMZ)
CF4.1, CF7.1, CF9.3, CF10.3

Desktop application
CF13.1, CF13.2, CF13.3, CF13.4

Destruction
SR1.2, SR2.2, CF2.3, CF3.2, CF3.3, CF8.5, CF8.8, CF16.4, CF18.1

Development
Environment(s)   CF17.2, CF18.3
Lifecycle   CF2.4, CF17.1, CF17.3, CF18.8
Management   CF17.1, CF17.2, CF17.3
Methodology(ies)   SG1.2, CF13.4, CF17.1, CF17.3
Process   CF17.2, CF17.3
Risks   CF17.3

Digital
Certificate(s)   CF4.2, CF5.3, CF5.5, CF6.3, CF8.4, CF8.6, CF10.3, CF15.1, CF15.2
Rights Management (DRM)   SR1.1, SR1.6, CF1.2, CF3.4, CF8.8, CF11.3, CF16.2, CF17.1, CF18.2, CF18.7
Signature(s)   CF1.2, CF3.1, CF5.3, CF8.4, CF8.6, CF8.8, CF15.1, CF15.2

Disaster(s)
SR1.2, CF7.5, CF8.6, CF16.1, CF18.4, CF20.1, CF20.2, CF20.4, CF20.5, CF20.6

Disaster Recovery
CF20.4, CF20.6

Disclosure
SG1.2, CF7.3, CF8.3, CF8.5, CF8.8, CF9.4, CF13.2, CF13.3, CF15.1
Non-   CF2.1, CF9.5, CF16.1
Unauthorised   SR1.3, SR2.2, CF3.1, CF3.2, CF3.3, CF4.1, CF4.2, CF5.2, CF6.3, CF8.7, CF14.1, CF14.2, CF14.3, CF14.4, CF14.5, CF20.1, CF20.7

Disposal
SR1.2, CF3.3

Document management
CF3.2

E

Electronic communications
CF2.3, CF3.1, CF15.1, CF15.2, CF16.1

Electronic documents
SR1.2, CF2.4, CF3.2, CF8.3, CF8.7, CF10.5

E-mail
CF10.3, CF15.1

Emergency
CF7.5, CF8.6, CF14.1, CF20.1, CF20.6
Access   CF11.3
Bypass   CF20.3
Conditions   CF2.5
Equipment   CF19.2
Fixes   CF7.6, CF11.3
Procedures   CF10.2, CF10.3, CF19.1, CF19.3, CF20.5
Response process   CF20.2
Situation   CF19.1, CF20.4

Encryption
SR1.2, SR1.6, SR2.1, SR2.2, CF2.4, CF4.2, CF7.4, CF7.7, CF8.4, CF8.6, CF8.8, CF9.3, CF9.6, CF10.4, CF11.4, CF14.1, CF14.2, CF14.4, CF14.5, CF15.1, CF15.2, CF16.3, CF16.4, CF18.2

End user environment
See Local environments

Environmental
Controls   CF20.6
Hazards   CF19.3

Escalation
SG2.2, CF10.6, CF11.1

Event log / logging
SR2.2, CF4.1, CF8.6, CF9.1, CF9.7, CF10.3, CF10.4, CF10.5, CF10.6, CF11.1, CF11.4, CF16.5, CF18.4

Evidence
CF1.1, CF11.1, CF11.4, CF14.2

Executive management
SG1.1, SG1.2, SG2.2, SG2.3, SR1.1, SR1.2, SR1.6, SR2.1, CF1.1, CF1.2, CF2.1, CF2.2, CF3.2, CF5.1, CF5.2, CF8.4, CF11.2, CF11.4, CF16.3, CF16.4, CF18.8, CF20.1, CF20.2, CF20.4, CF20.5, CF20.6, SI1.1, SI1.4, SI2.1, SI2.2, SI2.3

INDEX

External

Access   SR1.2, SR1.6, CF9.3
Assessment   CF16.2
Audit   CF16.1, CF16.2, SI2.1
Connections   CF9.3
Hard disk drive   SR1.2, CF3.4, CF11.3, CF14.3, CF14.4, CF16.2, CF19.1
Individuals   SR1.1, CF1.1, CF2.1, CF2.2, CF6.5, CF6.6, CF9.5, CF14.4
Locations   SR1.1
Networks   CF9.3
Service providers   SR1.1, CF7.7, CF10.4, CF12.3, CF16.1, CF18.6, CF20.3

External party(ies)

SG2.1, SR1.1, SR1.2, SR1.6, SR2.2, CF1.1, CF2.1, CF2.3, CF4.2, CF5.1, CF5.2, CF6.1, CF7.6, CF8.3, CF8.4, CF8.5, CF8.8, CF9.2, CF9.3, CF10.2, CF11.2, CF11.4, CF12.1, CF12.3, CF14.1, CF16.1, CF16.3, CF16.5, CF17.1, CF17.2, CF18.1, CF18.3, CF20.1, CF20.2, CF20.4, CF20.6, SI1.1, SI1.2, SI2.2, SI2.3

External supplier(s)

SG1.2, CF3.1, CF8.2, CF9.5, CF10.3, CF12.1, CF16.1, CF16.2, CF16.3, CF16.5

F

Fault tolerant

CF7.1, CF20.3

Firewall(s)

CF3.4, CF4.1, CF5.3, CF7.1, CF7.3, CF9.1, CF9.6, CF9.7, CF10.1, CF11.3, CF15.2, CF16.2, CF17.1, CF17.2, CF20.3, CF20.5, CF20.7
Log   CF9.3, SI2.1
Personal   CF5.1, CF9.3, CF14.3
Proxy   CF9.3, CF9.4
Stateful inspection   CF9.3, CF9.4
Web   CF9.4

Forensic

CF11.1, CF11.2
Investigations   CF1.1, CF1.2, CF2.4, CF10.4, CF11.1, CF11.2, CF11.4, CF12.2, CF14.2, CF16.5, SI2.2

H

Hardware

CF3.4, CF5.2, CF6.5, CF7.2, CF7.4, CF7.7, CF8.1, CF8.6, CF9.1, CF9.6, CF9.8, CF10.6, CF12.3, CF14.1, CF18.4, CF18.6, CF20.2, CF20.3, SI2.1

Hazard protection

CF19.3

High-level working group

SG1.2, SG2.1, SG2.3, SR2.3, CF8.1

I

Identity and Access Management (IAM)

CF1.2, CF5.1, CF6.3, CF7.1, CF8.1, CF8.2, CF8.8, CF16.5, CF18.2, CF18.4, CF18.7, CF20.5, CF20.7
Federated Identity and Access Management (FIAM)   SR1.1, CF1.2, CF5.1, CF5.2, CF8.1, CF8.2, CF16.5

Incident(s)

SG1.1, SG1.2, SG2.1, SG2.2, SG2.3, SR1.1, SR1.2, SR1.6, CF1.1, CF1.2, CF2.2, CF2.3, CF5.2, CF6.1, CF8.2, CF10.2, CF10.3, CF10.4, CF11.1, CF11.2, CF11.4, CF12.2, CF14.5, CF16.3, CF18.8, CF19.3, CF20.2, CF20.4, SI1.3, SI2.1, SI2.2

Incident management

SG2.1, SG2.3, SR1.2, SR2.2, CF1.2, CF2.4, CF5.1, CF7.7, CF10.4, CF10.6, CF11.1, CF11.2, CF11.4, CF16.3, CF20.1, CF20.2, SI1.4

Independent

Assessment / review   CF9.5, SI1.1
Audit   SI1.1, CF9.5
Confirmation   CF6.4, CF6.5, CF7.7
Expert / specialist   CF11.4, CF16.1, SI1.1
External Party   CF11.4, SI1.1

Information classification

SR1.2, CF3.1, CF3.3, CF5.1, CF6.1, CF8.8, CF11.1, CF13.4, CF14.2, CF14.3, CF17.1, CF18.1, SI1.3

Information leakage protection

CF8.7

Information risk

SG1.1, SG1.2, SG2.1, CF9.4, CF12.2, CF16.3, CF18.8, CF20.1, SI1.2, SI1.3, SI2.1, SI2.3
Analysis(es)   See Information risk assessment
Assessment   SG2.3, SR1.1, SR1.2, SR1.6, CF1.1, CF1.2, CF2.2, CF2.4, CF2.5, CF5.1, CF8.3, CF9.6, CF13.4, CF16.1, CF16.4, CF17.3, SI1.4, SI1.5
Assessment methodologies   SG2.3, SR1.1, SR1.2, CF12.2
Management   SR1.2, SR1.3, SR1.4, SR1.5, SR1.6, SG2.3
Reporting   SI2.2
Treatment   SR1.6

Information security

SG1.1, SR1.1, CF2.2, CF2.3, CF3.3, CF3.4, CF5.1, CF6.1, CF7.7, CF9.1, CF16.3, CF18.4, CF20.4
Arrangements   SG1.2, CF1.2, CF16.1, SI1.1, SI2.1
Assurance programme   SG2.3
Effectiveness of   SG1.2, CF1.2
Function   SG2.1, SR2.1, CF1.2, CF12.1, CF12.2, CF16.1, CF16.4, CF17.1
Managers   CF8.1
Principles   CF1.1, CF2.5
Responsibilities   CF2.1, CF2.4, CF12.1
Requirements   CF1.2, CF2.5, CF3.2, CF16.1, CF17.1, CF18.1, CF18.2, CF18.8, SI1.1, SI2.3
Strategy   SG1.1, SG1.2, SG2.1, SG2.2, CF1.2, CF2.1, CF20.1, SI2.1

Information systems
SR1.1, SR1.2, CF2.5, CF7.1, CF7.6, CF8.3, CF9.3, CF10.5, CF20.3, CF20.6, SI1.3

Information validation
CF4.3

Instant messaging
CF2.2, CF2.3, CF3.1, CF8.7, CF15.2

Integrity requirements
SR1.4

Intelligence information
SR1.1, CF1.2, CF20.3

Internal audit
SG1.2, SR2.1, CF8.3, CF20.4, SI1.1

Intrusion detection / prevention
SR2.2, CF1.2, CF3.4, CF7.3, CF11.3, CF12.3, CF16.2, CF16.5, CF17.1, CF20.5, CF20.7
Host (HIDS)   CF10.6, CF14.3
Network (NIDS)   CF10.6

Inventory(ies)
SG2.2, CF3.1, CF5.2, CF5.3, CF8.3, CF9.2, CF13.1, CF20.2, SI1.3

Information Risk Assessment Methodology (IRAM)
SR1.2, CF8.3, CF13.4, CF20.5, SI2.2
BIRT   SG2.3

IT
Facilities   CF11.1, CF19.1
Function   SG1.2, CF13.1, CF16.4
Projects   CF1.2, CF8.1
Specialist(s)   SR1.1, CF6.1, CF7.6, CF11.1
Staff   CF2.2, CF7.5, CF8.2, CF18.6, CF20.5, CF20.7

J

Job description(s)
CF2.1, CF12.2

L

Labelling
SR2.2, CF2.4, CF3.1, CF3.3, CF7.5, CF8.8, CF9.2, CF11.1, CF15.1

Legal / regulatory
Action   CF11.4, CF16.5
Advice   CF8.4, CF11.4
Bodies   CF11.4
Compliance   SR2.1, CF3.2, SI2.3
Function   SG1.2, SR2.1, CF8.4, CF16.4, CF16.5, SI2.3
Liabilities   SR1.3, SR1.4, SR1.5
Non-compliance   SR2.1
Obligations   SR1.3, SR1.4, SR1.5, CF1.1, CF3.1, CF6.1, CF8.3, CF8.4, CF17.1, CF18.1, CF20.5, CF20.6

Penalties   SI2.1
Requirements   SG2.3, SR2.1, SR2.2, CF1.1, CF3.2, CF3.3, CF4.2, CF5.1, CF5.2, CF8.4, CF8.7, CF10.4, CF10.5, CF11.4, CF14.1, CF16.1, CF16.3, CF16.4, CF17.1, CF20.1, SI1.3, SI2.1, SI2.3
Responsibilities   CF2.1

Legislation
SG1.1, SR1.2, SR1.6, SR2.1, SR2.2, CF1.2, CF2.1, CF5.2, CF8.7, CF11.2, CF11.4, SI2.3

License(s) / licensing
CF1.1, CF2.1, CF3.4, CF5.2, CF6.3, CF6.6, CF8.4, CF8.8, CF16.1, CF16.2, CF16.3

Local environments
CF1.2, CF2.3, CF3.3, CF12.1, CF12.2, CF13.1, CF13.4, CF20.1

Local security co-ordination
CF12.2

Logging
CF6.1, CF9.3, CF9.5, CF11.3, CF14.2, CF14.3, CF15.2, CF18.4, SI1.1, SI1.3
Security event   CF8.6, CF10.4, CF18.4

Login
CF1.1, CF2.2, CF2.5, CF7.1, CF9.3, CF10.4, CF16.5

Log off
CF2.3, CF2.4, CF7.2

M

Maintenance
CF1.2, CF6.3, CF7.7, CF8.5, CF11.4, CF12.3, CF16.2, CF20.3, SI2.1
Contracts   CF12.3
Remote   CF9.5, CF12.3, CF14.1
Utilities   CF7.2, CF9.1, CF14.1

Malware
SR1.2, SR1.6, CF1.2, CF2.3, CF4.1, CF5.1, CF5.2, CF5.3, CF6.3, CF6.4, CF7.1, CF7.2, CF7.3, CF7.4, CF7.7, CF8.3, CF8.8, CF9.3, CF10.2, CF10.3, CF10.6, CF11.2, CF14.1, CF14.2, CF14.3, CF14.5, CF15.1, CF15.2, CF16.5, CF17.2, CF20.5, CF20.7

Metadata
SR2.2, CF2.4

Mobile computing
CF14.1, CF14.2, CF14.3, CF14.4, CF14.5

Mobile device(s)
SR1.2, CF2.1, CF2.4, CF3.4, CF10.1, CF10.3, CF12.3, CF14.2, CF14.3, CF14.5, CF18.4, SI1.4
Management   CF14.2

Monitoring

SG1.2, SG2.3, SR1.6, SR2.2, CF2.2, CF2.4, CF2.5, CF3.2, CF4.1, CF7.1, CF7.2, CF7.4, CF8.2, CF8.3, CF8.7, CF8.8, CF10.1, CF10.2, CF15.1, CF15.2, CF16.1, CF19.3

Audit / review teams   SI1.5
Electronic communication   CF2.3
Information security   CF1.2, SI2.1
Information security compliance   SI2.3
Internet   CF4.2
Network   CF7.3, CF9.1, CF10.5
Performance   SG1.2, SG2.3
Software   CF10.5
VoIP   CF1.1, CF9.7
Vulnerabilities   CF1.2

Multifunction devices

CF2.4, CF3.3, CF3.4, CF10.1, CF10.3, CF11.3, CF12.3, CF16.2, SI1.2

N

Network

Address translation   CF9.4
Configuration diagrams   CF9.2, CF11.1
Connections   CF4.1, CF9.3, CF9.8, CF11.1, CF16.1
Devices   CF6.4, CF6.5, CF6.6, CF7.1, CF7.4, CF9.1, CF9.4, CF10.1, CF10.4, CF19.1, SI1.3
Device configuration   CF9.1, SI1.2
Documentation   CF9.2
Equipment   CF3.4, CF9.3, CF9.5, CF10.1, CF11.3, CF16.2, CF19.2, CF20.3
Gateway   CF9.3, CF20.5, CF20.7
Monitoring   CF10.5
Names   CF9.3
Owner   CF9.3, CF9.4, CF9.6
Services   CF4.1, CF7.7, CF9.4, CF20.5, CF20.6
Traffic   CF2.5, CF4.2, CF7.1, CF7.3, CF7.7, CF9.1, CF9.3, CF9.4, CF9.7, CF10.3, CF10.6, CF14.3, CF16.5, CF20.3

Network management

CF7.2, CF9.1, CF9.2, CF9.3

Network operations centres (NOC)

CF7.1, CF7.4, CF8.7, CF10.5, CF20.6

Network storage systems

CF7.4, CF10.1, CF11.3, CF16.2

Non-disclosure

CF2.1, CF9.5, CF16.1

Non-repudiation

CF5.3, CF8.4, CF15.1, CF16.4

O

Office equipment

CF12.3

Operating

Procedure   CF18.6, CF20.6
Standards   SR1.3, SR1.4, SR1.5
System(s)   SR1.1, SR1.2, CF1.2, CF3.4, CF4.1, CF4.2, CF6.4, CF6.5, CF6.6, CF7.4, CF8.6, CF9.1, CF10.1, CF11.3, CF12.3, CF14.1, CF14.2, CF14.5, CF15.2, CF16.2, CF16.5, CF18.4, SI1.2

Outsource / Outsourcing

SR1.1, SR1.6, CF1.2, CF5.2, CF12.1, CF16.1, CF16.3, CF16.4, CF16.5, CF17.1, CF20.1

Owner

Application   SR1.1, CF5.1, CF6.1, CF18.6
Business   SG1.2, SR1.1, SR1.6, SR2.1, CF3.1, CF3.3, CF5.1, CF7.1, CF9.4, CF10.5, CF11.3, CF12.2, CF14.5, CF16.1, CF16.3, CF16.4, CF17.3, CF18.2, CF18.6, CF20.2, CF20.7, SI1.2, SI1.4
Key   CF8.5
Network   CF9.3, CF9.4, CF9.6
System   CF6.1, CF8.2, SI2.1, SI2.2

Ownership

CF1.1, CF2.5, CF3.4, CF5.2, CF8.5, CF8.8, CF12.1, CF14.2, CF14.5, CF16.2, CF16.3

P

Password(s)

CF1.1, CF2.2, CF2.3, CF2.4, CF5.1, CF5.3, CF6.1, CF6.3, CF6.4, CF6.5, CF6.6, CF7.2, CF8.2, CF8.6, CF9.1, CF9.3, CF9.5, CF9.8, CF10.3, CF11.4, CF12.3, CF13.2, CF13.3, CF14.1, CF14.2, CF14.3, CF14.4, CF14.5, CF18.3, CF18.5, SI1.4

Patch management

CF7.1, CF7.2, CF7.4, CF7.7, CF9.1, CF10.1, CF14.1, CF14.2, CF18.4, SI2.1

Penetration tests

CF16.2, CF18.5, SI1.1, SI1.2

Personally Identifiable Information (PII)

SR2.2, CF2.3, CF5.1, CF5.2, CF12.1, CF16.3, CF16.4, CF16.5, CF18.1, CF18.4

Physical

Access   CF3.3, CF7.2, CF7.3, CF7.4, CF8.8, CF9.1, CF12.3, CF17.2, CF19.1, SI1.2
Assets   CF3.4
Controls   CF8.6, CF9.2
Material   CF19.1, CF19.2, CF19.3
Protection   CF12.3, CF19.1
Security   SG1.2, SR2.1, CF6.3, CF14.5, CF19.1
Token   CF2.1, CF3.4, CF5.3, CF6.3, CF6.5, CF6.6, CF16.2

Physical and environmental security

CF19.1, CF19.2, CF19.3

Policy(ies)

SG1.1, SG1.2, SR1.2, SR1.3, SR1.4, SR1.5, SR2.2, CF1.1, CF1.2, CF2.1, CF2.2, CF2.3, CF2.4, CF3.1, CF3.2, CF6.1, CF8.6, CF9.4, CF10.4, CF11.2, CF14.5, CF15.1, CF15.2, CF16.4, CF16.5, CF17.1, CF17.3, CF18.1, CF18.2, CF18.8, SI1.3, SI2.1, SI2.3

INDEX

Portable storage

Device(s) SR1.2, SR2.2, CF2.1, CF2.4, CF8.7, CF10.2, CF12.1, CF14.2, CF14.3, CF14.4, CF20.6
Media CF2.1, CF2.4, CF3.4, CF8.7, CF9.1, CF10.3, CF10.4, CF10.5, CF14.2, CF16.2

Post-implementation review(s)

CF18.8

Power

Loss of SR1.2, CF8.3, CF19.2
Supplies CF19.2

Privacy

Assessment SR2.2
Data SR1.6, SR2.1, SR2.2, CF1.2, CF8.7, CF14.1
Information SR2.2
Policy SR2.2

Protection of databases / spreadsheets

CF13.2, CF13.3

Public key

Certificates CF8.6
Infrastructure (PKI) SG2.2, CF8.6, CF8.8, CF18.2, CF18.4, CF18.7, CF20.5, CF20.7

Q

Quality assurance

CF17.3

R

Registration Authority (RA)

CF8.6, CF20.5, CF20.7

Remote

Environments CF2.3, CF14.1, CF14.3
Maintenance / Support CF7.2, CF9.1, CF9.5, CF14.1, CF14.2
Working CF14.1

Resilience

SG1.2, SG2.1, CF9.7, CF16.4, CF20.1, CF20.3, SI1.3

Risk

Acceptable level of SI2.1
Analysis SR1.1, SR1.2, CF8.3, CF13.4
See Information risk analysis(es), see also Information Risk Analysis Methodologies
Appetite SG1.1, SG2.1, SG2.3, SR1.6, CF20.1, SI2.1, SI2.2
Management SG1.2, SG2.3, SR1.1, CF1.2, CF8.7
Residual SR1.2, SR1.6, SI1.5
Treatment SR1.2, SR1.6, CF20.2, SI1.3, SI2.2

Roles and responsibilities

CF2.5, CF10.1, CF10.4, CF11.1, CF12.2, CF16.1, CF18.7, CF20.2, CF20.4

S

Security architecture

SG1.1, SG1.2, CF1.2, CF8.8, CF12.2, CF18.2, SI1.1, SI1.2, SI2.1
Principles CF4.1, CF7.1, CF8.1, CF8.3, CF9.1, CF9.4, CF16.3, CF18.2, CF18.7

Security assessment

CF18.6

Security audit

See Audit

Security awareness

CF1.2, CF2.2, CF2.3, CF5.1, CF12.1, CF12.2, CF14.1, CF14.5, SI1.4

Security direction

SG1.2

Security education / training

CF2.2, CF2.4, CF8.8

Security event logging

CF8.6, CF10.4, CF18.4

Security governance

SG1.1, SG1.2, SG2.1, SG2.2, SG2.3

Security monitoring

SI2.1

Security performance

SG1.2, SI2.1, SI2.2, SI2.3

Security policy

SG1.1, SG1.2, CF1.1, CF1.2, CF2.1, CF2.2, CF2.3, CF6.1, CF9.4, CF17.1, CF18.1, CF18.8, SI2.1

Segregation of duties

CF2.5, CF6.1, CF7.7

Sensitive information

SR1.2, SR1.3, CF1.1, CF2.2, CF2.3, CF2.4, CF2.5, CF3.2, CF3.3, CF4.1, CF4.2, CF5.2, CF5.3, CF6.4, CF6.5, CF6.6, CF7.3, CF7.4, CF8.4, CF8.5, CF8.7, CF8.8, CF9.3, CF9.7, CF10.2, CF10.5, CF11.2, CF12.1, CF12.2, CF12.3, CF13.1, CF14.1, CF14.2, CF14.3,CF14.4, CF14.5, CF16.1, CF16.2, CF16.4, CF16.5, CF17.2, CF18.2, CF18.5, CF19.1, CF20.1, CF20.7, SI2.2

Service interruptions

CF7.7, SI1.3

Service Level Agreements (SLAs)

SR1.2, CF1.2, CF2.5, CF4.2, CF7.7, CF12.3, CF18.6

Service providers

SR1.1, SR1.6, CF1.2, CF3.1, CF4.2, CF5.2, CF7.7, CF8.2, CF8.3, CF9.3, CF10.4, CF10.5, CF11.2, CF12.1, CF12.3, CF16.1, CF16.3, CF16.4, CF16.5, CF18.6, CF20.1, CF20.3, CF20.4
See external service providers

INDEX

Sign-on
Mechanisms   CF6.7
Process   CF5.3, CF6.7, CF8.2
Reduced   CF7.4

Smartcards
CF2.1, CF2.4, CF3.4, CF5.3, CF6.1, CF6.3, CF6.5, CF8.4, CF8.6, CF9.3, CF16.2

Smartphones
CF2.1, CF2.2, CF2.4, CF3.4, CF5.3, CF10.1, CF10.3, CF11.3, CF12.1, CF14.1, CF14.2, CF14.3, CF14.5, CF16.2, CF18.4

Social networking
CF2.3, CF2.4

Software
Configuration   CF9.3, CF14.1, CF14.2, CF18.4
Developers   CF8.1, CF17.1
Licensing   CF16.2
Malfunctions   SR1.2. CF8.3, CF18.4
Provision of   CF14.1, CF14.2
Tools   SR1.2, CF9.2, SI1.1
Unauthorised   SR1.2
Vulnerabilities   CF10.1

Specifications of requirements
CF18.1

Staff
SG1.2, SG2.2, SR1.1, SR1.2, SR1.3, SR1.4, SR1.5, SR2.2, CF1.1, CF1.2, CF2.1, CF2.2, CF2.4, CF2.5, CF3.1, CF5.1, CF5.2, CF6.1, CF7.2, CF7.4, CF7.5, CF7.7, CF8.2, CF8.3, CF8.8, CF9.1, CF9.3, CF9.5, CF9.8, CF10.1, CF10.5, CF11.1, CF11.2, CF11.3, CF12.1, CF12.2, CF12.3, CF14.1, CF14.4, CF14.5, CF16.2, CF16.3, CF16.4, CF16.5, CF17.1, CF17.2, CF17.3, CF18.1, CF18.3, CF18.4, CF18.6, CF19.1, CF19.3, CF20.1, CF20.4, CF20.5, CF20.6, CF20.7, SI1.4, SI2.1

Storage Area Network (SAN)
CF3.4, CF7.1, CF7.4, CF7.5, CF10.1, CF11.3, CF16.2, CF16.5

Storage media
CF2.1, CF2.4, CF3.4, CF8.7, CF9.1, CF10.3, CF10.4, CF10.5, CF11.4, CF14.2, CF16.2, CF20.3

System
Administrators   CF6.1, CF6.2, CF8.1, CF8.2, CF11.3
Build   CF18.3
Capabilities   CF6.1
Capacity   CF18.4
Configuration   CF4.2, CF7.6, SI1.2
Design   CF18.2, CF18.4
Documentation   CF6.1, CF17.2, CF20.6
Failure   CF4.1, CF7.1, CF8.1, CF18.1, CF18.4, CF18.7, CF20.3
Management tools   CF14.1, CF14.2
Monitoring   CF16.2
Promotion criteria   CF18.6
Utilities   CF7.1, CF7.2

System development
CF17.3, CF18.4, CF18.8
Environments   CF17.2
Methodology   SG1.2, CF17.1

System management
CF7.1, CF7.2, CF7.3, CF7.4, CF7.5, CF7.6, CF7.7, CF14.1, CF14.2, CF16.1

System / network monitoring
CF10.5

Systems development
CF2.4, CF16.1, CF17.1, CF17.2, CF17.3, CF18.2, CF18.3, CF18.8

System software
CF6.1, CF10.1, CF18.4

Systems testing
CF17.2, CF18.4

T

Tablets
CF2.1, CF2.4, CF3.4, CF10.1, CF10.3, CF11.3, CF12.1, CF14.1, CF14.2, CF14.3, CF14.5, CF16.2, CF18.4

Target environments
SR1.1, SR1.3, SR1.4, SR1.5, CF2.5, CF6.4, CF6.5, CF6.6, SI1.1, SI1.2, SI1.3, SI1.4, SI1.5

Technical infrastructure
CF1.1, CF8.1, CF8.3, CF8.6, CF8.8, CF9.7, CF10.1, CF10.4, CF11.3, CF15.2, CF16.1, CF16.5, CF18.2, CF20.1, CF20.2, CF20.3, CF20.4, CF20.5, CF20.6

Technical security infrastructure
CF4.1, CF8.1, CF8.2, CF8.3, CF8.4, CF8.5, CF8.6, CF8.7, CF8.8, CF16.4, CF18.2, CF18.4, CF18.7, CF20.5, CF20.7

Telephony and conferencing
CF9.8

Terms and conditions of employment
CF2.1

Testing process
CF18.4, CF18.5

Threat intelligence
SG1.2

U

Unavailability
CF8.3, CF20.2, CF20.6

Unique identifier(s)
CF5.3, CF6.2, CF6.3

User authentication

CF9.6

User authorisation

CF6.2, CF9.6

UserIDs

CF5.3, CF6.1, CF6.2, CF6.3, CF6.4, CF6.7, CF8.2, CF10.4, CF14.4

User requirements

CF9.4

V

Virtual

Desktop   CF3.4, CF10.1, CF11.3, CF14.2, CF14.5, CF16.2
Servers   CF3.4, CF7.3, CF10.1, CF11.3, CF16.2, CF16.4, CF16.5, CF20.3

Virtualisation

SG2.2, CF1.2, CF3.4, CF7.3, CF11.3, CF16.2, CF20.3

Virtual Private Network (VPN)

SG2.2, CF2.4, CF6.5, CF6.6, CF9.3, CF9.4, CF9.6, CF14.1, CF14.3, CF16.4

Visitors

CF9.6, CF19.1

Voice networks

CF9.2, CF9.8

Voice over IP (VoIP)

CF1.1, CF2.4, CF3.4, CF7.1, CF9.7, CF10.1, CF11.3, CF12.1, CF16.2

Vulnerability(ies)

SR1.2, CF8.1, CF9.1, CF10.1, CF16.2, CF18.5, CF20.5, SI1.1, SI1.3

W

Web

Browsers   See Web Browser Software, CF1.1, CF4.2, CF5.1, CF7.2, CF8.7, CF10.3, CF14.1, CF14.2, CF14.3, CF14.5
Server   CF4.1, CF4.2, CF10.3

Web application sessions

CF4.2

Web Proxy Servers

CF14.3

Wireless

Access   CF9.6, CF14.3, CF16.2
Access point   CF3.4, CF9.6, CF10.1, CF11.3, CF16.2
Devices   CF9.6
Network   CF1.1, CF2.4, CF9.4, CF9.6, CF10.5, CF12.1
Unauthorised   CF9.6, CF10.5